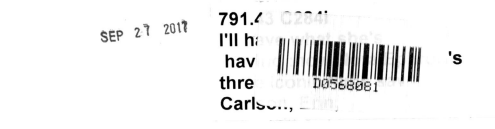

I'LL HAVE WHAT SHE'S HAVING

I'LL HAVE WHAT SHE'S HAVING

HOW NORA EPHRON'S
THREE ICONIC FILMS SAVED
THE ROMANTIC COMEDY

ERIN CARLSON

hachette
BOOKS
NEW YORK   BOSTON

Hachette Books
Hachette Book Group
1290 Avenue of the Americas
New York, NY 10104
hachettebooks.com
twitter.com/hachettebooks

First Edition: August 2017

Hachette Books is a division of Hachette Book Group, Inc.
The Hachette Books name and logo are trademarks of Hachette Book Group, Inc.

The publisher is not responsible for websites (or their content) that are not owned by the publisher.

The Hachette Speakers Bureau provides a wide range of authors for speaking events. To find out more, go to www.hachettespeakersbureau.com or call (866) 376-6591.

Library of Congress Cataloging-in-Publication Data

Names: Carlson, Erin, 1981– author.
Title: I'll have what she's having : how Nora Ephron's three iconic films saved the romantic comedy / Erin Carlson.
Description: First edition. | New York : Hachette Books, 2017. | Includes bibliographical references and index.
Identifiers: LCCN 2017014826| ISBN 9780316353885 (hardcover) | ISBN 9781478915706 (audio download) | ISBN 9780316353908 (ebook)
Subjects: LCSH: Romantic comedy films—United States—History and criticism. | Comedy films—Authorship. | Ephron, Nora—Crititicism and interpretation.
Classification: LCC PN1995.9.C55 C37 2017 | DDC 791.43/617—dc23
LC record available at https://lccn.loc.gov/2017014826

ISBNs: 978-0-316-35388-5 (hardcover), 978-0-316-35390-8 (ebook)

Printed in the United States of America

LSC-C

10 9 8 7 6 5 4 3 2 1

To Mom, Grandma Mary, and Grandma Marion,
my Noras.
To New York, my first love.
To Dave, my NY152.

Contents

Above all, be the heroine of your life, not the victim.

—Nora Ephron's Commencement Speech to
the Wellesley Class of 1996

MFEO
(Made for Each Other)

"God, are we gonna get away with this?"

So muttered Nora Ephron, smiling despite herself as she watched Meg Ryan traverse the Empire State Building observation deck to greet her destiny, Tom Hanks. In one corner of the set, painstakingly constructed to match the real thing, the director wore super-sized headphones and kept her eyes glued to the monitor.

It was the summer of 1992, and if Nora wanted to keep making movies, she really needed to pull off *Sleepless in Seattle*'s high-stakes last scene: a fantastical encounter between her stars that defied Hollywood convention. Studio executives quivered. *They don't meet until the very end! Would an audience accept the gimmick and sit through 90 minutes without a proper meet-cute? And can Nora Ephron, a neophyte director with one failed film under her belt, even be trusted to get away with this?*

What transpired when the camera started rolling would make cinematic history as the most romantic (and schmaltzy) moment she ever filmed, anointing Tom and Meg as America's Sweethearts—a

1

label at which they winced—and Nora the Queen of Romantic Comedy. But getting there was a battle. At one point, Tom got cold feet—*could he portray a wussy dad without committing career suicide?*—forcing Nora, anxious about keeping him happy, to persuade a fellow skeptic and know-it-all (and therefore a kindred spirit) to take a chance on her.

Sleepless is the second in a trilogy of Ephron-scripted romantic comedies that combined old-fashioned romance with hilarious truths about contemporary relationships (one word: *tiramisu*) to shape ideas and expectations about love, however pie-in-the-sky. According to *When Harry Met Sally*, you could get lucky and marry your best friend. Or, given the arcs of *Sleepless* and *You've Got Mail*, you might break your commitment to a blah suitor and delay marriage until Mr. Soulmate (who exhibits an uncanny resemblance to Tom Hanks) arrives to pledge his undying affection...as long as you both shall live. Like the great Manhattan-set romcoms of yore, from *The Apartment* to *Breakfast at Tiffany's* to *Annie Hall*, these romances stand the test of time: We get to experience the vicarious thrill of falling in love, a feeling at once intoxicating, addictive, and comforting, over and over again. But if you consider Nora a sentimentalist, you're mistaken: The mastermind yanking the heartstrings did not always sample the cherry-flavored Kool-Aid she served up.

Early in her career as a journalist, Nora cultivated a cutthroat, suffer-no-fools writing persona that skewered subjects from one-time idol Dorothy Parker to the staff of *Gourmet* magazine with bull's-eye precision. Back then, especially if you were a powerful media entity—or a ridiculous man, or a conventionally beautiful woman who complained about the downside of being born conventionally beautiful—you wanted to stay on Nora's good side and out of her line of vision. Later, when Nora turned her attention to filmmaking, she relied on her fierce wit and nimble social maneuvering to navigate the high highs and low lows of a male-dominated industry where women's stories typically play second fiddle. Though generous of spirit, she had the capacity to smear reputations and steer public opinion away from objects of her disapproval. And since she gave her point of view decisively and with such confidence, you took her word for it. You looked to Nora's bullshit detector to give it to you straight.

Nora, like a proto–Taylor Swift, channeled heartbreak into pop art with an autobiographical novel, *Heartburn*, exposing the bitter end of her second marriage to Watergate journalist Carl Bernstein. The film version, starring Meryl Streep and Jack Nicholson, would be her last cinematic take on divorce.

In a stark turnaround, her public image began to crystallize into a new Nora: someone who embraced the fantasy that a pair of perfect strangers, or mortal enemies, could be so MFEO. During the irony-drenched 1990s, when star-driven romances thrived anew, she found the ideal screen couple in two genre powerhouses whose sweet-and-tart sensibilities translated to sizzling chemistry, a merging of minds: Tom, an unlikely leading man who gained his sex appeal through clever delivery instead of a chiseled jaw, and Meg, a gifted actress trapped in the vessel of a Disney princess, forever struggling to earn the respect Tom came by effortlessly.

In hindsight, casting Meg as Sally Albright, her breakthrough role, was obvious. Faking the orgasm at Katz's Deli? Meg's idea. But other actresses turned down the part before she got to audition. On *Sleepless*, Nora initially doubted whether Tom, in career flux, had what it took to sweep Meg off her feet. On *Mail*, Meg expressed wariness toward playing adorable bookstore owner Kathleen Kelly. What changed her mind? And more importantly, what was an edgy up-and-coming comic named Dave Chappelle doing . . . *in a turtleneck?*

This is the story of how Nora and her collaborators shed inhibition to redefine the romantic comedy genre in a way that felt utterly new: wry, knowing, and urbane, but with an unabashed idealistic streak as well. And in the process, she came to also reshape the popular perception of the city she so loved: New York was just as much a character in her films as any of the romantic leads were, and her dialogue and cinematography betrayed her deep adoration of the town.

Recall the moment at a cozy Upper West Side café, where Shopgirl, rose tucked inside her well-worn copy of *Pride and Prejudice*, nervously awaited NY152 to walk through the door.

"I hear nothing. Not even a sound on the streets of New York, just the beat of my own heart. I have mail. From you."

Nothing, not least the city itself, would ever be the same again.

CHAPTER 1

It Was a Sign

Was the script trying to tell her something? Suddenly it all made sense. Her husband, she suspected, had been having an affair. She, Nora Ephron, had been duped.

"Read this," said Jay Presson Allen, the Academy Award–nominated writer, offering a screenplay by Frederic Raphael, who wrote the 1965 drama *Darling*. "You'll like it."

Nora was in New York, her adopted hometown, to meet Allen, a sharp-witted Texan who wrote her way out of her ho-hum first marriage to win prestige credits on scripts for Fosse's *Cabaret*, Hitchcock's *Marnie*, and the Broadway and big-screen adaptations of *The Prime of Miss Jean Brodie*, which scored Maggie Smith her best-actress Oscar in 1969. (Quoth Allen: "Male characters are easier to write. They're simpler. I think women are generally more psychologically complicated.") In 1979, the year Nora's second marriage went bust, she had started the transition from esteemed, if not handsomely paid, magazine writer to hired-gun screenwriter, a credit for a made-for-television movie called *Perfect Gentlemen* under her belt. "It was so awful," she said of the crime caper starring Lauren Bacall as one of three cash-strapped women outlaws who hold up a hotel safe. Its 1978 premiere had Nora, then expecting her first baby, paralyzed with fear and "really worried that this child was not going to live through this television screening."

Later, a silver lining developed upon discovery that the Bacall debacle inspired an older woman to rob a bank in Newton, Massachusetts. Nora's humiliation turned to bliss: "Forget journalism— that's power."

She cracked Raphael's script on the short flight home to DC, where she and her other half, Watergate hero Carl Bernstein, had an apartment at the Ontario, a Beaux Arts building that outlasted their crumbling relationship. He liked Washington; she loathed it. He was a notorious flirt who had vowed before marrying Nora to keep on the straight and narrow; she, caught up in Carl, willed away skepticism to instead look toward the future, thinking he'd changed. He had not. There she was, however many miles up in the air, absorbing the uncanny parallels between her life and the plot unfolding before her on page 8 of this screenplay she was reading.

"It began with a married couple at a dinner party," she later wrote. "I can't remember their names, but for the sake of the story, let's call them Clive and Lavinia. It was a very sophisticated dinner party and everyone at it was smart and brittle and chattering brilliantly. Clive and Lavinia were particularly clever, and they bantered with each other in a charming, flirtatious way. Everyone in the room admired them, and their marriage. The guests sat down to dinner and the patter continued. In the middle of the dinner, a man seated next to Lavinia put his hand on her leg. She put her cigarette out on his hand. The glittering conversation continued.

When the dinner ended, Clive and Lavinia got into their car to drive home. The talk ceased, and they drove in absolute silence. They had nothing to say to each other. And then Lavinia said: 'All right. Who is she?'"

All right, Carl. Who is she?

Nora Ephron, 38 years old and seven months pregnant with their second child, saw her carefully manicured world falling apart. She beelined from the airport to Carl's drawers, uncovering confirmation in the form of a "book of children's stories"—the audacity!—in which the Other Woman had scrawled "an incredibly stupid inscription about their enduring love." The Other Woman was Margaret Jay, the blond, doe-eyed daughter of Britain's former prime minister James Callaghan and wife of UK ambassador Peter Jay. Salt, meet wound.

She would write her way out of this. Maybe a book—one for adults, not children.

✳ ✳ ✳

Nora fell hard for New York City, and distance made the heart grow fonder. Even then it was clear that she could never live anywhere else. She didn't belong anywhere else. She felt discombobulated when her parents moved the family out of claustrophobic Manhattan, where she was born on May 19, 1941, and into a strange new world populated by strawberry blondes: Beverly Hills. Her five-year-old self wondered, *What am I doing here?*

What Henry and Phoebe Ephron were doing there: making it in showbiz. In 1943, the married screenwriting team landed a seven-year contract with 20th Century Fox amid the success of their play *Three's a Family*, a comedy about a miserable young mom who moves into her parents' West 110th Street apartment. Phoebe's idea. While she wasn't ha-ha funny, an irony observed by daughter Delia (who *is* ha-ha funny), Phoebe showed a comedian's instinct for spinning wackiness from unhappiness. She used her relatives as fodder. Her work became her identity. Speaking to a journalist during the couple's professional heyday, Phoebe proclaimed: "I don't go in the kitchen very often, except for ice cubes for a drink."

The Phoebe and Henry Ephron production *Three's a Family* lasted 497 performances on Broadway; Henry directed the stage show, but not the movie adaptation. Their creative collaboration had taken off when Phoebe—a restless stay-at-home mom who lived with Henry, baby Nora, and her parents in an apartment on 110th Street—became her husband's official writing partner.

"My dad had written a bunch of plays and I think Mommy got tired of his plays not selling and she said, 'I'll write one with you,'" Amy, the youngest of their four girls, relayed in the Nora-centric documentary *Everything Is Copy*, directed by Nora's son, Jacob Bernstein. "And it was sort of a hit. And then they moved to LA. And I think Mommy felt, and rightly so, that she'd broken some kind of glass ceiling."

They wrote the screenplay for the 1944 romantic comedy *Bride by Mistake*, starring Laraine Day as Norah Hunter, an heiress who pretends to be a secretary in order to fool gold-digging prospective suitors. Among their splashiest credits: the 1956 movie version of Rodgers and Hammerstein's *Carousel*, featuring Gordon MacRae and Shirley Jones as doomed but vocally gifted lovers, and 1957's *Desk Set*, a stylish battle-of-the-sexes romance that reunited Spencer Tracy and Katharine Hepburn as an IBM engineer and the equally brainy supervisor of a TV network's old-school research department at Rockefeller Center. Kate fears that Spencer, a productivity pro who means to install a computer in the office, will make her job irrelevant. It's no small thing, putting a nice lady out of business. Most inconveniently, an attraction grows.

Given Phoebe's disregard for traditional gender roles during a period when women were expected to stay home (and out of the workforce), it's fitting that she chose to name Nora after the iconoclastic heroine of the 1879 Henrik Ibsen play *A Doll's House*, which tells the saga of a soul-searching, independence-seeking wife who packs her bags and leaves her family behind. Phoebe, a Jane Austen fan, preferred that her young daughters read books about plucky female protagonists—Eloise, Madeline, and Dorothy Gale—and she passed down their stories like heirlooms. Nora's first memory of Phoebe was her mother teaching her how to read— and Phoebe's joyous response when she actually *could*.

In Beverly Hills, the Ephrons lived in a Spanish stucco home with 14 rooms on Linden Drive, just down the street from the property where gangster Bugsy Siegel was gunned down—a bit of trivia that fascinated Delia, the second eldest. Dinner was served nightly at six thirty, with the siblings swapping stories that entertained their parents. "That was when every time I said something funny, my dad said, 'That's a great line. Write it down,'" Delia wrote.

Phoebe, who recited poetry at the table, imparted a litany of rules: "Never buy a red coat." "Don't worship celebrities." "Don't join sororities."

Nora paid witness to Henry and Phoebe's insider-y parties, which drew boldfaced names like Dorothy Parker, the sharpest of the wits, as sparkling conversation and cocktails flowed.

Cut to 1957. Nora's prophetic interaction with the actor who practically invented the word *debonair*, the Mid-Atlantic accent, and the essence of George Clooney. The event: *An Affair to Remember*.

"My mother took me to a screening in Westwood, and I just lost it," Nora said. "There I was, a hopeless teenage girl awash in salt water, and we stood up to leave, and my mother introduces me to Cary Grant. I blubbered that this was the greatest movie I'd ever seen. I now look at this movie and say, 'What was I thinking?' But I could play the last 10 minutes of that movie for you now, and we'd be crying."

That was also the year Nora saw *Funny Face*, a romantic comedy that cast Audrey Hepburn as a winsome bookstore clerk turned model and Fred Astaire as an opportunistic fashion photographer. The 1950s prized hourglass shapes as a feminine ideal; Nora, the insecure 15-year-old Beverly Hills High School girl so desperate for bigger breasts that she once purchased something called a Mark Eden Bust Developer, was coming of age in a town where looks—the right look—meant absolutely everything.

She'd catch a matinee every Saturday around noon. She watched Marilyn. Doris Day. Jane Powell. She'd sit there thinking: *This breathy-voiced bombshell isn't me. This flaxen-haired ingénue isn't me.* Enter Audrey. "She was as close as you could get to someone who was interesting and quirky and smart," said Nora. "You saw her in that bookstore, in *Funny Face*, in that little black turtleneck sweater, and it was the most compelling article of clothing anyone wore in a movie when I was growing up."

Nora had a side job at a local bookstore (Martindale's, earning 75 cents an hour, once gift-wrapping a book for Cary Grant) and dreamed of lofty things. As the class of 1959's "Most Likely to Succeed"—she graduated number one out of 309 students—Nora wielded enough clout at her school newspaper to fire future billionaire Barry Diller, who would go on to run Paramount; launch a fourth broadcast TV network, Fox; and marry wrap-dress fashion icon Diane von Fürstenberg. Who knew?

Diller was 14 years old at the time. As an adult, he recalled, "There was not a lot of feminine about Nora...she had one eye that was kinda unevenly closed. Or open."

Still, she impressed the judges at an LA junior essay competition, winning first prize: a pair of tickets to the premiere of a movie starring Doris Day, that paragon of postwar conservatism.

While Phoebe's daughters swooned at the movies, she was making them. She took pride in an atypical path and urged the sisters Ephron to follow suit. Delia summed up Phoebe's ideology: "You will have a career like me. You will work. You will be a writer. You will leave Los Angeles. You will go to New York City. You will work. Career, career, career." Phoebe would repeat: "Everything is copy."

If everything was copy, then it had to be sugarcoated, scrubbed clean of self-pity, and played for laughs—or risk Phoebe's rejection. "If you came back to her with a sad story, she had no interest in it whatsoever," Nora said. "'Turn it into a funny story. Get back to me. I will be interested.'"

Nora studied, then mastered, the Tao of Phoebe: "When you slip on a banana peel, people laugh at you; but when you tell people you slipped on a banana peel, it's your laugh. So you become the hero rather than the victim of the joke."

She provided inspiration (and free material) for Henry and Phoebe's zippy 1961 play *Take Her, She's Mine*, which debuted to stellar sales at New York's Biltmore Theatre on 47th Street and referenced her letters home from Wellesley College. Precocious coed Mollie Michaelson, Nora's alter ego, proclaims: "He doesn't know it yet, but I have met a boy from Harvard who's going to marry me."

Not everything was fit for print. Concerned with decorum

(the table had to be set just so) and loath to show weakness, the emotionally distant Phoebe did not choose to make "copy" of her marital woes and self-destructive slide into alcoholism while Nora was in her teens. These could not be mined for laughs. Things got worse after Nora left the nest. Late at night, Phoebe and Henry (also a drinker) waged bitter verbal battles, traumatizing Delia, Hallie, and Amy (all of whom, like their big sister, became writer-subscribers to the "Everything is copy" mantra, in one form or another). "When she found out my father was fooling around with other women, she didn't walk out on him like Ibsen's Nora," said Hallie, writing in *O* magazine. She stayed, and stewed. "Alcohol ignited her anger, and sometimes they fought from midnight to dawn," Hallie continued. "By the time Delia and I were both in college, things got so bad that Amy ran away and ended up moving in with Nora and her first husband in an apartment near Central Park."

Henry and Phoebe returned to New York. Six years after the curtain fell on *Take Her, She's Mine*, the 1968 spectacle of *Hair*—a free-love, pro-nudity, antiwar rock musical—lit up the Great White Way. The Ephrons and their PG-rated collaborations were going out of style. "It was hard to change forty years of thinking that sex is a private thing," Henry wrote of himself and Phoebe in his memoirs. All the drinking wrecked Phoebe's liver. She died on October 13, 1971, when Nora was 30 and Amy 18; she was hospitalized with cirrhosis—immediate cause of death: an overdose of sleeping pills administered by Henry—and had remarked to Nora, "You're a reporter. Take notes."

The next decade, Nora took those words very seriously while chronicling the demise of her own messy marriage to a cheating partner in a roman à clef, *Heartburn*, which deployed comedy to share a painful personal story. "The truth is that if my father weren't my father, he would be one of the men he hates; he is incorrigibly faithless and thoroughly narcissistic, to such an extent that I tend to forget he's also capable of being a real peach," she wrote.

By 1993, Nora, partnering with Delia on *Sleepless in Seattle*, would undergo a decidedly unintentional rebrand as a specialist in the lost art of fairy-tale romance. Meg Ryan seemed an ideal mother figure and Tom Hanks the perfect father; together they embodied the kind of joie de vivre that Henry and Phoebe might have prolonged had darker realities not intervened.

"My sister Delia says this, and it's true," Nora recalled. "When we were growing up, we used to love to hear the story of how our parents met and fell in love and eloped one summer when they were both camp counselors. It was so much a part of our lives, a song sung again and again, and no matter what happened, no matter how awful things became between the two of them, we always knew that our parents had once been madly in love."

The retelling of their first date ended with a punchline.

Henry: Will you marry me?

Phoebe: Can I read your work?

❋ ❋ ❋

While attending Wellesley, Nora Ephron outlined requirements for her ideal husband: Loyal Democrat? Check. Reads the *New Republic*? Check. Plays tennis? Check. Speaks French? Check, check, and check.

A few years later, she fell under the spell of Dan Greenburg.

Twenty-five years and 11 months old, Nora said "I do" for the first time. Can you imagine if she waited one more month? It was

1967, and from Nora's perspective (which she'd grow to regret), a 26-year-old bride might as well be a 100-year-old bride.

Let's talk about the groom: early 30s. Chicago-born beta male. Acerbic, dry sense of humor. Magazine editor. Successful author. Unabashed cat lover. Catnip to a rising star *New York Post* reporter who had dreamed about (a) moving back to New York City, (b) becoming a journalist, and (c) dating a journalist, too.

Dan had a strong jaw, wide smile, and expressive, watchful eyes with Paul McCartney bedroom lids. If an actor were to play him in a romantic comedy, it might be a young Hank Azaria or Alan Alda, somebody who projects intelligence and quirk. In 1970, he went on *The David Susskind Show* and said he felt "anthropomorphic about things like wastepaper," so instead of throwing out wastepaper ("a rejection"), he saved sheets of it. Copy that for cardboard, string, and manila envelopes.

"I've always liked odd and interesting-looking men because I'm odd and interesting-looking myself, and I always figured I had a better shot at them than the conventionally good-looking ones," Nora revealed in *Heartburn*, spending several pages lampooning a Dan-inspired first husband character (Charlie) as a "low-grade lunatic who kept hamsters" (instead of cats) and had one cryogenically frozen when it died (correction: Dan never froze a cat—or a hamster for that matter). Charlie, according to narrator Nora, "slept with my oldest friend Brenda." (Hmmmmm.)

Dan and Nora got married in the Rainbow Room atop Rockefeller Center in a ceremony officiated by a rabbi. They shared a lavender apartment and several cats around whom they spoke in high-pitched voices. (This was before cats ruled the internet, and speaking to one's cat in a high-pitched voice was deemed generally acceptable, if not encouraged.)

Dan wrote the 1964 humor book *How to Be a Jewish Mother,*

which also happened to be the bestselling nonfiction book of 1965, an accomplishment that most certainly appealed to Nora. It was easy to succumb to the charm of an interesting (and interesting-looking) male writer, a Clark Kent to her Lois Lane, who thought being smart was sexy.

"We would have dinner parties," Dan said, "and Nora would go up to celebrities she had never met and say, 'Hi, my name is Nora Ephron; if I invited you to dinner to my house, would you come?' And she was so adorable and so appealing that I don't think anybody ever said no. And so we got to run with a very fast crowd. We had Mike Nichols over to dinner. We had Buck Henry. Joan Didion."

Writing features and essays for *Esquire* and *New York*, Nora rode the wave of New Journalism that swept up Didion, Tom Wolfe, and Gay Talese, voice-y writers who flouted the traditional who-what-when-where-why rules of news reporting and made themselves part of the story. What Nora had in spades that many of her equally driven peers did not was a point of view that engaged (and sometimes enraged) the reader; an unrelenting itch to shake things up, cause trouble, and undo emperors and empresses whom she found to have no clothes; a voice demanding to be heard that people actually wanted to listen to. Hers was simultaneously warm and icy, winking and withering. She could be brutal, eviscerating her subjects with wry detachment—and if she suffered fools in person, she rarely suffered them on the page. As a cultural and media critic, she spared no one, no woman: an *Esquire* profile of Helen Gurley Brown stung the pioneering *Cosmopolitan* editor as oversensitive, "Almost but not quite tasteless," yet also celebrated Brown as totally genuine in her motivation to help women succeed as she had. *Post* publisher Dorothy Schiff, her ex-boss, was "silly," "frothy," and "giddy." Dorothy Parker, whose fame she sought to emulate early in her career, had an "almost unbearably girlish sensibility." While Gloria Steinem represented "the only remotely chic thing" about the women's movement, Betty Friedan threatened to undermine it through her petty, "thoroughly irrational hatred of Steinem."

Among Nora Ephron's biggest targets: Nora Ephron. In May 1972, she achieved what she considered her breakthrough as a real Writer with a capital *W*—a confessional, self-deprecating, angry, funny column in *Esquire* that lamented the small size of her chest and zinged women who whined about their fuller busts. "A Few Words about Breasts" described an obsession that had its roots in adolescence. "If I had had them, I would have been a completely different person," she wrote.

In July of that year, she informed the magazine's predominantly male readers that she had a rape fantasy involving "faceless" men tearing her clothes off. The startling, shock jock–ish confession riled second-wave feminists fighting the good fight but drew attention to a gray area that confused Nora: "So many of the conscious and unconscious ways men and women treat each other have to do with romantic and sexual fantasies that are deeply ingrained, not just in society but in literature. The movement may manage to clean up the mess in society, but I don't know whether it can ever clean up the mess in our minds."

She slipped on banana peels, telling everyone.

"I am skinny and have a long face, long chin, and dark hair and a snaggletooth that I've worked very hard to get," she banana-peeled to a writer doing a profile on her, writing a physical description *for* him. "My hair droops over my left eye so no one will notice my left eyelid droops."

It's hard to believe in this age of digital overshares, but such candor was deemed radical. People on the outside of clubby New

York media circles began to care what this young, fearless writer had to say about women's issues, about other women, and, especially, about herself.

In the meantime, she and Dan had drifted apart. As her *Heartburn* doppelganger would divulge, those "Charlie" quirks had begun to grate. She wrote, "At first I thought he was charming and eccentric. And then I didn't. Then I wanted to kill him. Every time he got on a plane, I would imagine the plane crash, and the funeral, and what I would wear to the funeral and flirting at the funeral, and how soon I could start dating after the funeral."

She initially tested the bit on *The Dick Cavett Show*, looking glamorous in a black jumpsuit and deflating Dan in her nasally drawl: "He's like on this plane—it's terrible—and then I get to marry Mike Nichols!"

Nora partly pegged her stifling disinterest to the times, leaving Dan off the hook. Sort of.

"My first husband is a perfectly nice person, although he's pathologically attached to his cats," she remembered in her 2006 essay collection, *I Feel Bad about My Neck*. "It's 1972, the height of the women's movement, and everyone is getting a divorce, even people whose husbands don't have pathological attachments to their cats. My husband is planning for us to take a photo safari through Africa, and I say to him, 'I can't go on this trip.'"

She changed her mind. Off they went. "It's a wonderful trip. When we come back, I tell my husband that I want a divorce."

Goodbye, Dan Greenburg.

* * *

The signs were there from the very beginning. Before Nora Ephron met the man who would be her second husband, at Marie Brenner's party in 1973, Carl Bernstein had something of a reputation as a ladies' man—a fun, sexy ladies' man with warm brown eyes; full, kissable lips; and thick, shaggy black hair. His look conveyed 1970s rebel cool, but his resume read Washington Establishment: Carl became a celebrity overnight as one-half of the *Washington Post* reporting team that scooped Watergate through intel from a shadowy source nicknamed Deep Throat and helped link Nixon's dirty tricks to the June 17, 1972, break-in at the Democratic Party's National Committee headquarters. Two years later, Woodward and Bernstein published a bestselling book about the scandal, *All the President's Men*, and two years afterward, Alan J. Pakula directed a film adaptation that starred Dustin Hoffman as Carl (the less disciplined but better writer) and Robert Redford as Bob (the methodical workhorse who, for a time, made better life choices). It won four Oscars, including best supporting actor for Jason Robards, who played the legendary *Post* editor and newsroom lion Ben Bradlee.

Naturally, Nora was in the thick of it.

She loved to be at the center of things, around the very people who were making things happen, especially if they were fellow writers, authors, thinkers, doers, movers, and shakers who shared her New York energy, liberal views, and elite status as a media socialite who hopped from dinner party to dinner party, crossing New York City lines for the Hamptons and gossiping all the way there. At that moment, Carl was a prince. Barely 30, the University of Maryland dropout managed without a college degree to make his name as the hottest sleuth at the hottest newspaper in the nation at the hottest time to be a journalist; like Nora, he was a social animal. Each had a sense of blurry boundaries between the personal and the professional; their work defined them, and so did the company they kept. Sure, talent stood for something, but so did showing up at the right party. You might encounter your next Deep Throat. Shake the hand of a producer who wants to make your next screenplay. Lock eyes with your future wife.

Marie Brenner, a New York–based investigative journalist with a warm, sophisticated presence, briefly dated Carl starting in May 1972. The flirtation ended when Watergate began. The next year, he found himself at Marie's Manhattan shindig chatting up Nora Ephron. He jotted down her digits.

"I was dazzled, and I did not really know who [she] was in terms of her work," said Carl in *Everything Is Copy*. "We had this amazing conversation. I said I would call her in a few days. And I didn't wait a few days. I called her the next day."

The next day: Marie Brenner gets a phone call from Nora.

"Are you really, really finished?"

"Oh yeah, long ago."

Nora felt a gravitational pull, and Carl did, too. They were similar in several ways: she an atheist Jew by way of Beverly Hills and he a secular Jew by way of Silver Spring, Maryland. She a daughter of alcoholic Hollywood screenwriters who wrote popular films that appealed to mainstream America while operating an erratic, sometimes terrifying, household behind the scenes; he a son of a progressive lawyer father and activist mother whose affiliations with Communism in the 1940s led to heavy, sometimes terrifying, FBI scrutiny during the McCarthy era. (The Feds even crashed Carl's bar mitzvah.) Like Nora, Carl had been married before, to former *Post* reporter Carol Honsa.

Childhood drama and childless first marriages aside, he represented what Nora doubtless deemed an equal match. The missing piece of a power couple puzzle, a partner who could make life fun and exciting. Because being single was *the worst*. She found the notion of going dateless to a dinner party a distraction. Carl solved that problem. He could also persuade this true-blue New Yorker to do the unthinkable: move to Washington. And she hated Washington with a passion.

"As happens in great love affairs, you want the other person to know who you are at the most intimate and deepest levels," Carl said. "I think we came very quickly to a deep understanding of who the other person was."

Back to the part about his wandering eye: It was an ill-kept secret that Carl Bernstein was something of a Casanova, even before Watergate fame lured women who were turned on by the whole "bringing down a president" thing.

Carl was "so intense in his aura that you would be swept away kind of in his ferocity, in a kind of enchanting way," said Brenner. "I don't think she questioned him. I think they fell madly in love. They were just absolutely, at that period, made for each other."

In a 2003 interview with *Washingtonian* magazine, Chuck Conconi, a former newsman at the *Washington Star*, recalled an awkward brush with young Carl's first wife: "One day when I was at the *Star*, I was sent to cover a dinner where Lyndon Johnson was speaking at the Shoreham Hotel. I ran into Carl, and we chatted for about five minutes. Three or four days later, I ran into Carol and she said to me, half-joking, 'I didn't like how you kept Carl out that late the other night.' I looked at her strangely. Then I got it, but it was too late. She just said, 'Oh,' and walked away."

Nora's close friend Liz Smith, the famous gossip columnist, observed Carl flirting up Lucie Arnaz, daughter of Lucy and Desi, at her Bridgehampton dinner party. "Carl! Nora is right across the room," she declared. There was also the time when the newlyweds attended a Tavern on the Green charity event, and a photographer captured Nora—apparently mortified—looking away while another woman sat on Carl's lap. A picture, as they say, is worth a thousand words. Look no further.

People talk, and people said Carl saw other women when he and Nora were dating. She pulled the plug. He vowed to stay true, and she took him back.

"It seemed to me that the desire to get married—which, I regret to say, I believe is fundamental and primal in women—is followed almost immediately by an equally fundamental and primal urge, which is to be single again. But there was Mark," she revealed in *Heartburn*, her novelistic account of Carl's betrayal, transforming Carl into fictional political columnist Mark Feldman: "Forever and ever, he said. Forever and ever and ever, he said.... For a long time, I didn't believe him. And then I believed him. I believed in change. I believed in metamorphosis. I believed in redemption. I believed in Mark. My marriage to him was as willful an act as I have ever committed; I married him against all evidence. I married him believing that marriage doesn't work, that love dies, that passion fades, and in doing so I became the kind of romantic only a cynic is capable of being."

After two and a half years, the pair made it official on April 15, 1976, in a Manhattan civil ceremony that took place shortly after Nora's group therapy session with celebrity psychologist Mildred Newman. Afterward, she laid into the limo driver for taking Third Avenue rather than the FDR on the way to their reception at the St. Regis. Bob Woodward, an Illinois-raised straight arrow who never really clicked with Nora nor fully understood her focus on details he considered frivolous, witnessed the nuptials. He once told the *Washingtonian*: "I remember I heard Nora talk about being at some dinner and holding a discourse on the kind of lettuce that had been served: 'Can you believe they served that lettuce?' There was just this sense that she had been offended. People agreed with her, and maybe I agreed with her, but it just wasn't the way I lived."

Friends and enemies alike gazed curiously and with envy at what they perceived to be a lucky matrimonial merger between two writers who'd achieved resounding success. ("They had the perfect life," an unnamed source—not Deep Throat—observed in the March 1983 issue of *New York* amid the *Heartburn* fallout.) When it turned out that Carl, like the president he helped bring down, was up to dirty tricks, these friends and enemies shared deep satisfaction in watching the castle crumble and the queen being humiliated in the worst way imaginable. You could cut the schadenfreude with a knife.

"She was really a well-known journalist and she was really successful at it and a lot of people were jealous of that," Delia has said. "And then, lo and behold, Carl, you know, that awful thing happened when she was pregnant, and people thought, Oh, she's just gonna go down. And they were all very excited about it. People do get excited about things like that, especially when it's a woman who's gotten uppity."

By 1979, Nora had written four well-received collections of her journalism, columns, and musings on the media—including *Wallflower at the Orgy, Crazy Salad,* and *Scribble Scribble*—and dipped her toes into screenwriting. It was in her DNA. At one point, she and Carl had tried, and failed, to retool William Goldman's original *All the President's Men* script.

"One scene from it is in the movie, a really nifty move by Bernstein where he outfakes a secretary to get in to see someone. And it didn't happen—they made it up. It was a phony Hollywood moment," said Goldman dismissively in *Adventures in the Screen Trade*, his half memoir, half manual for screenwriters.

Nora and Carl's script was rejected, and Goldman won an Oscar for *All the President's Men*. In hindsight, Nora admitted that she and Carl should not have attempted to revise an expert's draft. On the other hand, she learned a lot about technique. Goldman, gushed Nora, "does things so economically that you can't believe it."

Nora and Carl's joint effort, though a failure, opened doors for Nora and led to *Perfect Gentlemen*, the TV movie with Lauren Bacall she'd rather forget. Intriguingly, Nora wrote a mother-daughter rock musical that never saw the light of day. The premise, via the journalist Rachel Abramowitz: "the daughter of a singer who outdoes her mother by becoming a rock star." (Entertainment executives, if you're listening, it is never too late to greenlight this movie. It demands to be seen.)

Also stashed away somewhere: *The Eastern Shuttle*, Nora and Carl's romance about lovers commuting each weekend between New York City and Washington on the Eastern Airlines shuttle, now defunct. Lynn Nesbit, the literary agent who repped Nora, shared the script with her colleague Bob Bookman at International Creative Management (ICM). Though it wasn't Nora's best work, Bookman thought the main characters "shared an easygoing equality of status" that seemed original and contemporary.

While *Eastern Shuttle* never flew, Nora and Carl were working on a family. Nora embraced her latest role as mother to son Jacob Bernstein, born August 22, 1978, and prepared to welcome baby number 2.

Shortly after Nora discovered the children's book with Margaret Jay's declaration of love, she gave birth prematurely to Max Bernstein on November 16, 1979, at New York's Mount Sinai Hospital. Carl, in the doghouse but keeping up appearances, patronized incestuous writers' hang Elaine's on Second and 88th following hospital visits. In a gossipy *People* dispatch (titled "Can Carl Bernstein Handle Deep Troth?"), an anonymous source (not Deep Throat) blabbed, "Nora could forgive him. But she is down and broken up by it. She went a little crazy over the whole thing."

The news startled close friends like *New Yorker* writer Ken Auletta and *Washington Post* columnist Richard Cohen. Auletta and wife, Amanda "Binky" Urban, had recently hosted Nora and Carl for dinner at their Bridgehampton home. They seemed over the moon.

Nora's antenna had raised the past several months. She reportedly questioned Carl that summer about his friendship with Margaret, which he played down as nothing. But as friends and family can attest, Nora was often right; if she smelled smoke, there was probably fire. Indeed, she had also unearthed the existence of an antique porcelain box (inscription: "I Love You Truly").

Out for revenge, she dialed up Liz Smith to dish the dirt. "One day Nora rang me up and said in her characteristic determined kind of way: 'Liz, I have a story for you. Carl and I are going to divorce! Please write it,'" Smith recounted in her memoir, *Natural Blonde*. With a heavy heart, Smith published the news a few days before Christmas. "One night at a party I ran into Carl and he forced me up against a wall, started weeping, and told me I had ruined his life," she said.

Meanwhile, Knopf editor Bob Gottlieb and his wife, actress Maria Tucci, opened their New York town house to the newly single mom. She brought her boys, a baby nurse, and a Saul Steinberg painting. "My heart was broken," she said. "I was terrified about what was going to happen to my children and me." Her shrink, Mildred Newman, author of the 1970s self-help bible *How to Be*

Your Own Best Friend, remarked, "You have to understand something: You were going to leave him eventually."

* * *

When one love affair dies, another sprouts anew: take the serendipitous missed connection between Dennis Quaid and Meg Ryan on Manhattan's Upper West Side circa the 1980s.

"We didn't know each other at the time, and he was walking— I remember this day, although I don't remember him—and I had on a long, strange green sweater," Meg said. "And he remembers seeing me walk up Amsterdam Avenue to this health food store, and the way I swung my arms in this sweater. This is, like, five years before we met!"

Doing press for *Sleepless in Seattle*, Meg used Dennis's memory to illustrate her belief in romantic destiny. A seedier story she told about her early days in the city involves getting attacked at knifepoint. It underscored the true grit beneath the giggle. There she was, 21 or so, when a mugger brandished a blade to her neck in the foyer of her walk-up apartment building. Marveled Meg: "I just took my head and smacked it into his stomach. I couldn't scream or anything. I was just kicking and biting and punching— it was unbelievable! And he ran away. And after that, I knew that about myself, which is a great thing to know."

November 19, 1961. Sixty miles away in Fairfield, Connecticut, Margaret Mary Emily Anne Hyra arrived crying on cue. Her parents, math teacher Harry and housewife Susan, called her Peggy. She had an older sister, Dana, and two younger siblings, Annie and Andrew. She was a popular and magnetic student at Bethel High, a vision in crewneck sweaters, preppy collars, and soft curls.

Skirts weren't her jam. "Usually in high school, when a beautiful, smart person arrives, you want to hate her," said Tracy Parsons, Meg's friend from way back when. "You want to scratch her eyes out. There was something about her that stood out from the day she walked in, a charisma thing. Everybody wanted to be her friend."

These credits you won't find on IMDb: National Honor Society. Class secretary. Conehead (she played one in a *Saturday Night Live* spoof). Homecoming queen (she'd remind you that the original queen was kicked out of school, and only then did she, the runner-up, assume the crown). Alongside her yearbook photo, a note: "Inane Happiness."

To the outside observer she led the perfect life. Or so it seemed.

In 1976, 15-year-old Meg watched her guilt-ridden mother, Susan—as if channeling Nora Helmer in *A Doll's House*—make the unorthodox move to divorce Harry and leave the kids with their father until she found her footing. Meg said Susan fled to chase an acting career in New York. No way, responded Susan, giving her version to *Vanity Fair*: "My husband told me when I told him I wanted to have a divorce that he could not support the children or the house if he had to be the one to leave it. He said, 'I can't afford to rent an apartment for myself and support you and the children, so their whole lifestyle is going to be ruined.' That's why I left—*honestly*."

What transpires when you're a teenager can linger into adulthood as a defining—motivating—chapter in your autobiography. "The thing I want to be clear about is that it has nothing to do with something that happened when I was 15," Meg said of her rift with Susan. "I'm over it. It's this long-running personality, character thing."

Susan had a role in Meg's early ingénue days. In the late 1970s she began teaching English and theater history at the New England boarding school Choate Rosemary Hall (MVPs: John F.

Kennedy, Edward Albee, Glenn Close). Previously, she assisted a casting director, connecting Meg to agents. Meg changed her last name from Hyra to Ryan. She dropped out of New York University's journalism program. She got commercials, her first movie (George Cukor's *Rich and Famous*, playing Candice Bergen's daughter), and a soap opera (*As the World Turns*, breaking hearts as Betsy Stewart, whose candlelit church wedding to Steve Andropoulos drew 20 million viewers).

Yes, she could cry on cue. But you never saw the wheels spinning. An open and giving performer, Meg ripped open her soul and laid it bare. The fact that she wore a frilly Little Bo Peep dress of nightmares to deliver fake vows? Irrelevant. You still believed every word she said and every tear she shed. There was no Meg Ryan. There was only Betsy Stewart.

The Susan Lucci route was not for Meg. Nothing wrong with a cushy, New York–based soap gig, but Meg had bigger fish to fry out in Hollywood. *Top Gun* proved a catch. As Goose's fun-loving wife, Carole, she pushed the "bubbly" button and kept her finger firmly on it, memorably yelping: "GOOSE, YA BIG STUD! TAKE ME TO BED OR LOSE ME FOREVER!"

Off camera, she dated movie husband Anthony Edwards. The baby-faced character actor appeared in *Revenge of the Nerds* and *The Sure Thing*, Rob Reiner's 1985 romantic comedy introducing John Cusack in his first leading role. Cusack, then 18, played a charmingly obnoxious college freshman who desperately pines for an uptight bookworm out of his league. Meg auditioned, but Daphne Zuniga, with her cool glare, was deemed the best fit. A couple years later Meg read for Princess Buttercup in the Reiner-directed fantasy *The Princess Bride*, based on William Goldman's novel. Goldman declared Buttercup "the most beautiful woman in a hundred years."

"Rob said, 'If William Goldman had written that Buttercup were the most adorable girl in the world, she'd be perfect,'" says casting director Jane Jenkins. "He thought that he needed more than adorableness, and as pretty as she is, she just wasn't the most beautiful girl in the world."

Rob wanted Robin Wright for Buttercup. Adorable girlfriend roles continued in Meg's direction. She met Dennis in Los Angeles on their 1987 sci-fi comedy *Innerspace*; he played a pilot, shrunken as part of a science experiment, with Meg his adorable girlfriend. "I remember thinking I had to stay away from him," she said. "You know, *him with the women.*" Then she stole a glimpse of Dennis's six-pack. "He was in a trailer getting body makeup on. All of us were there staring at his abs going, 'Is there a sound those things make?'"

Look but don't touch: Meg was seeing Anthony, and Dennis was involved with *Back to the Future*'s Lea Thompson. Little did they know what the future would bring; Lea was not it. "We went to dinner, I think once, as friends," Dennis said. "I really liked her and was convinced that she didn't like me—of course. Then on *D.O.A.*, we were both free. And it happened. When you fall in love, there's that immediate realization that you're in love and you go, 'Oh *no*! Not now! *No.*' I'm sure she had that—she couldn't believe she was falling in love with someone like *me*. I'm from Texas; I come from a different style than what she came from."

It was no secret that Dennis, brother of actor Randy Quaid, liked to party and have a good time. His cocaine use had intensified. Meg was in the dark. "By the time I was doing *The Big Easy*, in the late 1980s, I was a mess," said Dennis, writing about his addiction in *Newsweek*. "I was getting an hour of sleep a night. I had a reputation for being a 'bad boy,' which seemed like a good thing, but basically I just had my head up my ass. I'd wake up, snort a line, and swear I wasn't going to do it again that day."

Their next film, *D.O.A.*, a middling thriller, starred Dennis as murder-target college professor Dexter Cornell and Meg as a student whose arm he superglues to his. Preposterous! But their chemistry crackled: There was a real sexual charge that audiences felt, especially as a fan blew air into their faces during a steamy kiss. "She matches Mr. Quaid's ability to make third-rate dialogue sound better than it is, but even they can't make this sound better than second-rate," wrote the *New York Times* in its review.

Lightning struck on the movie's Austin shoot. Enjoying a night off, Dennis and Meg wound up sitting side by side in the sort of raucous establishment where revelers boogie on tables, *Coyote Ugly*–style. He reached out and touched her.

✳ ✳ ✳

As a twice-divorcée, one of Nora's biggest fears was following in the path of so many other former wives who vanished to Connecticut, sliding off the grid and into obscurity. She actively avoided a quiet life in self-imposed exile.

Scouting apartments in February 1980, she stumbled upon perfection on the Upper West Side. "Head over heels. This was it. At first sight. Eureka. Ten steps in and I said, 'I'll take it,'" she relayed in the essay "Moving On," her love letter to the Apthorp.

It was a sight to behold. Erected after the turn of the 20th century, the Italian Renaissance Revivalist residence at the bustling intersection of 79th and Broadway achieved landmark status in 1969; it drips Old World glamour, boasting a charming, cobblestoned courtyard with a fountain at the center and an ornate wrought iron gate accented with gilded gazelle heads, a touch of Liberace meets Lake Como. It's the kind of place that might attract very fancy ghosts as houseguests. It's the kind of urban sanctuary where Nora could confront—and finally exorcise—the ghosts of husbands past.

From her five-bedroom abode on the fifth floor (rent: $1,500 per month, a steep price for 1980 but so worth it), she supported the kids and herself with moneymaking screenwriting jobs. That meant she could afford to spend four months out of the year and summers on Long Island, finishing the novel that she'd proclaim a "male nightmare." She dedicated *Heartburn* to Bob, her editor, and his wife, Maria. She created a fictional Nora, a successful cookbook author and TV personality named Rachel Samstat, who—seven months into her pregnancy—discovers her husband, Mark, is having an affair with their friend. The words, like tiny daggers, drew blood: Carl's, Margaret's, and also her own.

Of Carl, or "Mark Feldman," she sneered, "the man is capable of having sex with a venetian blind."

Margaret, aka Thelma Rice, was a "fairly tall person with a neck as long as an arm and a nose as long as a thumb and you should see her legs, never mind her feet, which are sort of splayed."

Nora, aka Rachel, gets told by a producer that her on-camera presence is similar to that of Howard Cosell, riffing: "'Too New York' is what the last network that was approached about me responded, which is a cute way of being anti-Semitic, but who cares? I'd rather be too New York than too anything else. Anyway, I don't belong on a network. I have the kind of odd and interesting features that work out all right in real life but not at all on the screen, so I'm far better off on public television, where the producers and cameramen are used to Julia Child and are pathetically grateful that I'm not quite as tall."

Nora dreamed of being Barbara Walters. She auditioned in 1973 for a co-anchor role on the *CBS Morning News*; she was passed over for Sally Quinn, her friend and fellow journalist and the future Mrs. Ben Bradlee. Sally, a blonde with a dazzling smile, inspired *Heartburn*'s nosy Betty Searle. She lasted six short months at CBS, detailing her ordeal in another talker of a book, *We're Going to Make You a Star.* In her debut *New York* column—title: "A Star Is Born"—Nora dissected her disappointment, quoting Lillian Hellman: "I was just jealous of women who took advantage of men, because I didn't know how to do it."

Published by Knopf in 1983, the 179-page truth bomb titillated the literati among whom Carl and Nora had moved, all the hype helping to churn the book from esoteric gossip fodder into national page-turner. It would touch a nerve among women (and men!) who saw *Heartburn* as a kind of catharsis. Most readers could not find Elaine's on a map, but they understood heartbreak and humiliation.

"I think probably the feeling I like least in the whole world is feeling dumb," Nora explained. "If your mom loves you for being smart, you feel idiotic being dumb—and I feel dumb about that marriage."

Many in New York's chattering class decided the writer had gone too far. "I want to see her crawl over broken glass," sniped an unnamed enemy (most likely not Deep Throat) to *New York* magazine.

Said Liz Smith: "I'm 100 percent for her having written the book, but I'm a little in awe of how she's not too worried about what the effect's going to be. I think she's probably made a problem for herself."

Said Carl: "Obviously, I wish Nora hadn't written it. But I've always known that Nora writes about everything that happens in her life. And I think the book is just like Nora—it's very clever."

He would later publicly blast the book as having a "kind of Joan Rivers sensibility," "a nasty tone," and an undignified, unserious approach to marital troubles in contrast to works by Philip Roth and Woody Allen. In an interview with *Vanity Fair*, Nora would argue: "There is barely an American writer in the last 50 years who has gotten divorced and not written something about it, so give me a break. I just don't see anybody attacking any of them—but they're all men. It was quite fascinating to me that when a woman did it, everyone started worrying terribly about the poor children."

The following year, Nora and Alice Arlen earned an Oscar nomination for co-writing the script for the Mike Nichols drama *Silkwood*, which starred Meryl Streep as Karen Silkwood. The real-life nuclear whistleblower perished in a car accident. Or was it murder?

The liftoff had been rough. But it helped that Meryl was keen on playing the working-class Oklahoma rebel. And who better than Nora Ephron to Hollywoodize the story with a journalistic eye? Accuracy here was key, lest lawyers pounce. Nora needed research help, so she recruited her friend Alice, a skilled screenwriter drawn to stories about underdogs. She also happened to know the lawyer on the Silkwood trial. "Nora had visited our ranch and thought I knew more about rednecks than she did," Alice, married to writer Michael J. Arlen, told me. "Our deal was that I would get paid half of what she did unless it was made into a movie in which case we would each get 50 percent," she said.

Arlene Donovan, an agent at ICM, suggested Nora to her agency colleague and boyfriend Sam Cohn, who at one point repped Nora, Meryl, *and* Mike Nichols. ICM had a potential client "package" on its hands. But ABC Motion Pictures controlled the rights to a Karen Silkwood film.

"Meryl wanted to do it and then Mike Nichols wanted to do it because Meryl wanted to do it," Nora said. "But even then the studio did not want to make the movie; they were dragged kicking and screaming into making this movie, because they realized that if they didn't make it some other studio would obviously make it with those two elements attached to it."

Meryl, a double Oscar winner for *Kramer vs. Kramer* and *Sophie's Choice*, was a no-brainer for the meaty role. But Nora, fairly new to screenwriting, was untested. Mike, the guru behind *The Graduate*, was on Hollywood hiatus following the double disappointment of *The Day of the Dolphin* and *The Fortune* in the 1970s.

"We weren't able to get an answer out of Sam Cohn, Meryl Streep's agent at ICM, as to whether she would commit to the role of Karen Silkwood," Bob Bookman, then heading production at ABC Motion Pictures, recalls. "While Sam kept us at bay, we quietly approached Sissy Spacek and made sure that Sam found out. When he did, he presented us with the package of Meryl, Karel Reisz as director, and Nora and Alice Arlen as screenwriters, all clients of his. I had never heard of Alice Arlen at that time. And we had a big fight with Sam because we didn't want Karel Reisz as the director. He ultimately put forth Mike Nichols who at that time had burned just about every bridge burnable in the business. One more flop or one more misstep and he was in movie jail with a long sentence. We took a chance that he was aware of that and would be Mike at his best on *Silkwood*, which he was."

Silkwood marked Mike's return to movies after an eight-year absence. He "was supposed to direct a Broadway musical instead, but it all fell through because he was betrayed by a close friend who was involved with the show," wrote Nora in *I Feel Bad about My Neck*, referring to said friend as "Jane Doe."

Mike worked with Nora and Alice to tweak the screenplay, "suggesting scenes for the movie that involve Karen Silkwood's being betrayed by a close woman friend," which Nora shot down, saying: "Mike, Jane Doe did not kill Karen Silkwood."

She admired how the curious, reflective Nichols—another follower of Mildred Newman and her husband, Bernie Berkowitz, also a shrink—leveraged psychoanalysis to relate to a character and help actors do the same. For example: "It's like when you were in high school and nobody would choose you."

Nora had a tough time nailing down Silkwood's personality. Then she read the transcript from an interview with Drew Stevens, Silkwood's ex, who said she once flashed him at work. *Bingo.* Karen was no angel. She was a troublemaker.

Mike allowed the screenwriters in on the casting process—a revelation for Nora. The right actor, she learned, can tell you which lines work and which don't. The right actor can make the scene. The right actor can surprise you. Or make you nervous. "I couldn't believe what Meryl wanted to wear as Karen Silkwood," Nora said. "And the first day Cher improvised a line, I practically had to take five aspirins."

It takes a village to make a movie, with lots of chefs in the kitchen. A scribe accustomed to controlling her own narrative may curse the script-to-screen compromises—and Cher ad-libs—to be made. Not one to toss out a juicy bit of dialogue, Nora "thought like a cook and would refer to lines as leftovers we can use some other time," Alice told me. "I see the whole experience as a magic time: working with Nora and her making me omelets, working with Nora and Mike Nichols at the Carlyle Hotel. Taking location trips. Being on set. Hanging out in the wardrobe department. All very exciting for a first-time film writer. As to Nora herself, she became my best friend and was the funniest, most entertaining person I've met outside of my husband." The drama was a hit with audiences and critics, launching Nora into the same A-list screenwriting echelon as William Goldman.

The collaboration was such a hit that Nora and Mike wanted to keep the magic going. Mike, for one, was thoroughly entertained by *Heartburn*. Did Nora consider it movie material? Not at the outset. But Mike did. He helped her bring the infidelity tale to the cinema in 1986. And he gave her an office at Fox Movietone studios on West 54th Street, where filming took place. She personally supervised the catering. On the defense, Carl vented to *Playboy*'s Tony Schwartz:

> *I think he must have been hallucinating when he bought this thing. When Nora decided that she would sell this as a movie and Mike decided to buy it, I called him and said, "Let's have lunch," because we've been friends for a long time. So we went to the Russian Team Room and I said, "I can't believe you're going to do this."...Well, the other night, I was at a Lincoln Center gala for Elizabeth Taylor, watching clips from* Who's Afraid of Virginia Woolf?, *which was directed by Mike Nichols. And it suddenly occurred to me that Mike, who knows both Nora and me very well, saw in us this kind of titanic, classic male-female struggle. Which is nuts! Because what you see when you see this movie is a very little story, a very silly story. It's no epic.*

Mike cast Meryl as Rachel Samstat. The director asked Dustin Hoffman, who had played Carl in *All the President's Men*, to star in a sequel of sorts. Dustin declined out of respect for Carl. Mandy Patinkin took the part, but he proved a bad fit for the role; Mike replaced him with Jack Nicholson, who showed more swagger. Carl was said to be "ecstatic" about the casting. Here he is again:

> *I think we both came to believe a little too much of what we were reading in the papers about the marriage. We had come to expect that it had to be storybook perfect, and when one of us wasn't Cinderella or Prince Charming, it created havoc of a degree totally out of proportion to whatever the event would have been in an ordinary marriage. I read recently a comment Nora made that I thought was telling. She referred to the "chemistry" between Jack and Meryl on screen being like that of Tracy and Hepburn. Perhaps Nora had that idea about us.*

It certainly seems odd to us today that a newspaper or a national publication like *People* would report on the love lives of two writers like they were Tom Cruise and Katie Holmes. Carl and Nora were journalism's TomKat, making headlines after the divorce was long over. Everything they said about it was copy. Commented Bob Gottlieb:

> *They were a celebrity couple which clearly they allowed to happen or perhaps they wanted it to happen. If she had a failing, for me, it was her overwhelming need to have success. Maybe that had to do with the fact that her parents got there but didn't get there.*

After much back-and-forth, Carl—who tried to kill the film, complaining it would harm their sons—scored script privileges as the exes hashed out a divorce settlement. The terms prohibited Nora from turning Carl and the boys into extra copy. She also stated that he would be "portrayed at all times as a caring, loving and conscientious father." Carl won the right to review screenplay drafts and make suggestions, but Nichols retained the right to decide whether he would *take* those suggestions. The Carl character's last name was tweaked from Feldman to Forman; given how Nora had correctly guessed Deep Throat's identity long before Mark Felt revealed himself in 2005, it could be wagered that the name Mark Feldman had been Nora's idea of a hint.

The final product divided critics. The *Times* praised Meryl and Jack, but not the "barely there" characters and plot. Denouncing *Heartburn* as a "bitter, sour movie," Roger Ebert suggested Nora "had too much anger to transform the facts into entertaining fiction." Pauline Kael snubbed Rachel as a "bratty narrator." Suffice it to say Rachel was far from Meg Ryan, who would play Nora's Sally Albright in *When Harry Met Sally* with a hefty dose of sweetness to balance out the bite.

"Nora told me she wasn't pleased with *Heartburn*," Carrie Fisher has said. "I guess it was the restrictions imposed by her ex-husband. His character couldn't scream, 'You know why I fucked someone when you were pregnant? I was terrified!' A lot of men do that. She married a man not known for his fidelity. A known hound....She needed to have children. Nora never copped to that. It was implicit."

But while Nora's attempts at marriage backfired, an ambitious young actor named Tom Hanks had managed to get it right on the second try. The object of his affection: Rita Wilson.

A few weeks before marrying Rita, the woman he credited with saving his life, Tom escorted her down the aisle of the Zanuck Theater at 20th Century Fox Studios. She wore a white windbreaker; he a White Sox hat tucked down low on his head. It was a very special occasion: a test screening for *Big*, a buzzy comedy-drama about a 12-year-old boy who wishes to be "big" and wakes up a 30-year-old man. Tom had yet to see the movie. Among the 476 seated guests were Jim Brooks, *Big*'s producer, and Penny Marshall, its director. The actress initiated a foray behind the camera on the 1986 Whoopi Goldberg picture *Jumpin' Jack Flash*; with *Big*, she would become the first woman filmmaker to surpass $100 million at the box office.

At first, Tom had turned down the role, as did Dennis Quaid and Kevin Costner, but regained interest in man-child Josh Baskin after Robert De Niro accepted the offer. "Once Bobby wanted to do it, then Tom wanted to do it," Penny said. "Bobby gave me believability or credibility."

De Niro backed away and Tom stepped in, shedding his ironic side to step fully into Josh's sneakers. When Penny asked for "insh"—innocent and shy—he carried out a sweet, earnest, and empathetic performance that yielded his first Oscar nomination in 1989 and deep respect for the character he considered a role model. "He was such a great kid, and it was wonderful to be him and I wish I was still him now in a lot of ways," Tom told Barbara Walters at the time. "This kid had no ego, he had no competition. And that's an aspect of me that I wish I could shake—I think I'm awfully competitive. I have this tendency to state categorically what it is about something. It's just my opinion. I say, look, here's the scoop here. It's like *this*. Anything beyond that is not worth talking about, OK?"

Curtain. Josh and his boss duet on "Heart and Soul" and "Chopsticks" at FAO Schwarz, making the older man feel young again. (Lump in throat.) Josh, a rising star at MacMillan Toys, attends an office party in a white matador suit and nibbles a baby corn like it's a normal corn. (Hahahaha!) Josh, back to his younger self thanks to fortune-teller Zoltar, waves farewell to first love Elizabeth Perkins and returns home. (Waterworks.)

Both Tom and Rita were brought to tears. He lifted her up and nuzzled her neck. "It's just a movie, hon. You'll get over it," he reassured, adding, "What a sweet movie. I didn't expect to cry."

The year 1988 announced the arrival of Tom Hanks the Serious Actor: *Big* was big. *Punchline*, his dark turn as a stand-up comedian, was well received. The *Newsweek* cover was a hoot. He held up the September 26 issue ("Hanks Hits It Big: The Dazzling Actor Scores Again in 'Punchline'") while hosting *Saturday Night Live*, telling studio 8H: "I'm glad my movies have met with some success, but, jeez, the things these interviewers and reporters are going on and on about me being such a nice guy. It makes me feel sorta silly.... Nobody gets this kind of press. It's embarrassing. Nobody can be that nice." His monologue then cut to vignettes where Tom talked a meltdown-having Phil Hartman off the ledge and researched Nora Dunn's family tree out of the kindness of his heart. While the self-deprecating, self-assured star mocked the media's Mr. Nice Guy coverage, he seemed not to mind a bit—he was, after all, a famously nice guy.

"I don't threaten any man's sense of virility, or any woman's sense of security or decorum," Tom once said of his genial, nonpolarizing image. "I think I'm a gentleman, you know. But a sloppy one!"

Born on July 9, 1956, in Concord, a town north of San Francisco, Tom was a child of divorce. When Amos Hanks, a cook, ended his marriage to wife Janet, he took five-year-old Tom and older siblings Sandra and Larry while six-month-old Jim stayed with his mother. The gang moved around a bunch; Amos married and divorced a second wife, eventually settling down in Oakland with the third and last Mrs. Hanks, Frances Wong.

In high school Tom—voted Male Class Cutup—was "horribly, painfully, terribly shy," he said. "At the same time, I was the guy who'd yell out funny captions during filmstrips. But I didn't get into trouble. I was always a real good kid and pretty responsible." He gravitated toward the stage, donning a grass skirt to croon "There's Nothing like a Dame" as Luther Billis in *South Pacific*. "I was attracted to acting because it was fun," he explained. "I'd rather laugh all day long than anything." He met soulmates backstage: "Nobody on my track team was funny; no one was looking to crack up; no one got me the way my theater friends got me."

He graduated from Skyline High to study at Chabot, a Bay Area community college, and after two years transferred to California State University at Sacramento, majoring in theater. He dropped out, took a job as a technical director at a local theater, and tackled the Bard in an acclaimed run as the villain Proteus in *The Two Gentlemen of Verona* at Cleveland's Great Lakes Theater Festival. Next came a move to New York City, where he earned $800 for a minor role in the Staten Island–shot horror flick *He Knows You're Alone*. The city was a financial drain. "You see pictures of it: Frank Sinatra dances in the streets of New York, things like that," he joked to Johnny Carson. "But I realized as soon as we got there, New York gives you no choice. First of all, because as soon as you get off the plane, they have agents of the state that put a vacuum cleaner hose in your pocket to suck out all your money."

Back then, Manhattan wasn't just expensive—parts beyond Woody Allen's Upper East Side were grimy and dangerous. The number of murders rose during the 1970s, when the city suffered financial problems coinciding with an increase in the crime rate and the migration of thousands of New Yorkers out of the city. Movies like *Taxi Driver* reflected the hard edges and shaped public perception of Gotham as a concrete jungle where dreams are snuffed out. Meanwhile, "I lived around the corner from Broadway, but I couldn't even get arrested," said Tom. "I didn't know how to dance, I hadn't taken a voice lesson, and I wasn't feeling confident."

Shortly after the birth of their son Colin, Tom, then 21 years old, wed Samantha Lewes in 1978; they struggled to make ends meet. "We were young and impetuous," he told *Premiere*. "It was a very fervent time.... It was just the greatest thing that [Colin] was healthy. 'Cause if he'd got sick—if we'd had to take him to a clinic—that just would have been hell. We didn't have the money."

Los Angeles offered more opportunity, especially on television. In a lucky break Tom snagged a role on ABC sitcom *Bosom Buddies* as New York adman Kip Wilson, who dresses in drag to afford a flat at an all-female apartment building. Tom and co-star Peter Scolari began a lifelong bromance. They commiserated over their not-great married lives, and even shared some brief screen time with a young Rita Wilson, whom Tom found delightful. The actress guest-starred as Scolari's devil-worshipping date Cindy. Watch the 1981 episode "All You Need Is Love": Tom emits what appears to be a real guffaw, not a canned one, after Cindy—a vivacious brunette with Precious Moments blue eyes, dark curly hair, and a megawatt smile—reveals, matter-of-factly: "I worship Satan. You know, Beelzebub. Prince of Darkness."

The next year *Bosom* got the boot—but Tom's career propelled upward. He'd hone his charming wiseacre shtick as a *Tonight Show* guest, grab a recurring role as Michael J. Fox's uncle Ned in *Family Ties*, and, best of all, cross over into movies with the 1984 rom-com *Splash*, a sleeper hit that made $70 million. Tom—funny but not too far out; handsome but not beautiful—played the straight man to Daryl Hannah's fish out of water. His salary: $100,000.

"He came in wearing these 501 Levi's and construction boots and a T-shirt—he wasn't nervous at *all*," said producer Brian Grazer. "And here's a guy who'd never had a major movie. I thought, 'Why is this guy so calm?' But we read him, and we liked him, and we hired him right away."

As an actor, he was intelligent, hilarious, pathetic, and relatable. As a husband, he was disconnected. He and Samantha separated in 1985, divorcing two years later. "You can't put all the blame on the film business," he has said. "It's just as hard working at a bank and staying happily married as it is in the movies. For a long period of time you go through this period of swearing you will never make the same mistakes as your parents. But then you realize that they didn't really make mistakes. They just did what had to be done. That's just the way it works out sometimes."

Tom immersed himself in work. He and Rita reunited on the set of daffy comedy *Volunteers*, in which his character—a lockjawed blueblood running from debt collectors—disappears into the Peace Corps in Thailand (actually Mexico). Rita played his grounded, do-gooding love object. A bond formed. They laughed together. At first her character despises his—Lawrence Whatley Bourne III is kind of a garbage person—but there's a heart in there somewhere, and by the second act they're slow-dancing to "As Time Goes By."

"It was very *When Harry Met Sally*," said Rita, who was then engaged to a man she didn't love. "We had a slow, gradually building friendship, which blossomed into a wonderful relationship."

Back in LA and single again, they started dating. Once when the pair was in New York, on the corner of 58th Street and Fifth Avenue, "we were holding hands and we were waiting for the traffic light to change," said Rita, "and he looked at me and he said, 'You know, I just want you to know that you never have to change anything about who you are in order to be with me.'"

Tom popped the question on New Year's Eve 1987 in St. Bart's, and that April, he wed Rita, who's got Greek roots and a tight-knit family, at Saint Sophia Greek Orthodox Cathedral in LA.

"It's odd, but even as a child, all the change I experienced at home made me feel ahead of everybody else," he said. "I thought it was a great way to live and that people who lived in the same house all their lives were slow, dull, and uninteresting. The downside of this is that once I was on my own, I found it impossible to root myself anywhere and continued to move every six months for years. It wasn't until my second marriage that I began to get comfortable with the idea of home. Everything made sense for the first time, but that was a long time coming."

Inside the church, bride and groom circled a ceremonial table once, twice, three times. After the third time, they were married.

❋ ❋ ❋

The third time's the charm.

Nick Pileggi had a thing for Nora Ephron. He heard she was seeing the perennially single real estate and media mogul Mort Zuckerman, an obstacle that did not deter the affable crime reporter from pursuing a date. No longer in competition: Joe Fox, the irreverent Random House editor she went with post-Carl. (Before their breakup, Nora told Maria Tucci: "I realized I don't want to die with Joe Fox.")

In *I Feel Bad about My Neck*, Nora recalled: "I'm having dinner at a restaurant with friends. A man I know comes over to the table. He's a famously nice guy. His marriage broke up at about the same time mine did. He says, 'How can I find you?'"

Nick, a born-and-bred Brooklynite and son of Italian immigrants, worked alongside Nora at *New York* magazine back in the

43

'60s. He specialized in covering the Mob, and his good-natured, gentlemanly manner doubtless helped gain the trust of made men in smoky rooms throughout the city. Easy to laugh, with wide-set eyes and apple cheeks, Nick carried himself like a grown-up. He could get a table at Rao's. In 1986, he wrote the nonfiction book *Wiseguy: Life in a Mafia Family*, which became a Martin Scorsese movie (*Goodfellas*) four years later.

"Not unlike Henry Hill, I grew up in Bensonhurst," he explained. "I knew those guys. I saw the power they had. I saw the influence they had. I saw the benevolence of some of them. And I saw that a lot of these young guys I was growing up with who were going in that direction were really mean guys....I was curious to learn more about them for myself. Why wasn't I one of them? Why was I going to school and trying to be a writer?"

As for Nora, "By the third date I had no questions. She's like the kind of Italian mama I grew up with: they make a house really a home."

Speaking to *Vanity Fair*, literary agent Binky Urban characterized Nick as "the walking wounded" after the demise of his first marriage. Nora was a second chance, and she adored him. Nora later said that Nick "instantly caught pinkeye" from four-year-old Jacob and three-year-old Max at the start of the courtship; again, he was not deterred.

Nick and Nora had a surprise wedding at their Apthorp apartment on March 28, 1987, when she was 46 and he 54. The 40 or so guests thought they were going to a dinner party. Her two regrets: she hated her wedding dress, and she didn't get to cook because Nick advised against unnecessary multitasking.

"She had fallen in love with and married a man who was as fastidious about presentation as she was," wrote Jacob Bernstein, a journalist. "All sorts of men had rejected her when she was younger as cute but not beautiful. She wrote about it, turned it into a comic riff—everything is copy—but privately, it was heartbreaking for her until this noble man came along and made her feel that she was as fabulous to look at as she was to talk to."

He would do the most romantic things for her, like come home with a bag of subway tokens because she was always losing them. In her pithy autobiography for the Six-Word Memoir book series, Nora devoted all six words to Nick:

"Secret of Life: marry an Italian."

Against all odds, and even her own expectations, she had found True Love. Soon Nora Ephron, the Queen of Snark, would get the chance to bring an indomitable faith in couplehood to the masses. But first, she'd have to figure out her own answer to an impossible question: Can two best friends become lovers?

CHAPTER 2

Transitional People

It was an autumn day in 1984 when Rob Reiner and Andy Scheinman greeted Nora Ephron at the Russian Tea Room next door to
Carnegie Hall. In October the Hollywood producers phoned the
Silkwood screenwriter's New York superagent, Sam Cohn, to set
up lunch. They had a movie pitch: would she bite? The Tea Room,
with its exuberant red banquettes, rich green walls, gold tinsel-
dressed chandeliers, and borscht and beef Stroganoff on the menu,
was a fabulously kitschy place to find out.

The past spring Rob released the brilliant rock satire *This Is
Spinal Tap*, his first as a film director. He cast himself as Marty
DiBergi, a documentarian—meta—shooting behind-the-scenes
footage of the pretentious heavy metal group Spinal Tap, fronted
by Brits Nigel Tufnel (Christopher Guest) and David St. Hubbins
(Michael McKean). They invented their own dialogue. ("He died
in a bizarre gardening accident some years back," says David of a
former drummer. Nigel replies, "...the authorities said, you know,
best leave it unsolved, really.") The mockumentary opened in just
206 theaters, grossing $4.5 million, but its portrait of a band

staging an unsuccessful comeback tour spread like a secret among Nigel-quoting fans who felt *they'd* discovered Spinal Tap and were the only ones hip to the humor.

So there sat Rob Reiner, a guy known for being hip to a funny story, attempting to sell Nora Ephron a not-so-funny courtroom drama. The plot revolved around a lawyer and a class action lawsuit. She rejected the concept immediately. (In hindsight, Rob said he pitched too soon. Better to wait 'til the coffee portion of the meal.)

"I remember being slightly perplexed about whether to say straight off that the idea didn't interest me or whether to play along for an hour so as not to have that horrible awkwardness that can happen when the meeting is over but the lunch must go on," Nora wrote. "I decided on the former; and we then spent the rest of the lunch talking about ourselves. Well, that isn't entirely true: we spent the rest of the lunch talking about Rob and Andy."

Close friends since the 1970s, Rob met Andy at the Hollywood Indoor Tennis Club, where the former was a member and the latter a pro. "You know, you're the funniest person who doesn't get paid for it," Rob said to the slim, low-key University of Virginia law school graduate. Andy, more comfortable behind the scenes than in front of the camera, became a regular at the fratty Encino home Rob had shared with then-wife Penny Marshall; it doubled as a writer's room for joke-swapping, pot-smoking, sweater-wearing comedians, most of whom were men.

In Nora's presence the pals made amusing, off-the-cuff observations about bachelorhood. "I'd been single for almost 10 years at that point," recalls Rob, "and I was making a complete and utter mess of my personal life."

She was paying attention.

A few weeks passed. Rob flew back with some new pitches, inviting Nora to meet at his hotel room on Central Park South.

Nora vetoed the first pitch, then the second. Next came a sexier proposition, something Rob was mulling that concerned men and women. This is what he said: "Two people become friends at the end of the first major relationship in each of their lives and they make a decision not to have sex because it will ruin the friendship. *And then they have sex and it ruins the friendship.*"

Nora's antenna raised. *Sold.*

"I can do that," she told Rob, watching the narrative flash before her eyes. These two people would collide over time, in five-year increments. A meaningful love connection would be delayed. Rob, who knew from missed love connections, would direct.

A trained reporter, Nora took notes. For a few days in February 1985, she listened in horror as Rob and Andy revealed disturbing insights into the heterosexual male psyche: for instance, a man's impulse to skirt postcoital cuddling and escape a woman's bedroom. "You're totally passionate and then, literally 30 seconds later, you're going, 'Boy, I'd love a sandwich right now but I don't want to...,'" Andy says. "It's not that you dislike the person, and you could be in love with the person, it's just in my experience— and Rob had the same experience."

A man and a woman can't truly be *friends*, they said, because the sex part gets in the way. Nora, who begged to differ with that assertion and certainly could not work in Hollywood without befriending men like Rob, recorded the good, the bad, and the ugly.

"She took all of this as the grist for the film," says Rob. "Initially we called the film *Scenes from a Friendship*. I wanted to do a similar thing that Bergman had done with *Scenes from a Marriage*, which is to really explore male-female relationships and what goes on between [the sexes]....I knew that I needed a woman to work with me because I knew what my point of view was, I know what men think but I don't know what women think and I needed to get a woman's perspective.

I thought of Nora because not only is she a great writer but she's a great observational writer with a wonderful ability to observe human behavior, so I thought the combination would be good."

To Andy, she might as well have been a unicorn. "I didn't know that many women who were really funny," he confesses.

Rob, outwardly gregarious and outgoing, waxed nonstop about his depression. A perpetual raincloud seemed to hover above his bearded dome, and yet he tossed aside the umbrella, stretched out his arms, and soaked up the droplets of despair. He was happy when it rained. He splashed in puddles and slipped on banana peels.

"I think I'm not ready for a relationship," he told Nora, "when you're as depressed as I am.... If the depression was lifted, I would be able to be with someone on my level. But it's like playing tennis on a windy day with someone who's worse than you are. They can do all right against you, they can win a couple games, but there's too much wind? You know what I mean?"

Oh, she could use that.

"You know how women have a base of makeup. I have a base of depression. Sometimes I sink below it. Sometimes I rise above it."

That too.

Rob clarified the project further, ruling out "chase scenes" and "food fights" and conventional happy endings. "We're talking about a movie about two people who get each other from the breakup of the first big relationship in their lives to the beginning of the second," he said. "Transitional on some level. Who are friends, who don't have sex, who nurse each other and comfort each other and talk to each other and then finally do it and it's a mistake and recover from it and move into second relationships."

Harry and Sally's fate would echo that of Alvy Singer and Annie Hall—the final frames bittersweet, naturalistic—with brushes of Ingmar Bergman. The director's talky *Scenes from a*

Marriage, first aired on Swedish TV in 1973, followed a lawyer wife (Liv Ullmann, serious) and professor husband (Erland Josephson, serious) undone by infidelity, among other (serious) problems. They remarry but find themselves drawn back together. Seriously.

Forget the movies, John Cusack and Daphne Zuniga, man and mermaid. This was how it happened in real life.

Before Rob and his raincloud drifted to Oregon to make *Stand by Me*, Nora gathered her notes and went to work. For Harry Burns, the fatalistic political consultant, she used Rob as a model; she even saw Rob pulling double duty and acting the part. Clearly he was qualified for the job. "He is the all-time gloom-and-doom guy, but he's funny," she said. "Now, not all gloom-and-doom guys are funny. Woody Allen is a gloom-and-doom guy who's not funny in real life." Infusing Harry with Reiner's essence was strategic. A control-craving screenwriter, beholden to the powers that be, could witness her words sliced, diced, and rewritten until nothing remained but her byline. A female character—one who existed on the page and on the screen—was often at risk if the male director could not identify with her as Mike Nichols had with Karen Silkwood. To protect her material and ensure the movie got made, Nora sought to invest Rob in Harry's side of the story by crafting dialogue and language—*the transitional person*—from his surprising, specific, and highly personal confessions. While Rob focused on Harry, the odds were greater that Sally Albright could survive— and one day steal a scene or two, right from under Harry's nose.

All Nora had to do was look in the mirror. She made Sally a journalist with a defiantly glass-half-full disposition; mathematically speaking, she required several spoonfuls of sugar to balance her foe's saltiness. "I'm not precisely chirpy, but I am the sort of person who is fine, I'm just fine, everything's fine," said Nora, describing her attitude even when things are not. She gave Sally a couple of BFFs: Marie, a frank, worldly Marie Brenner avatar; and Alice, a happily married Alice Arlen alter ego. Real-life Alice's maiden name? Albright.

In the earliest stages, "she was Jewish and he was Gentile," said Nora of her characters. "And then Rob fell in love with [Elizabeth McGovern], so Elizabeth McGovern was going to play it. So we had to change it because there was no way that she could play...so I switched their last names."

✳ ✳ ✳

Like Sally, Nora had days-of-the-week underwear that were missing Sunday. Sally had a boyfriend, Joe, modeled on a college beau who reentered Nora's life some six years after their relationship, "every single time saying horrible things." Sally scoffed at the prospect of marrying a man who runs a bar—even if that man is Humphrey Bogart in *Casablanca*. "Which is such a stupid thing to say but she is so stupid at the beginning of that movie," opined Nora, admitting: "I think I actually used to believe that."

Like Harry, college-age Nora once pondered the worst-case scenario to befall a New Yorker: a lonely death. The sort "where nobody notices for two weeks until the smell drifts into the hallway." She shared with Mr. Negative the conclusion that taking someone to the airport signals the start of a relationship and thus exerts pressure upon the chauffeur to keep up the good deed when things fizzle out. "That's why," he says, "I have never taken anyone to the airport at the beginning of a relationship."

A debate between married friends Ken Auletta and Binky Urban over a wagon-wheel table became a sparring match for Marie and Jess, Harry's best friend who romances Marie—and defends the decorative eyesore from which she recoils. (Said Binky: "Once she put it in the movie, I couldn't throw it out.") Nora admonished Rob for a lack of filter, as did Sally to his counterpart: "Harry, you're going to have to try and find a way of not expressing every feeling that you have every moment that you have them."

"This is a romantic comedy where certain rules—that probably began in *The Taming of the Shrew*—apply," said Nora. She gave Shakespeare and Jane Austen shout-outs for popularizing the love-hate dynamic between two equal but opposing lovers co-opted by Golden Age filmmakers from Frank Capra (*It Happened One Night*) and Ernst Lubitsch (*The Shop around the Corner*) to George Cukor (*Adam's Rib*).

"All of the guys I know, including Rob, have slept with a friend that they shouldn't have slept with and pretty much ruined the friendship, and the women I know have done the same thing. So we had that operating. In some sense what you're hoping for is that it's everybody's autobiography."

As she sat down to write, to flesh out that narrative in her head, to flavor it with her lemony voice, to relate it back to Rob, to add elements of her own biography, Nora looked inward and outward to consider a struggle all too real: dating in New York City. *Heartburn* covered the territory, Nora's running commentary a retort to every well-meaning but tone-deaf pep talk from someone with no clue, like your serially monogamous co-worker who organizes monthly "girls' nights" as if to ignore the fact that your life is one big long girls' night. *There are millions of singles here—is it really that hard?* Consider when a complete stranger winks at Rachel Samstat on the subway:

> *I immediately wondered whether he was single, and if so, whether he was a college graduate and straight. Then I thought of how awful it would be to be single again, how*

awful it would be to be back on the market with the old New York ratio going against me, 200 single women to every single straight man, packs of Amazons roaming the streets looking in vain for someone genuinely eligible and self-supporting who didn't mind a little cellulite.

Marie voices this fear while urging a reluctant Sally to rejoin the singles circuit just days after her breakup with Joe, a lawyer and human Ken doll. She warns: "I'm saying that the right man for you might be out there right now and if you don't grab him, someone else will and you'll have to spend the rest of your life knowing that someone else is married to your husband."

No pressure at all. Although, if you're not quite ready to get out there again, spending the majority of your free time with a decidedly platonic substitute boyfriend could be a welcome diversion.

In her essay "When Harry Met Sally dot dot dot," Nora removed a first-draft leftover from the fridge for readers to chew on. Sally tells Harry, "I think we should write a movie about our relationship.... Two people become friends at the end of the first major relationship in their lives and get each other to the next major relationship of their lives." The scene is "too self-conscious" yet also conveys her intent, she said. An excerpt:

HARRY: What happens to the friends when each of them gets to the next major relationship of their lives?

SALLY: They're still going to be friends. They're going to be friends forever.

HARRY: I don't know, Sally. You know what happens. You meet somebody new and you take them to meet your friend,

and you want them to like each
other as much as you do, but they
never do, they always see the friend
as a threat to your relationship,
and you try to stay just as good
friends with your friend but
eventually you don't really need
each other as much because you've
got a new friend, you've got someone
you can talk to *and* fuck—

SALLY: Forget I mentioned it, OK?

They smile at each other.

HARRY: I love you. You know that.

SALLY: I love you too.

HARRY: When I say, "I love you," you know
what I mean—

SALLY: I know what you mean. I know.

Friends without benefits, Harry and Sally's strong fondness masked a deep need for the comfort of cross-sex companionship. There was a tension, a weirdness. At the same time Harry seemed to view Sally as a fleeting non-girlfriend of sorts, a buffer until a real-deal *girlfriend*-girlfriend took her place. This dynamic plays out everywhere, from the Big Apple to a small town to a college campus. Men and women float in and out of each other's lives like butterflies on the breeze. One day you're talking and the next day you're toast.

"We met again and decided that Harry and Sally belonged together," said Nora, tweaking draft number 2 to reflect the change of heart. She and Rob would remain skeptical. The "true" finale, they acknowledged, ended with the couple parting ways. Forever. From a marketing perspective, Rob the businessman understood what he had to do in order to peddle a $14.5 million mainstream romcom that charted familiar terrain—boy meets girl, boy loses girl, boy wins girl back—but Rob the director, partial to the offbeat and the honest, sniffed BS. Besides, he said, "I couldn't imagine how they could ever get together or how a man could ever get together with a woman!"

As for Nora, she disputed the notion that you could suddenly develop sexual feelings for a friend toward whom you've never felt sexy. "I think for the story it really doesn't feel right," conceded Nora. "I do think that if two people meet each other and they don't do it, it's because something's missing. And it's hard to make up for that."

Throughout the revision process, a thought crossed Nora's mind: What if Rob dropped Harry and Sally...and she took them on? As the director? Despite her alpha ambition, for a time she wasn't interested in running a film set—"First of all, how was I going to do it with my kids?"—but this a rookie could handle. It was two hyperverbal urbanites walking and talking and eating.

✳ ✳ ✳

Jeff Stott was looking for Rob Reiner.

The Castle Rock production boss dispatched assistant Hwei-chu Meng to deliver the message to Rob's office. It was January 1988, and Hwei-chu, a few days into her new position as employee number 11 at the Century City–based entertainment company, saw no sign of her hero—she revered *Stand by Me*—so she asked Rob's secretary to tell Rob that Jeff needed him.

The secretary, typing away on an IBM typewriter, rolled her eyes.

The "secretary" was Nora Ephron, working on a rewrite of *The Untitled Rob Reiner Project*, known alternatively as *Boy Meets Girl*, which was to be Castle Rock's debut feature film.

Noooooooooooooooooooooooooo.

After the incident, Hwei-chu was embarrassed whenever she glimpsed the screenwriter in the hallway.

In July 1987 five friends—Rob, Andy, Martin Shafer, Glenn Padnick, and Alan Horn—formed Castle Rock out of a mission to create quality content untainted by corporate brass and bureaucracy. Though Rob's movie *The Princess Bride* seduced the darkest of souls, film critics included, the feeling was that the studio, 20th Century Fox, had mishandled its marketing. Alan, who had recently resigned as Fox president amid differences with boss Barry Diller, became CEO; Rob and Andy tag-teamed on project development.

Alan's octogenarian father, Sol, a California retiree married to wife, Marjorie, since 1939, unwittingly sparked Rob's idea to document real couples, not actors, telling the stories of how they met in *When Harry Met Sally*. Rob would sprinkle those interviews throughout the picture to suffuse the narrative with extra humanity and psyche the audience for Harry and Sally's inevitable reconciliation. (Later, Rob hired seasoned actors to tell those couples' stories.)

"Sol Horn was sitting quietly, and all of a sudden he lit up, he got excited, he was animated, he was sitting like a lox for a long time," said Rob, whose question—*How did you meet Marjorie?*—spurred the one-time Queens bartender to relive the love-at-first-sight episode. "He was sitting in a [Horn & Hardart café] and this girl walked in— he'd never seen this girl before in his life. And he turned to his friend and said, 'You see that girl? I'm going to marry that girl.'"

Alas! Marjorie was engaged to someone else! Not for long. Shortly afterward she accepted Sol's hand, and then they had Alan.

Good story, right? Rob wanted more. His casting director, Jane Jenkins, notified agencies, saying, "If you have parents or relatives, if you know of anybody." Feelers were sent to elderly hot spots, like retirement homes.

Those innocent audition notices, however, excluded any mention of what would become the most stimulating scene in the movie.

* * *

"What about fake orgasms?"

Although Nora received sole credit for proposing that women feign sexual climax, Rob and Andy peg the source as model and actress Dani Minnick, who starred in a series of Virginia Slims cigarette ads during the 1980s. ("According to the THEORY OF EVOLUTION, men evolved with fat, stubby fingers and women evolved with long, slim fingers," purred 1984 advertising copy, curving around Dani's lithe, tanned form to seduce its intended target: female smokers who wanted to look like Dani Minnick. "Therefore, according to the THEORY OF LOGIC, women should smoke the long, slim cigarette designed just for them. And that's the THEORY OF SLIMNESS.")

Dani was also the sister of Andy's girlfriend. They were having lunch at the Ivy on Robertson Boulevard. Andy discussed his writing dilemma: Rob wanted Sally to reveal something outré about women that would shock men like the director's bachelor confessions had appalled Nora. That's when Dani had an explosive idea.

"Andy brought that back the next day," says Rob. "He said she mentioned this thing and Nora said, 'Absolutely, that's great. That's what we should do.' And I said, 'What are you talking about? What do you mean faking orgasms? Women are doing this?' And she said, 'Absolutely, that's a thing.'"

The director—who saved room at the production table for the screenwriter, making her an associate producer—was genuinely blindsided. According to Nora, Rob "went thundering into the bullpen where they kept all the poor women who worked at

Castle Rock in the unwindowed area" and summoned "six terrified-looking women" to his office.

"DO WOMEN FAKE ORGASMS?"

Yes, they each admitted.

"And like, half the guys said, 'No' and half the guys said, 'Probably, yeah, a girl's faked an orgasm with me but I don't know,'" Andy recalls of male employee response to the unscientific poll. "We said, 'This is perfect' and we worked that right into the scene."

Later, Rob phoned Nora and voiced that scene aloud. "I loved it," she said. "It went into the script."

But it was all foreplay, no action; all talk, no table-thump. Sally would take longer to climax, but when she did, no thick, meaty pastrami sandwich compared to her ecstasy.

Well, depends what kind of pastrami sandwich.

✱ ✱ ✱

Rob and Andy watched Nora order lunch with overly detailed instructions bordering on the absurd.

"It was avocado and bacon and sprouts and cheese," said Nora, the sandwich details fresh. "But I wanted half of it on the side... you know, it was just unending. It was the 19th time I had done my horrible ordering."

The bread she required "toasted and slightly burnt," the "bacon crisp."

My God, thought Rob, *this has to be in the movie!* You had to agree that Nora's demands, redolent of her controlling nature, managed to elevate a standard avocado sandwich into a yummier combination of taste and texture.

"I just like it the way I like it," she explained.

Satisfied with the script, his number one priority, Rob turned attention to wrangling his Harry Burns. Someone bankable, preferably a movie star whose wattage guaranteed ticket sales. The industry prioritized male actors—considered box-office breadwinners in comparison to actresses—and *The Untitled Rob Reiner Project* was no exception. He approached a number of popular leading men. Michael Keaton, whose ghoulish comedy *Beetlejuice* opened that spring of 1988, horrifying the nation's children, turned him down. So did Tom Hanks, about to blow up bigger in *Big*. "I don't think Tom ever regretted not doing it, because he just never knew how to play it," said Nora. "That part really was very much out of Rob's own kind of Jewish self-obsessed thing that I don't think Tom has a clue about."

Nora noted that unlike Harry, Tom wasn't gloomy over his divorce. She hoped that Rob, so funny acting out the parts, would see the light and cast himself. Not interested. Instead he went to buddies Albert Brooks and Richard Dreyfuss. Albert, Oscar-nominated for his charming role in the Jim Brooks romantic comedy *Broadcast News*, worried the screenplay was too Woody Allen. Albert and Allen were of the same nerdy-neurotic type, and given Allen's godlike hold over cinephiles, Albert thought it wise to pass. Dreyfuss, who bled boomer-nostalgia as adult Wil Wheaton in Rob's *Stand by Me*, boarded the "no" bandwagon.

"Richard Dreyfuss turned it down in front of me," said Nora. "Richard—who is a nightmare, a total nightmare—said to Rob, 'God, it's too bad you don't want to direct the movie I really want to do'—*Let It Ride*. He said, in front of me, 'It's the opposite of this situation. That has a great script and no director.'...What am I going to say, 'How dare you say that, Richard?' I will love Rob forever for this. Richard said, 'I want to know more about these people's jobs.' Well, Rob and I had been through this a million times, and that was not what we were doing. We were doing a thing about friends. And it wasn't about work. There is no director living on this earth who wouldn't say to an actor, 'Hmm, that's an interesting idea, we'll think about that.' And Rob said, 'Well, I don't.' It was like a man on a white horse. It was just great the way he stood up for it."

Where Nora bristled—Richard was insulting her work!—the actor's complaints rolled off Rob. "I don't care why they turn it down, I don't listen," Andy quotes the director as saying. "Yes or no, that's all that matters."

(*Let It Ride*, a comedy starring Dreyfuss as a gambler on a winning streak, tanked at the box office in the summer of 1989.)

Ego bruised, Billy Crystal waited in the wings. "Rob never mentioned it to me, but I knew from agents and managers that he had met with almost every male actor my age, except me," wrote Billy in his memoir, *Still Foolin' 'Em*. "I was not happy about that, but what could I do? We were the closest of friends, and I thought he was a great director, but if he didn't think I was right for it, then so be it. I didn't want to jeopardize our friendship by pushing the issue."

Neither did Rob. He says, "I was also nervous about going to Billy because he was my best friend and I thought, 'Oh, God, if this doesn't work....'"

Despite Billy's growing celebrity, when Hollywood compiled its shortlists for romantic leads, his name was nowhere near the top. Did B-list Billy have the goods to play, you know, The Guy? To that end: Would audiences buy him as The Guy?

Rob, empowered to make casting decisions, was willing to place that bet. He dialed Billy, explaining: "I had to see everybody. I had to go through the process just to make sure you're the perfect guy."

"I haven't read it yet. What if I don't like it?"

"I guarantee you'll like it. You'll hear your voice in it."

Script in possession, Billy didn't wait to consult his people. He said yes.

Once Rob and Elizabeth McGovern put a lid on their love affair, the director reopened his Sally search.

The shortlist included Helen Hunt (*Project X*), Meg Tilly (*The Big Chill*), and Meg Ryan, whom Jane and partner Janet Hirshenson had cast in a pair of films that turned out to be duds: the John Candy comedy *Armed and Dangerous* and the Sean Connery drama *The Presidio*. Molly Ringwald, the striking ginger muse of *Sixteen Candles*, *Pretty in Pink*, and *The Breakfast Club*, was up for consideration, though too young for the part. Susan Dey, starring as attorney Grace Van Owen in *L.A. Law*, declined.

"Rob went to Debra Winger for Sally," says Andy. "She was a big, hot actress then. She goes, 'I like it but I'm not sure.'...So she kept saying, 'I don't know. I'll decide.' Rob would keep calling her agent. He said, 'Rob, let me put it this way. She hasn't really committed emotionally to do *An Officer and a Gentleman* yet, and it's been in theaters for three years. She's insane. If you wait for her to get an answer, it could take forever.' Rob said, 'I have to move on.' By the way, she's a great actor but thankfully that happened."

Meg Ryan, neither *The Sure Thing* nor *The Princess Bride*, prepared to prove Rob wrong this time. She tested with Billy and turned out to be an adept improviser, returning the funnyman's serves, Jane Jenkins recalls. The two were chemically balanced. "It was always, 'Well, she could do it. She could do it. She'd be great. She'd be great.' And then Meg came in and we didn't even read a scene, and we all knew it was her," said Billy. "It's just one of those indefinable things that when we started talking we were them already, you know?...There was no mystery. We just hit it off."

After Meg left the room, Rob decreed: "She's perfect." An uncommon elixir of comedy chops, acting talent, and adorable.

And, she was fluent in Nora's language. "There was a really particular rhythm on the page," Meg has said of the writer's style. "Very, very short sentences....There wasn't a lot of dialogue, but it was rapid. Rat-a-tat-tat, rat-a-tat-tat."

She was young—all of 26—but looked like 40-year-old Billy's peer. Just one *minor* problem: Meg was supposed to play Sally Field's chronically ill daughter, Shelby, in *Steel Magnolias*, a six-woman ensemble piece with an emotionally devastating, Oscar-bait deathbed scene. Meg backed out of the movie and signed with Rob and Castle Rock. Her *Magnolias* role went to an actress named Julia Roberts, who had made an impression in *Mystic Pizza*.

Since breaking out in *Top Gun*, Meg had looked for a romantic comedy—but not just any old romantic comedy. One that could last. Like *Splendor in the Grass*, the timeless teen melodrama starring Warren Beatty and Natalie Wood, a (decidedly unfunny) favorite of Meg's. "What I love best about the movies is watching difficult choices being worked out—love versus duty, intelligence or passion," she said. "I could never figure these things out. Bogart and Bergman, Warren and Natalie did."

Now was the chance to sink her teeth into a nuanced relationship story with lasting potential. She felt she had played interesting and varied roles but never the main character. "And that's a real luxury because you have a lot more time to show your stuff," said the newly minted leading lady. "For the first time in my life I don't play *the girl*."

Meg's casting announcement hit the trades on May 16, along with news that Carrie Fisher and Bruno Kirby would play wingpeople Marie and Jess. Right around this time, Meg joined Billy, Rob, Nora, and Andy as a collaborator, dropping fresh insights into the stew, stirring the pot and bringing up the boil. One day, during a read-through, the orgasm scene came up. On the page, the dialogue involved Sally breaking the news to an incredulous Harry that women fake orgasms.

"Well, why don't I just do it?" Meg asked.

"Would you do that?" went the collective response.

Meg later recalled of her bold concept, a stunt so out of character but impossible to resist, Sally "doesn't necessarily have punchlines in that script, but she's behaviorally funny. It came out of understanding that."

Meg also hatched the scheme to fake it in an incongruous place. If Sally meant to humble Harry, who crudely questioned her sexual experience when they first met, then she was going to expose his folly and show him who was boss. Loudly and in public.

Billy suggested a restaurant. "I don't know if we can get away with this," he said to Rob, "but a woman says, *I'll have what she's having."*

Now to track down the right older Jewish woman—the kind who might order the brisket, a hot dog, an egg cream at her local deli, and ultimately get the last laugh. Billy knew such a woman.

"How about your mother?"

Estelle Reiner, in her early 70s, was long known as the wife of Carl, with whom she raised two sons and a daughter; *The Dick Van Dyke Show* creator used Estelle as a basis for Mary Tyler Moore's Laura Petrie. But she was also an accomplished vocalist, painter, and character actress; a student of Viola Spolin and Lee Strasberg, she filmed minor parts in comedies like 1983's *The Man with Two Brains*, directed by Carl, and 1980's *Fatso*, starring Dom DeLuise. At 65 years old, her nest empty, Estelle embarked on a second act as a blues-jazz singer. She recorded songs and performed in clubs. She could dispense a saucy riposte. Asked how she and Carl managed to stay together so many years, she'd reply: "Marry someone who can stand you."

Rob rang her up. "Mom, we got a scene here that I think is gonna be very funny. Billy wrote the last line which we think is gonna be the big topper." However, he warned, "If it's not the topper you could wind up on the cutting room floor."

"I don't care as long as I get to spend a day with my son," she answered. "I'll come, I'll have a hot dog."

A lean operation, Castle Rock planned on filming seven weeks in Los Angeles, one in Chicago (where postgrads Harry and Sally clashed egos, for the worse), and two in New York (where yuppies Harry and Sally reconnected, for the better). Rob hired Jane Musky, the woman responsible for Patrick Swayze and Demi Moore's airy, aspirational SoHo loft in *Ghost*, to re-create Manhattan on studio lots and palm tree–lined streets. "I spent about a month scouting LA, trying to figure out how to make it work," says Jane. "While I was doing that we were actually losing time in pre-production." Jane and location manager Donna Bloom corralled Rob back east, taking him on a "whirlwind" site tour and showing him the difference between the sort of "fake" New York they could build on a Hollywood soundstage and the real deal. "His eyes opened wide and he goes, 'Oh my God, no comparison at all.'" Rob's partners gave their blessing, and he added seven weeks in Gotham.

Rob advised Jane: "I don't care that much about what neighborhood Billy lives in, as much as I think he needs to feel lost in his space." Jane and Donna found Harry a bachelor loft off Broadway and 11th Street, near New York University, with high ceilings, dramatic rounded windows, and a romantic view of neighboring rooftops. Wait. Wasn't the place above Harry's pay grade? Outrageously impractical? Rob erred on the side of realism; Nora touted the fantasy.

"Nora was great," Jane remembers. "She tried to remain as neutral as she could because she wasn't directing it; she was the writer. But every once in a while she'd say, 'Rob...' [and he] would always say, 'No, no, no, that'd be too rich; they can't do that.' That's when we had this whole 'Come to Jesus' moment where I said, 'Yeah, but we want to make it like a major motion picture.' I think just in general, in a romantic comedy, you want to help it out a little; you want to have the audience believe they could be there with their girlfriend or boyfriend. 'Wouldn't that be great with those big windows.'"

Rob relented. Per his request, Jane would sparsely decorate the apartment to reflect the fact that Harry's ex-wife, Helen, took everything in the divorce. The poor guy—tossed aside for *Ira*—owned just a few pieces of furniture. And a rug. Rob saw the rug and thought Harry and Sally could unroll it together.

Castle Rock enlisted Cheryl Shuman of Starry Eyes Optical Services to supply eyewear for Meg Ryan. During a production meeting, Cheryl remembers, Nora said Sally needed specs to correct a visual imbalance: "Well, we have to have glasses for the character because... Meg's a lot more attractive than Billy is."

Nora requested a single pair that "does it all" and blended business and sex appeal. *"It can't be nerdy,"* the team told Cheryl. *"It can't detract from her beauty, but it's got to soften it a little bit."*

At a fitting with Meg, Cheryl brought in 200 frames; she detected the actress was "nervous because she still wanted to look pretty." She quotes Meg as saying, "I'm really sorry and I don't mean to be disrespectful but I'm not in love with any of them. I really like the ones that *you* have on."

Cheryl was wearing a one-of-a-kind La Roche frame with a 14-karat-gold base that cost her some $5,000. She handed hers to Meg, who tilted her head to the side and slipped the glasses down her nose, seeing herself clearly in the mirror. "These actually do look cute on me," Meg said.

"She kept them on," says Cheryl. "She said, 'Oh I can't just have them?' I said, 'Actually, those are mine and my prescription.' She was trying to walk off with them. Not to steal them, you know, celebrities are used to getting everything for free....I said, 'I really need them' and I looked across the room and I saw Peter Schindler, who was the guy who brought me in. He gave me this look, like 'Are you fucking kidding me? You want your glasses back from Meg Ryan?' It was a 'Give her the fucking glasses' kind of look. I looked over and Nora and Rob had that same look and I laughed this nervous laugh. I said, 'What am I thinking, Meg? I would be honored if you would take my glasses.'"

Roughly 20 metallic clones were ordered in La Roche's horn-rimmed MOD.55s style, with blue-speckled marble accents near the eyes. Sally would peer through the anti-reflective lenses to spy Harry browsing Shakespeare & Co.'s "personal growth" section.

MARIE: He's cute.
SALLY: You think he's cute?

Gloria Gresham took Meg shopping on Fifth Avenue and below 14th Street, scouring SoHo and the Village for Sally's wardrobe. The two consulted popular magazines—Gloria partial to *Life* versus *Vogue*, real people versus glossy excess—and spotted an odd wide-brimmed hat that could belong to Annie Hall, J. Peterman, or Pharrell. It repelled Rob but grew on him later. Gloria, who dressed John Travolta in *Urban Cowboy*, Kevin Bacon in *Footloose*, and Sigourney Weaver in *Ghostbusters II*, worked primarily on corset-free contemporary pictures. She formerly assisted *Annie Hall* designer Ruth Morley, styling Diane Keaton's menswear-inspired androgyny. For Sally, Gloria unpacked a fitted red turtleneck sweater, a boxy gray blazer, classic straight-leg jeans, and loose-fitting pleated pants that harkened back to the 1940s. At night, Sally stepped out in an off-the-shoulder black cocktail dress. Prim, practical, appropriate. But her hat, like that spontaneous orgasm, was a surprise; just when you think you've pinned her down, Sally peels back another layer of her identity. With Harry—prone to fishermen sweaters and kvetching—what you see is what you get. "I don't think we thought of her as chic, but as individual," Gloria said of Sally. "She dresses to please herself."

Nora, meanwhile, told hair and makeup that it would be funny if Sally's tresses got younger as she grew older. Her feathered Farrah Fawcett 'do and helmet bob reeked of Aqua Net, aging the twentysomething. But in her 30s, Sally loosened up—and so did her curly mop of hair.

After less than two months of prep, principal photography (industry speak for the stage when a movie is filmed) got going in Los Angeles on August 29, 1988. "*When Harry Met Sally* was probably close to the easiest movie I ever made, 'cause it was so well organized," says Aaron Barsky, the first assistant director. Rob, Nora, and the actors rehearsed at Raleigh Studios, blocking out "almost everything that we were going to do," he adds. "There was a lot of spontaneity because of the personalities we had, but they had a pretty good idea of what they wanted each scene to *say*." As a result, a scene stood solidly on its own; strung together, there were no weak links.

When it came time to film the Pictionary game—Bruno Kirby yelling "Baby fish mouth!"—the set hosted a reunion of sorts for members of Rob's extended family. Bruno was on an industry softball league with Rob and Billy, and known for his scratchy rasp, a result of vocal damage from singing high tenor in glee club at New York City's Power Memorial Academy. "He had a way of going through life with a sense of humor," veteran LA acting coach

John Kirby says of his brother, who died of leukemia in 2006. "He loved telling jokes and he had a way of telling them where you didn't know if he was setting up a joke or not, but you were always taken in and surprised. Deadpan. He liked to put me on the spot; he liked to put a lot of people on the spot."

Carrie Fisher—a turbo-talking heir apparent to screwball comedienne Rosalind Russell—was the jaded foil to Bruno's Jess, a sweet, if self-serious, Jimmy Breslin fanboy. "Talk about opposites," says John. "Two very wonderfully opinionated people, right? Strong views on anything, both of them. I think it worked. I think it became this wonderful odd couple. And yet, in spite of their differences you believed they loved each other. . . . I don't want to say beautiful misfits, but in a sense they were a little. And that made for the perfect match. It was amazing because they let their brilliant minds work for the character, but not dominate the character where their smarts got in the way of their off-beat-ness. That's why it was genius to put them together. And they're not predictable."

It had been 11 years since Carrie kicked stormtrooper butt as Princess Leia. A cultural icon, she operated on two levels: Hollywood insider (social butterfly, connector of power players, and daughter of Debbie Reynolds) and outsider (brainiac, truth teller, and burst of fresh air in a town where honesty is rarer than a forehead wrinkle). In this way she was similar to Nora, another intellectual at the cool kids' table. Post–*Star Wars*, she acted in Woody Allen's *Hannah and Her Sisters*, played Tom Hanks's wife in *The 'Burbs*, and wrote a bestselling novel, *Postcards from the Edge*, mining her drug addiction and time in rehab. Of *When Harry Met Sally*, she said, "It just fit my personality. . . . I didn't have to act." She was practically a sister to Penny Marshall, her best friend and Rob's former wife. "There was no weirdness," says Andy Scheinman. "And Carrie . . . listen, when you're Debbie Reynolds's kid, this is nothing."

If there was any weirdness, it involved Rob Reiner and Penny's 24-year-old daughter, Tracy, whom Rob adopted when they were still married. Rob asked Tracy to join the baby fish mouth scene in a tiny role as Harry's short-term girlfriend, Emily, aka "Aunt Emily," who runs a Mrs. Fields–esque baking empire. As Rob put it to Tracy on the phone: "Could you come? I need you to kiss Billy."

She was taken aback. "I said, 'What? This is someone I've known since I was a child,'" she remembers. "I was like, 'Kiss Billy?' He goes, 'Well, he's really more embarrassed than you. And here's the situation. And if you could come, we need you to play this girl, 'cause he would feel comfortable'—which is also weird!"

Billy agreed with Tracy. "This scene was slightly awkward for me because of Tracy Reiner, because I knew her since she was a little girl and now I have to date her in the movie," he grumbled later. Though Billy and Kim Greist locked lips in *Throw Momma from the Train*, Tracy says Billy—married 18 years—was apprehensive about kissing Meg. Tracy became a buffer "so when he did have to kiss Meg it wasn't going to be too weird and Janice [Crystal] wouldn't be weird. It would just be like…*pecking Tracy.*"

A kiss is still a kiss, but theirs lacked tongue. "It wasn't even like a *kiss*, you know, thank God," she adds.

For Sally's turn at Pictionary, "We improvised our way into the scene and were shouting made-up answers when Bruno Kirby hurled his three magic words: Baby. Fish. Mouth. It was like the heavens opened up to receive us," said Lisa Jane Persky, who played Alice. "As tremendous as Billy and Meg and Carrie are in the film—and they are the greatest of great, just perfect—when Bruno appears, onscreen movie-happiness amps up to the proverbial 11. He had an authority that carried him and everyone else to a greater level in their work."

Meg drew with gusto, tossing her curly mane and directing stink eye to the gang on the couch. In person her loopy gestures could seem micro. "She's not doing anything," thought Kyle T. Heffner (Alice's husband, Gary) at the time, echoing the immediate first impressions of several actors who watched Meg up close. "But the camera's tight and her eyes are so expressive and beautiful and she was working very small and all of that stuff translated right into the audience's heart. I think her ability to open her heart and show her vulnerability was why the audience latched onto her so much. She was very focused, and you couldn't really talk to her in between scenes. She was sitting there with her Walkman on... she wasn't screwing around in between takes. She kind of dropped into this zone and stayed there to allow her to reveal so much of herself on camera."

❋ ❋ ❋

"It felt like a boys' set, which is funny because in retrospect I think of it as Meg Ryan's movie," says Harley Jane Kozak (Harry's albatross, Helen). "But I remember feeling like the girl on a boys' set, which is why I'm pretty sure Nora was not there for that scene. I think she was enough of a presence that it would have tipped the scales."

Harley got the sense that Meg, too, felt like "the girl": "The adored 'girl,' the 'we're happy you're here girl' but 'the girl' on a boys' set."

Her instincts weren't mistaken. "While Ephron was amused and content enough to watch the often humorous banter between Reiner and Crystal, Ryan couldn't seem to find a niche for herself in the film's pseudo-family," wrote Rachel Abramowitz in her book

Is That a Gun in Your Pocket? Women's Experience of Power in Hollywood. Gossip from the set:

> *Crystal incessantly beseeched Reiner to give him encouragement ("How did I do? Did you see my dailies?"), and Reiner stroked his ego assiduously, often ignoring his leading lady, says one close observer. Ryan, who has a reputation as hardworking, self-sufficient and extremely professional, was often left to figure things out on her own. "I felt like I was doing my work in my trailer," acknowledges Ryan. Rapport between the [co-stars] quickly degenerated. On occasion, they were barely talking.*

Referencing Meg's alienation, Billy told the *Los Angeles Times* in 1989: "There were times for her it was hard in the beginning. But we're really open people. Meg, we just opened our arms to." Admitted Meg to the paper, "If they ever thought they intimidated me, it would shock them. But their stature in the comedy world is awesome, so that was intimidating. They were very conscientious about making sure I felt OK, because it was very much like a pre-fab relationship that I'd come into. Usually, everyone comes in and negotiates their respective positions on a movie. That didn't happen on this one."

Meg and Carrie became friends off the set. Billy has said he "resented that the girls would say, 'It was a boys' club.' We invited them to everything. They didn't want to go to a football game."

Witnesses describe a focused young woman who was more gentle than loud, but always had her say. She could seem aloof or cautious. Actors slip into their roles; perhaps she was internalizing Sally, who lets down her guard as the movie progresses.

"I never thought she was necessarily standoffish," says Todd Henry, camera operator on the movie. "When actors keep to themselves, my reaction is: they're into the role.... The first couple days are very, very awkward. You're feeling people out."

One person who was on set every day recalls, "I know that by the time we finished she was pretty at home with things. I think for a while there it was just a little bit—you know, she would do more watching than talking. Let's put it this way: She talked more and more to the director as the show went on. She became more and more open."

Rob, more verbal than visual, liked an actor to deliver certain lines as he heard them in his head; he would sometimes give readings. On occasion Rob instructed Meg: *Try to do nothing.* Listen and react. "It's really not about you," she said, summing up his advice. "It's about the other actor. And try not to make it about you. Make it about the other person.... Even in a bigger way it's not about you, in the sense that you're an instrument for storytelling. It's not about me, Meg Ryan.... It's about the audience."

Her professional attitude impressed the crew. If you asked Meg to show you which mark she intended to hit in a given scene, she'd happily oblige, and if she was comfortable around you, she might discuss Dennis Quaid, her recent *D.O.A.* co-star.

"They were going out," one crew member tells me. "She said, 'I know this guy Dennis. He's really crazy about me. But I don't know what to do.'" She wondered: "Should I get married? Or, what should I do?"

In Todd Henry's front-row view, her performance grew more impressive as Sally warmed to Harry and the leads' chemistry bubbled to the surface.

"I didn't think in the movie that Meg was brilliant," he says. "I gave her the credit as being a good actress.... But I think that when the magic started happening between them, then it was easier to see that it was working."

Along the way, Meg discovered the Easter eggs Nora laid out for Sally. She'd take a harmless line, like "I need a Kleenex," and render it extraordinary—the saddest, funniest, she-needs-a-huggiest. Meg, as thin and pretty as any basic nightmare, did not alienate Everywoman in row 15. Through Sally, she reflected Everywoman's doubts and fears, hopes and hang-ups. Everywoman and her daughter, Everygirl, saw an ally. *That's me.* And that's how teenage Nora connected to Audrey Hepburn in *Funny Face*. Meg, like Audrey, was a fun face and girlish grace. She didn't seem in love with herself.

But, as they say, the camera loved her.

"There is no question that everyone who complains about how little Hollywood cares about women characters is telling the truth," said Nora. "For instance, though I had a great experience with Rob on *When Harry Met Sally*, it was a big shock to him that the movie was as much Sally's as Harry's. Harry had more jokes but he was a less complex character. I knew this when I wrote it but he didn't know it, so when Meg began to work in the movie they were all stunned since she kept stealing scenes. But those scenes were all there in the script ready to be stolen by the right actress."

Nora later said that everyone knew they'd struck gold the first week of filming. Meg was a discovery, a trove of buried treasure, "that thing you almost never see: somebody who is as beautiful as she is funny." Where had she been hiding, and how did they get so lucky?

CHAPTER 3

The Orgasm and the Aftershock

Scene: Katz's Deli. October 1988. The worst day of Rob Reiner's life.

In hindsight, it would not go down as the *worst* day of Rob Reiner's life, but at the time, it looked like it. The director seemed to collapse into a puddle of sweat and crippling self-doubt. The level of perspiration was such that he laid a dishcloth atop his balding head to soak up the moisture. "What was I thinking?" he repeated. As if to ward off an anxiety attack, Barry Sonnenfeld, his cinematographer, remarked that the shoot was "going kind of good." To which Rob replied: "I'm directing a woman on how to fake an orgasm in front of my mother? Is that 'kind of going good' to you?"

That morning, production manager Steve Nicolaides stopped by Rob's trailer and found him "all in a tizzy." Perhaps Rob was nervous about Meg and whether she could pull off the faux O?

"Don't worry, man," Steve reassured. "She's gonna nail this."

"I'm not worried about her," said Rob. "I'm worried about the look of my mother."

Meg, meanwhile, had been in "happy denial" leading up to Sally's public climax. Blinders off, she suffered stage fright—*could she mimic bedroom noises with everybody watching?*—forcing Rob, himself tense, to play down the mortification of it all.

"What's Dennis going to think?"

"Meg, it's in a deli. It's not a sex thing. It's comedy."

A Lower East Side mainstay since 1888, Katz's Delicatessen on Houston Street supplied pastrami, salami, and franks to locals including the neighborhood's vibrant Jewish immigrant community that coalesced in the beginning of the 20th century. When that population declined—greener, more suburban pastures an idyllic option compared with cramped apartments—the 1960s wrought an era of crime-ridden urban decay. Katz's stood still. But times were tough. Many customers steered clear after dark. Others stayed away because of rebuilding on the Williamsburg Bridge in the late 1980s.

"It wasn't just the bridge; New York was in a pretty bad recession at the time," says Katz's co-owner Fred Austin. "The real-estate market collapsed; Wall Street was down. Our clientele was different. We appealed a lot to local people. People on their way home to Brooklyn or Queens would stop and take the Williamsburg Bridge, and with the bridge out we lost about a third of business then. You'd see it at 4 to 6 p.m. at night. The store was a lot quieter than it was previously."

Katz's was second choice. Rob and his crew wanted Carnegie Deli, the famed pastrami purveyor farther uptown, but failed to make a deal due to cost and schedule restrictions. They needed a full day; Carnegie wasn't prepared to close up shop for some movie. Next, they approached Fred and his fellow owners—father-in-law Martin Dell and brother-in-law Alan Dell—and won permission to rent out the institution. "When we were all talking about it, we knew it had to be someplace where there were a lot of tables and a big crowd," recollects Jane Musky. "And it couldn't be fancy because it had to feel like they just stopped there; it was not expected. They were just meeting up."

They hired extras to be servers. "For continuity's sake, you need to have the same people in the same position—and our staff was too wild to contain," explains Fred, half joking.

Fred had no idea what the scene, let alone the movie, was about. He would be in for a surprise, that's for sure. Although, is anybody surprised by what happens in New York?

Setup began around eight a.m. Lightbulbs were changed, tables moved, an actress mollified. Meg assumed her position across the table from Billy. She didn't like what she was supposed to wear, so she slipped on Billy's dark gray sweater. The co-stars were comfortable enough by this point to recap a day's shoot by phone on the regular; the previous night, Meg had expressed her jitters to Billy. The actor, off the hook, was sympathetic—and excited. Rob had the two rehearse. Meg underwhelmed.

"She did it kind of half-heartedly at first," Rob tells me. "I said, 'Meg, it doesn't work unless you go full out. You've got to do it.' And she tried a couple of times. I said, 'Let me show you what I want' and I sat down opposite Billy and I started acting it out. I started pounding the table and yelling and all this stuff." *Oh, oh God! Oh God!* "Billy said it looked like he was on a date with Sebastian Cabot, this guy with a beard that was on a TV series. So I did that, then Meg saw and she did it. And she did way better obviously than anything I could have done."

Rob's loud panting lesson incited applause. Fred Austin was amused at the demonstration. Estelle Reiner watched a few tables away, a willing bystander. "I made a mistake," the director divulged to Billy, referring to the matriarch in their midst. "I shouldn't have done that."

From Fred's vantage point, Meg's orgasm went on and on, take after take, stretching out into the afternoon. It improved each time.

"She was very focused," he says. "Everybody else was friendly and open. She, I guess—because of the embarrassment of having to do that scene—was very closed. During each break she'd run to her trailer out front."

While Meg wailed, adding hot, convincing sound effects, Billy adjusted his reactions accordingly. He appeared to enjoy every moment. "During breaks he'd run over and get some sour tomatoes and hot dogs," says Fred. "He was eating all day long."

Barring his climactic tutorial, Rob was "very quiet," remembers the bald, blue-eyed, white-goateed restaurateur. "What was funny was Rob and I looked very much alike at the time. People kept coming over to me and asking me directorial questions and were coming over to him and asking him delicatessen questions. So I answered as best as I could, as did he."

Estelle mastered her famous line in two takes. Afterward, she told Rob the story of a friend who regretted fooling a guy she was dating. Spoiler alert: he became her husband. According to Rob, "They had sex, and she faked an orgasm, and she was all upset. And I asked why. And my mother said, 'Because she made him think that's the way it was. Then she had to do it every time.'"

It was all over by six p.m. Lightbulbs reinstalled, tables returned to rightful places, an actress relieved and out the door.

Fred could not have predicted it then, but the orgasm would go on forever, outlasting Wall Street collapses, bridge closures, and needle-strewn sidewalks. Luxury hotels, mojito bars, and Carrie Bradshaw. Tourists, mostly women, would come to sample what Sally had. To sit at her spot and squeal.

✳ ✳ ✳

"When we were in New York, she was on set almost every day," Aaron Barsky, the first AD, says of Nora. "She always had something to say about everything."

For instance, she was adamant that the taxis' lights be turned *on*—signaling a vacancy—while Harry struggles to flag one down on Sixth Avenue during New Year's Eve, the worst time to catch a cab in New York. Isn't it more ironic that way?

"I think that Nora kind of came into her own once we started shooting and Rob realized she was a real asset as a producer," Jane observes. "She really had great ideas every day on the set. Since they were great friends I think Rob embraced it because he's kind of mensch-y that way. Rob had a strong mother. I think that he grew up in a household where everybody did their thing and I think that that's the way he was. He expected that you got it done. I think with Nora, because they were best friends, I don't think he gave her the credit to help her out. I think he truly felt like, 'I couldn't have done this without you.'"

Nora, boasting bigger clout than your average screenwriter, spoke often to Meg and Billy about their characters. As for Billy, "He was very insecure about it being his first real leading role and who he was and what he looked like and if the stuff he was doing looked like anything. He was concerned about his voice," Barsky says. "I think Rob talked him off of it a little bit, and I think he was just in a situation where he had to go with it. And he did a lot of talking with Nora. A lot."

Nora and Meg convened before Sally's tragicomic crying jag. It was to precede what we all knew would happen: sex with Harry. Meg was to sob uncontrollably, crescendoing into one of her best lines ("And I'm gonna be 40!"), bereft because Joe's marrying his paralegal. ("She's supposed to be his transitional person; she's not supposed to be The One!") Billy was to proffer Kleenex, moral support, and...one thing leads to another.

The hookup scene put each star on the spot: Billy would have to take one for the team and kiss Meg Ryan; the actress would have to melt into a puddle of tears.

Rob filmed around 30 takes of her comedy cry. Meg let loose her inhibition and released the floodgates; she'd do anything for a laugh. Off to the side, the director, who mouthed dialogue and ruined takes by laughing, mimicked her facial contortions in sympathetic solidarity. He could be distracting.

Jane constructed Sally's uber-feminine bedroom on a soundstage at Silvercup Studios in Queens: "Hers was as sweet as sweet could be. The scale was brought down. I had April Cornell fabrics; she was like, Miss Buttercup. And also I think it had to be because when they finally make love and they wake up the next morning, he just has to be like, 'Where am I?' So we just went really over the top with that sweetness."

Harry's expression: *What have I done?* He has one foot on the floor—Billy's idea. Sally wraps on her robe, exposing bare back. "That's as sexy as I get in any of my movies," Rob said.

While Harry bolts for the door, paralyzed by commitment angst, Rob happened to meet the woman who flipped his disastrous love life upside down—and gave him a reason to stick around.

"When we were in pre-production, Barry Sonnenfeld was the DP [director of photography] and there was a copy of *Premiere* magazine lying around the office," Rob tells me. "Michelle Pfeiffer was on the cover of the magazine. I had seen and met her a few months earlier, we had a lunch, a professional kind of thing. I read somewhere that she was getting divorced. So I said to Barry, 'Maybe I should call her.' I was like, an idiot, you know, grasping at straws because I had been single for so long. Barry said, 'You're not going to call her. I have a [photographer] friend in New York whose name is Michele Singer. You're going to marry *her*.' And I said, 'Does she smoke?' and he said, 'Yes.' And I said, 'Well,

I don't even want to meet her.' I'd been married to someone who smoked a lot and I just didn't want it.

"Time goes by and we're three quarters through shooting the movie and we're shooting the scene outside the brownstone on the Upper West Side, the wagon-wheel coffee table scene," says Rob. "We're just about to break for lunch and I look across the street and see Barry's girlfriend Susan, who's now his wife, and she's standing with this very attractive woman. I said to Barry, 'Who's that woman with Susan?' And he said, 'That's Michele Singer.' I said, 'What is she doing here?' He said, 'We're just going to have lunch.' I said, 'Maybe I'll join you.'"

So Rob wormed his way into lunch, with Nora, Billy, Carrie, and Bruno along for the ride.

"Nora was sitting next to Michele," Rob recalls. "We went to this place Docks on 90th Street. I hear Michele say to Nora, 'I can make better vichyssoise than this' and I'm thinking, 'Wow, what a bitch.' But I'm really attracted to her. Then lunch is finished, then we're walking back to the set. I walked over to her and chatted for a little bit, not a lot. After she left I said to Barry, 'Find out if it's OK to give her a call.'"

Rob was giddy, and everybody noticed.

"Afterward he goes, 'Boy, she was really great, huh? She's really something.' And I didn't think anything," says Andy Scheinman, at Docks that day in early October. "I thought, 'She's nice, she's attractive' but I didn't think, 'Wow or not wow.' I just thought we were having lunch. But he was smitten from the first second and it was really funny. Especially, since she told Barry Sonnenfeld, 'Don't do this movie, do the other one.' . . . Rob had sent the script to Barry, and he's out on Long Island with [Susan] and their friend Michele Singer. And he had *When Harry Met Sally* and another script. His wife kind of liked *When Harry Met Sally* and Michele liked the other movie, and said, 'Don't do that movie.' So it was up in the air and if Barry had listened to Michele, she would have never met Rob."

Barry got the OK from Michele, and Rob began to court her while he was making the movie. At one point, on a double date, Barry observed this exchange between the two:

> **ROB:** You know, you really shouldn't smoke. It's not good for your health.
>
> **MICHELE:** And you shouldn't be so fucking fat.

Despite Rob's disdain for cigarettes, Michele kept him on his toes. "She's got a really great edge to her," he gushes. "Everything about her. She's funny and she's got all these great qualities. For me, I could never be with somebody bland. I need somebody that has a little edge to them and she has that and she's incredibly smart and beautiful."

Not coincidentally, Rob recovered some joie de vivre after they hooked up. "He was very serious, very emotional, very in touch with his emotions," says cameraman Brian W. Armstrong. "There were definitely times when he may not have such a great day. But the last half of the movie he was very content, very happy."

Though Rob and Nora decided Harry and Sally belonged together, Rob changed his mind during filming. The meant-to-be couple weren't an item in an early cut.

"They ran into each other in New York," Andy reveals, "and they walk off and you think, 'Oh, maybe they'll be together; maybe they won't be together.' Just like the rest of the movie, it was like another five years. It was five years after the current ending would have taken place."

When Rob screened this bittersweet spin on *When Harry Met Sally* for various pairs of fresh eyes, the ambiguity was taken badly. "If they had tomatoes they would have thrown them at the screen," remembers Andy, adding: "They loved Harry and they loved Sally and they wanted closure. Rob felt it wasn't honest, but at the end he wasn't very comfortable with it."

A script given to actors in mid-August, shortly before filming, had closed with Harry sprinting to Sally on New Year's, delivering a line to rival *Jerry Maguire*'s "You complete me": "I came here because when you realize you love someone and you want to spend the rest of your life with them, you want the rest of your life to start as soon as possible." (This was written by Andy Scheinman, who's had a number of relationships but never been married. "You write really romantic lines for someone who's so shitty at romance," Rob pointed out.)

But rather than pay tribute to Sally's lovable qualities, and what makes her so great, Harry blurts the L-word (and the *Jerry Maguire* speech) as if that would be enough. "See, that's just like you, Harry," she says, furious. "You say things like that, and you make it impossible for me to hate you. And I hate you. I hate you, Harry, I really hate you."

(She so does *not* hate Harry. But the "hate" is important: When Sally refuses to say *love* during Harry's grand gesture, she denies her selfish admirer the satisfaction of hearing her say aloud what he knows to be true. Power move!)

Nora had pulled for Harry to look up from his navel and focus on Sally. "We had a huge battle about this," she said. "Rob wanted him to say basically, 'I've been thinking it over and I love you.' I wanted him to talk about her. I said, 'This guy has been a narcissist for the entire movie. It's time for him to talk about what it is about her that's important.' It was a gigantic fight, and the result is a scene that has both of those things in it."

And so the ending that we all know and love commences shortly before midnight: Harry dashes into the party and declares "I love you" in a flat tone of voice, as if to assume Sally would blithely share his enthusiasm. But as the countdown begins, an irate Sally explains: "I'm sorry, Harry. I know it's New Year's Eve, and I know you're feeling lonely, but you just can't show up here, tell me you love me, and expect that to make everything all right. It doesn't work this way!"

She walks away, prompting Harry to offer up specifics instead of vague pronouncements:

"I love that you get cold when it's 71 degrees out. I love that it takes you an hour and a half to order a sandwich. I love that you get a little crinkle above your nose when you're looking at me like I'm nuts. I love that after I spend a day with you, I can still smell your perfume on my clothes. And I love that you are the last person I want to talk to before I go to sleep at night. And it's not because I'm lonely, and it's not because it's New Year's Eve. I came here tonight because when you realize you want to spend the rest of your life with somebody, you want the rest of your life to start as soon as possible!"

Sally is that missing puzzle piece that renders Harry whole— the Michele Singer to his Rob Reiner—and now he must honor her quirks and how much she means to him. Though Sally unconvincingly declares her hate, her saucer eyes transmit joy. How romantic to learn that your best-friend-turned-lover adores you for *you*. Your personality! Your eccentricities! Your high-maintenance sandwich order! Nora vouched for a reconciliation worthy of our heroine because the writer had actually placed herself in Sally's sensible shoes, asking, *If a man were to quasi-propose, and I quasi-hated him, what could he possibly say to win me over?*

Rob filmed an unsuccessful version of the big finale at the Puck Building down in Nolita. The day after, Nora walked home in high spirits. She had just been to Cafe Luxembourg on West 70th Street to watch Bruno and Carrie nail her trademark quotables "Pesto is the quiche of the '80s" and "Restaurants are to people in the '80s what theater was to people in the '60s."

This movie is going to be good.

Later, around six or seven p.m., she caught the dailies— footage in the raw—from the previous night.

"It was the first time we shot the last scene in the movie," said Nora. "We shot it many times. And it was the worst thing I've ever seen. And I went home and thought, 'This is going to be a grotesque personal disaster.' That's what it is when you make a movie. And that's just from the writer's point of view. It's a whole other thing when you're the director."

One problem was the extras. Harry and Sally were lost in a sea of them. On a positive note, they were nicely animated and sang the hell out of "Auld Lang Syne"—not surprising, given New York's abundance of wannabe Broadway babies hoping for a big break (or small paycheck). Overall Rob felt it lacked emotional impact.

These are definite reasons for a director to exclude such a scene and replace it with that flash-forward alternate ending nobody liked in his early cut. Coming from the TV sitcom world, where pragmatic trumps precious, Rob was merciless in critiquing his films. *If something's not working, change it.*

He ordered a reshoot on a smaller Los Angeles soundstage. As Jane Musky recalls, "No one knew it was going to be a huge success, so you've doled out the money.... I wish there were 100 more extras and the place was three times as big."

In between Total Disaster and Total Recovery, there were rewrites. Billy, noticing the trait in Meg, came up with the nose-crinkle bit. The actor had been a fierce proponent of the dramatic entrance.

"He was saying, 'No, no, no, I have to tell her. I have to run to her,'" Jane recollects. "He thought he really had to go for it at that point. He also really wanted to do that whole thing where he would run like the Dickens. We started the run in New York up 6th Avenue and cut to him turning the corner on Wilshire Boulevard. It worked pretty well. I remember how tired he was because he had to do it over and over again."

It worked. Sally melted. Aaron Barsky, who handled the extras, partook of some mezcal. (His production assistant from Vegas downed the worm.) That was a wrap.

After considering several different titles—*Boy Meets Girl*; *It Had to Be You*; *Harry, This Is Sally*—Rob would finally settle on *When Harry Met Sally*. To Nora's chagrin, and mine as a writer, he added ellipsis points...

Columbia Pictures chose to release *When Harry Met Sally* on July 12, 1989, one week after *Weekend at Bernie's* and *Lethal Weapon 2* and two weeks before Tom Hanks's *Turner & Hooch*, a love story between a man and his Dogue de Bordeaux, and *Friday the 13th Part VIII: Jason Takes Manhattan*. In June, Tim Burton's *Batman* hurled into theaters; in May, *Indiana Jones and the Last Crusade* roped the box office.

It was a master stroke of summer counterprogramming that Nora adopted for *Sleepless in Seattle* in 1993. Audiences fatigued by male buddy action comedies, caped crusaders, and even Harrison Ford would be in the mood to escape the escapism. *Why don't we go see a nice romantic comedy?* The poster showed Meg and Billy standing atop a shrunken New York skyline. It teased a provocative subject: "Can two friends sleep together and still love each other in the morning?"

Word of mouth was essential to anoint a commercial win for Castle Rock. No Bat-Signal could alert the masses. Michael Keaton and Jack Nicholson were stars. Meg and Billy were not. Given that fact, a preview screening was necessary to test reactions and help spread the message. For better or worse.

Rob held his at Pasadena's UA Marketplace Theater on May 31. He was nervous. Billy was apprehensive. Thirtysomething women dominated the crowd.

"You never know what an audience is going to relate to," says Steve Nicolaides. "Something you put a lot of time into. And the lights go down and up comes the movie. And when Billy gets in Meg's car at the University of Chicago and pops the seeds in his mouth and turns to spit them out the window and the windows are closed, he says, 'Next time I'll roll the window down,' the audience started laughing and they didn't stop laughing until the movie was over."

They just about lost it when Estelle Reiner quipped, "I'll have what she's having." The shrieks bounced off the walls; the sound, rapturous. Billy and Rob—hidden near the back—grabbed hands. *Oh my God.*

As Nora suspected, the scene would play uproariously, causing women to convulse and men to shift uncomfortably in their seats. This made her happy.

No way was Nora going to miss *When Harry Met Sally*'s Beverly Hills premiere, held July 13 at the Academy of Motion Pictures Arts and Sciences. Look, Demi Moore and Bruce Willis! *Is that Maria Shriver and Eunice Kennedy Shriver?* There's Charlton Heston! Carol Kane! John Cusack! Judd Nelson! Shelley Long! Scott Baio! *O.J. Simpson and Nicole Brown Simpson.*

Billy and Janice smiled for the cameras. Rob escorted wife

Michele Singer, whom he married in Hawaii on May 19, some seven months after meeting her on the movie. Funny how things work out, even for a chronic pessimist.

At the Beverly Hilton after-party, the director urged hundreds of merrymakers to stop what they were doing and listen to a young, butterscotch-voiced jazz musician named Harry Connick Jr., who sang on the soundtrack. A woman shouted: "He must be 12!"

Meg Ryan, belle of the ball, skipped the entire event. Her excuse? She was stranded on the Hawaii set of *Joe Versus the Volcano*, a romantic comedy co-starring Tom Hanks. Hurricane Dalilia was headed toward the Big Island. (Very convenient, should one aim to avoid endless orgasm questions.)

Partygoers mobbed Rob and others in the cast and crew. The schmoozing extended into the night.

Nine days later, *When Harry Met Sally* opened nationwide after playing in just 41 theaters across the country. Expanding to 775 theaters, it soared to third place behind number one champ *Lethal Weapon 2* (1,830 theaters) and runner-up *Batman* (2,201). Harry and Sally ultimately reached 1,174 screens in the United States, racking up $93 million in ticket sales. They'd collect another $100 million overseas.

Previously, popular romantic comedies like 1987's *Broadcast News* ($51 million) and 1988's *Working Girl* ($64 million) and *Moonstruck* ($81 million) received winter openings. They never made as much money.

Practically overnight, Nora was solicited as an expert on relationships and love. "You seem quite wise," she said. "You give the impression that you knew what you were doing all along. You become an expert on friends, on the possibilities of love, on the differences between men and women. But the truth is that when you work on a movie, you don't sit around thinking, *We're making a movie about the difference between men and women.* Or whatever. You just do it."

Not that she lacked an opinion on the differences.

"The truth is that men don't want to be friends with women," Nora wrote in 1990. "Men know they don't understand women, and they don't much care. They want women as lovers, as wives, as mothers, but they're not really interested in them as friends. They have friends. Men are their friends. And they talk to their male friends about sports, and I have no idea what else."

✳ ✳ ✳

When Harry Met Sally polarized reviewers, with a sizable swath nitpicking similarities to Woody Allen. Atypical of a screenwriter, Nora's name was mentioned equally to the director and actors. She assumed a chunk of the blame in negative critiques. Otherwise cordial to the movie, the *Los Angeles Times*' Sheila Benson handed credit to Rob and Billy, implying that Nora—whose *Heartburn* "had an undertaste so nasty you could be puckered for a month afterward"—was too snotty to write a tender romantic comedy. "Wherever it came from, the results are charming," said the critic.

Over at the *New York Times*, Caryn James pointed out the Woodyish opening credits (white font against black background), dreamy New York cinematography, and Gershwin-inflected melodies, calling it "the sitcom version of a Woody Allen film, full of amusing lines and scenes, all infused with an uncomfortable sense of déjà vu." She deferred to Woody: "Gently mocking his own romanticism, Mr. Allen gives his films depth and a believable, astringent undertone. But Mr. Reiner has a simple faith in fated love, which makes his film cute and sentimental rather than romantic and charming."

Roger Ebert, who egged *Heartburn*, gave the screenwriter a thumbs-up, saying, "Ephron's dialogue represents the way people would like to be able to talk.... The dialogue would defeat many actors, but Crystal and Ryan help it to work; their characters seem smart and quick enough to almost be this witty."

Newsweek's David Ansen observed, and rightly so, that "Ryan gets stronger as her character grows. She strains in the 1977 scenes and sometimes oversells her cuteness, but she blossoms into a comedienne of dazzling charm."

In the *Washington Post*, Rita Kempley raved: "Ryan is summer's Melanie Griffith—a honey-haired blonde who finally finds a showcase for her sheer exuberance. Neither naif nor vamp, she's a woman from a pen of a woman, not some Cinderella of a Working Girl. She's feisty and eccentric and more than holds her own against Crystal's irascible, charming, George Burns nouveau."

On November 11, 1989, Meg found herself face-to-face with the Princess of Wales at *When Harry Met Sally*'s London premiere. Sloane Ranger by day and screen siren by night, Diana turned heads in a floor-length scarlet chiffon number with matching shoes and clutch. Her other accessories: diamonds, a suntan, and a smile. At this event, Meg—four months younger than the princess—might have posed as her sister, the casual Pippa to her ceremonial Kate. Unrestricted by royal dress codes, Meg the pre-grunge gamine veered to clothing that embraced simplicity and eschewed fuss, emitting the faintest whiff of "I don't care...too much." She rarely showed skin. The actress's clothes so appalled bitchy fashion pundit Mr. Blackwell that he crowned her "rag doll of the year" on his 1987 list of the top 10 "Worst Dressed Women," next to Diane Keaton, Lisa Bonet, and Cher.

To meet Princess Diana she pulled up to the West End theater in a brown velvet frock, two strands of white pearls, and dewy no-makeup makeup. The tuxedo on her arm: Dennis Quaid. As the lights darkened, a question loomed: *How would Diana react to Meg's uncivilized showstopper?* "When the orgasm scene starts, she was laughing so hard, just belching it out," said Billy, also in royal company. "She had the kind of laugh where if you were on a date, you'd never want to see her again. Then she grabbed my hand and said, 'So naughty.'"

Princess Di asked to screen the movie privately with friends—at Buckingham Palace.

While princesses giggled, airliners clutched their pearls. Censors gutted the 'gasm for the in-flight edition. Nora happened to be on a plane showing a sanitized cut—she wasn't fully paying attention, as she'd seen it all before—when she heard a hum of boos echo throughout the aircraft cabin. The passengers had spoken: *Where's the scene? Prudes!*

The Motion Picture Association of America slapped an R rating on the movie because of the scene. Nora was baffled. I mean, if you go around killing people, like Batman and Indiana Jones, you got a PG-13, but if you weren't violent and merely *verbalize* lovemaking instead of *showing it*, then the MPAA brands you unsuitable for under-17s? Ironically, Sally's fearless creator would strip the racy sex talk from *Sleepless in Seattle*, explaining to Meg Ryan, *You're a Republican who's never had an orgasm.*

A reinvention was afoot.

CHAPTER 4

This Is Her Life

If you were a celebrity in the 1990s, and you needed a place to stay in New York City while filming a movie, you called Boaty Boatwright. Or Boaty Boatwright called you.

So it seemed. The prominent talent agent, then at William Morris, which represented Tom Hanks until his defection to Creative Artists Agency, rented out her apartment at the Apthorp to the actor and his pregnant wife, Rita, while he filmed *The Bonfire of the Vanities* in the spring of 1990.

At the Apthorp, the couple befriended the screenwriter Nora Ephron on the elevator. She introduced herself and told them the best neighborhood spots for bagels, lunch, and food delivery. (Tom would return to those places in *You've Got Mail.*) They'd see Nora's sons, Jacob and Max, heading off to school. They met her friends—and fellow Apthorpians—Bob Balaban, the actor, and Tony Walton, the Broadway set designer. They met people with dogs. Says Tom, "It was kind of like living on Elm St. USA, except it was the Upper West Side. And we were the new people that were staying in town for a while."

Imposing on the outside, the Apthorp fostered comfort, community, and creaky charm within. For years its spacious units and stabilized rents attracted a largely middle-class assortment of tenants, including artists and small business owners who claimed vacancies in the 1960s and 1970s amid the city's devastating economic crisis. Prostitutes prowled Broadway, as did drug dealers. And when the yuppie invasion of the 1980s cleaned up the avenue, clearing room for upscale condos, Starbucks, and Barnes & Noble, many residents stayed put against worries they'd be pushed out. Joe Crackhead moved on to a new gutter; Joe Fox moved into 152 Riverside Drive. It wasn't all bad. Tom and Rita were "perfect tenants," says Boaty (real name: Alice), adding: "Nora was a delightful neighbor, and we had fun sharing parties and guests together. Her cooking, which she did, was far superior to mine, which was either catered or takeout!'"

A few years later, the Hankses bought a crash pad across Central Park, on posh Fifth Avenue. The Upper East Side is the staid, WASPy cousin to the Upper West. Close to but a world apart from the Upper West Side, which maintains its lefty-intellectual core with Columbia University, Hayden Planetarium, and Lincoln Center on the premises, the East Side possesses high-toned arts like the Met, the Guggenheim, and Bemelmans Bar at the Carlyle. Shockingly, Nora, the consummate Upper West Sider, would switch sides in 2002 as the Apthorp, under new management, jacked up rents—adding a marble nude statue that scandalized low-key denizens—in a bid to lure the superrich. "She gave us the list of the places to get the greatest salami and the place that would fix your zipper," says Tom. "And the place where you could get your prescriptions and they always remembered you and never even asked you to sign anything. It was the same sort of thing. She just moved a couple of towns over."

Tom Hanks has no memory of Nora's 1989 visits to the set of *Joe Versus the Volcano,* his first romantic comedy opposite Meg Ryan. Part of it was shot on location in Hawaii and the other half on Soundstage 30 at Warner Brothers Studios in Burbank. The movie marked the directorial debut of John Patrick Shanley, who wrote the winsome Cher–Nicolas Cage romp *Moonstruck,* for which he won the 1988 Oscar for best original screenplay. Cher, irresistible as the Italian American Brooklyn widow who falls for her fiancé's brother, beat Meryl Streep in the best actress category, accepting the award in a black beaded, barely there Bob Mackie. She was the first actress in a romantic comedy to win since Diane Keaton's 1977 victory for *Annie Hall.* Another romcom nominee Cher's year was Holly Hunter for her role as an ambitious TV news producer in *Broadcast News,* written and directed by Jim Brooks. While *Broadcast News* ended on a realistic note, with Hunter's character choosing neither Albert Brooks nor William Hurt, *Moonstruck* embraced a deep and abiding faith in love that the next wave of romances would continue in earnest. The time was ripe for Tom and Meg to finally hook up, with Shanley at the helm.

At the urging of Steven Spielberg, 38-year-old Shanley would make a go at the genre as both director and writer. His imaginative *Joe Versus the Volcano* tells the story of Joe Banks, a down-on-his-luck office drone whose terminal illness—"brain cloud" is the diagnosis—frees him to quit his job, buy some natty threads, and see the world. Embrace life as he wouldn't otherwise. Joe's journeys lead to the South Pacific island of Waponi Woo, home of the Waponi tribe, whose teeth have rotted from drinking too much orange soda. There, he must jump into a volcano to honor a cash-for-suicide deal made with a shadowy industrialist who needs clearance from the natives to mine a rare mineral. The Waponis require a volunteer to pacify a volcanic deity; none will apply. By the time he reaches the edge, Joe has fallen for Patricia, a sultry sailor; before Patricia he meets insecure LA heiress and self-described "flibbertigibbet" Angelica; before Angelica he musters the courage to ask mousy co-worker DeDe on a date. He is dying, with less than six months to live, and that freaks her out.

Joe was autobiographical—at least in terms of the characterization—for the first-time director. Like his character, a former fireman with PTSD-related hypochondria, Shanley experienced intense fear of death. As a young man, the Bronx-born Irish Catholic, who won the Pulitzer for his play *Doubt: A Parable*, about a nun who suspects a priest of inappropriate behavior toward an altar boy, drudged along in the advertising department of a "very depressing" company that made medical supplies. A New York University dropout, he returned to school following a tour with the Marines; he graduated valedictorian of his class in 1977. (He has never leaped into an active volcano.)

Tom admired the script and the idea of a guy who awakens from a zombie state to embrace life and love. When Shanley was casting Joe, "His lawyer, agent, his everybody called at the same time, basically, said Tom wants the role," he says. "And after a brief discussion with Steven Spielberg, who was one of the producers of the film, I embraced that as a great idea. He is kind of Everyman and I would feel more than comfortable having him represent my best self."

Shanley wanted one woman to play DeDe, Angelica, and Patricia; he thought it would be an easier route to attract top-tier talent than by offering three separate cameos. Besides, using a single actress would bring "emotional continuity" to the narrative.

"I read Julia Roberts. I read Diane Lane," he says. "And Julia was incredible. It was before she got cast in *Pretty Woman*. Within a few months she was cast in that. Diane was great, and all kinds of people came in. And then Meg came in. And as soon as she started reading, I was like, nobody else can play this role. She was so charming, she was so fluid, she was so bold. She had no problem. Some of the other people who read were terrific at one of the roles. What they had to offer was their personality, which was terrific. But they couldn't transform particularly. So they'd be better in one role than the other role. Meg could just fluidly enter any vessel and inhabit it. She was just luminously beautiful. And at the same time didn't seem like a distant celestial orb. She seemed like somebody you might know who just happened to be very beautiful. And idiosyncratic at the same time. And I knew as soon as she started reading that her and Tom would be fantastic together."

Shanley immediately made an offer. "And she took the weekend, I remember," he continues. "Because there was another role that she kind of wanted to play, which was a very dark role. And that was always the thing with Meg, that here she was projecting this incredible, luminous, well-adjusted, 'I love life' persona. But inside she also was really aspiring to be edgy, and be dark. And thought that that side of her had not gotten its day in court. When her manager, I think it was, told me she was struggling over whether to do this or—I think it was *Jacob's Ladder*—I just basically thought she was crazy. And I was deeply alarmed. Not that it meant something negative about her but that she might, in her aspiration to do something edgy and dark, choose this other film. She actually demonstrated to me in her audition that she was irreplaceable. Good news, on Monday she came back and they accepted the role and we were off and running."

Meg welcomed the triple-part challenge. She thought that each character, a part of the whole, represented a woman's growth through risk-taking. Joe Banks might be the main attraction, but he wasn't the only one doing the growing. As DeDe, she wore a brown wig and contacts, Staten Island accent, and a sheepish innocence; as Angelica, the pill-popper with daddy issues, she projected low self-esteem in vibrant red curls and a breathy voice somewhere between Cher Horowitz and Holly Hunter; as Patricia, her last incarnation, she let down her long, blond hair, and her natural smolder, as the confident captain sailing Joe to his doom. While Sally Albright mirrored women, Patricia enchanted men. Here, Meg Ryan became the dreamgirl next door—wise, supportive, sexy—whom Joe Bankses everywhere longed to "wife." She could heal your broken wings and make you fly again. She'll even follow you into a volcano:

> **PATRICIA:** Joe, nobody knows anything. We'll take this leap and we'll see. We'll jump, and we'll see. That's life.
>
> **JOE:** I saw the moon when we were out there on the ocean. Shining down on everything. I'd been miserable so long, years of my life wasted, afraid. I've been a long time coming here to meet you. A long time on a crooked road. Did I ever tell you? The first time I saw you, I felt like I'd seen you before.

"They just had instant chemistry," Shanley says of his two leads. "They were very easy with each other and sparkly with each other, whether they were in the scene or just talking. Meg was very humble...always seemed to be startled when she was treated well. I didn't know exactly what that was about, but I remember noticing it and being charmed by it. I remember one time I made her a cup of espresso coffee—I had gotten an espresso machine for my trailer—and I invited Tom over for one. And I invited Meg. And she just seemed kind of startled to be included. I'm like, I don't know what's been going on in these other films that she's been doing!"

The actors were extremely prepared, open to direction, and adaptable to change. Good thing, too: Hurricane Dalilia delayed the Hawaii shoot two days; in an ironic twist, Tom and Meg filmed during a (fake) typhoon back at Warner Brothers. There were rain machines. Fog machines. Wind machines the size of plane propellers. Swept up in adrenaline, Joe kisses Patricia. Lightning strikes. The ship's hull whacks her overboard. Joe, knight in a Hawaiian shirt, dives to the rescue.

It must be a bizarre feeling to see your husband kiss another woman, but Rita and Meg struck a close friendship, cushioning the blow. ("Meg is one of the all-time great people I know," Rita affirmed. "It's a lot nicer when you know that it's your good friend kissing your husband.") Nora, a regular visitor to Shanley's set, approved the pairing. "She got sort of a crush on Tom Hanks and Meg Ryan together," says Shanley. "She just couldn't get over how terrific they seemed as a couple. And I think that was part of her inspiration for casting them when she made her films."

Meanwhile, over at Stage 24, she had been watching director Herbert Ross fumble *My Blue Heaven*, a comedy she wrote and executive produced about a New York mafioso hidden in suburban California as part of the witness protection program. Steve Martin was Vincent "Vinnie" Antonelli and Rick Moranis the meek FBI agent assigned to keep the flamboyant Vinnie from blowing his cover. It's a bromance, with lessons learned on both sides, and a lighthearted poke at the Mafia genre of which Nora's husband was a verified expert; Nora absorbed Nick's passion via osmosis. Organized crime was filled with intriguing customs, folklore, and the myth of concrete shoes. And characters. Nora kept a framed picture of John Gotti, on trial for murder, leaving the courthouse, his smile an exercise in self-control: "Don't let them know what you're really feeling."

Thanks to Harry and Sally, the screenwriter was extra-hot. She won best original screenplay at the 1990 British Film Awards over Steven Soderbergh (*Sex, Lies, and Videotape*), Tom Schulman (*Dead Poets Society*), and Ronald Bass and Barry Morrow (*Rain Man*). And she was the only member of her romantic comedy to receive an Oscar nomination.

Meanwhile, the snub of Meg in *When Harry Met Sally* from the Academy of Motion Picture Arts and Sciences remains a huge unsolved crime. For best actress nominees they selected Jessica Tandy, Jessica Lange, Michelle Pfeiffer, Isabelle Adjani, and Pauline Collins, British star of a 1989 romantic comedy called *Shirley Valentine*. Like the genre in which she thrived, the actress would continually be excluded from the most prestigious of ceremonies.

It was 22-year-old Julia Roberts's first time attending the Academy Awards. In 1990, she earned a supporting actress nod as Shelby in *Steel Magnolias*—the role Meg turned down to play Sally. Julia lost to *My Left Foot*'s Brenda Fricker, but still there was cause to celebrate: her romantic comedy, *Pretty Woman*, in which she played the proverbial hooker with the heart of gold, had debuted at number one three days before. She was hands down the biggest female star Hollywood had seen in years—and the Academy would invite her back the next year as a leading-actress nominee. Director Garry Marshall had approached Meg to play sex worker Vivian Ward. She passed. Additionally, she rejected *Ghost*, that year's top-grossing movie, as well as 1991's *Silence of the Lambs*, which brought Jodie Foster her second Oscar in three years. As excellent as Meg might have been, she would not be better than Julia or Demi or Jodie; like all memorable per-formances, you can't imagine anyone else playing their parts. "It wasn't a druther situation—it wasn't like, 'Oh, I'll turn this down in order to do this,'" Meg explained. "They kinda came along and, again, the script is everything and I have absolutely no regrets about any of those things." As for *Silence of the Lambs*, "I felt it was dangerous and a little ugly. I felt it was too dark. For me."

Casting decisions spelled agony. *Which parts to accept and which to reject? What should I do? What do I want to do? How do I reconcile my needs and my wants while also pleasing the fans?* Without their love, an airborne actress loses fuel. Without box office, she free-falls back to earth. Though Meg seemed to rely upon gut instinct and personal interest, she was doubtless not immune to the money question: *What if I say yes to a stinker and no to a sensation?* After *Joe Versus the Volcano*, she chose one serious role (Jim Morrison's companion Pamela Courson in *The Doors*) and one light (Alec Baldwin's wife in *Prelude to a Kiss*). At least directors were knocking on her door and sliding scripts underneath. It's safe to assume many were stinkers.

"I'm barely able to contain a guffaw when a reporter asks me what drew me to a role, as though there is a rainbow of well-written female leading roles," Meryl Streep stated onstage at a Screen Actors Guild women's conference in August 1990. "There's very little work for women. And when we do work, we get paid much less than our male counterparts. And what work there is lately is odd." Given the proliferation of big-budget action flicks—which Nora termed "Guys Chasing Guys"—and the popularity of *Pretty Woman*, Meryl said you'd think "the chief occupation of women on Earth was hooking, and I don't mean rugs."

Either you surrendered to the market or you disappeared—and, after 40, you might as well be invisible. The statistics were troubling. The Screen Actors Guild reported a widened gender gap in 1989, with men seizing 71 percent of feature film roles and 64 percent of TV roles. Male actors outearned female actors $644 million to $296 million. Desperate to snatch international dollars, Hollywood courted young men from Boston to Beijing who overwhelmingly preferred Guys Chasing Guys—rather, Arnold Schwarzenegger Raining Bullets—over gender-balanced fare that focused on character, words, and women. Meryl, drawn to a spectrum of shape-shifting female characters, lamented, "the crackling wit and stylish verbal surprise which characterized films of the past has been crushed under the wheels of blockbusters."

The casualties included *Joe Versus the Volcano*. Shanley's final cut—philosophical, surreal, transcendent, with the wonderful original song "Marooned without You"—defied simple categorization. It stumped Warner Brothers' marketing division. Ebert lavished praise, writing, "my heart began to quicken, until finally I realized a wondrous thing: I had not seen this movie before....Hanks and Ryan are the right actors to inhabit it, because you can never catch them going for a gag that isn't there: They inhabit the logic of this bizarre world and play by its rules. Hanks is endearing in the title role because, in the midst of these astonishing sets and unbridled flights of fancy, he underplays. Like a Jacques Tati, he is an island of curiosity in a sea of mystery."

The *New York Times*' Vincent Canby likened *Joe* to the big studio flop *Howard the Duck*. "Many gifted people contributed to it," he wrote, "but there's no disbelieving the grim evidence on the screen." One dismal review following the other and—*kerplat!*—the film was tagged a failure. It underperformed at the theater. Shanley took a lot of heat in New York. "It always surprises me how conventional the critical establishment is," he says, "because if something comes out that's not like other stuff, they're like, *what's this?* ... I guess because it was my directing debut, because I was a writer as well, they thought it was some kind of ineptitude on my part. But, in fact, everything in that film was exactly what I intended to shoot. And I had a very definite vision, which you could either share or not."

Little by little, over a period of 10 years or so, *Joe* began to amass a cult following. Viewers responded to its messages about self-actualization and romance. "It takes courage to love," says Shanley. "And there's always going to be problems. And you have to have a certain faith that the problems will be solved."

* * *

Meg Ryan and Dennis Quaid intended to marry in Montana, but postponed their wedding after Dennis confessed his cocaine addiction in 1990. He entered rehab. She went into therapy and Al-Anon. Meg recalled: "I was probably as aware as a lot of people who were in that situation are—you sort of know, but you don't know. ... In one way it was very complicated because I thought, 'This is so brave of him to be telling me'—so incredibly brave. And then I felt furious. If I had found out some other way maybe we wouldn't be together."

One week before *The Doors* premiered in Los Angeles, Meg married Dennis in their room at the Hotel Bel-Air on Valentine's Day 1991. It was spur of the moment. Now or never. Randy Quaid and his wife, Evi, witnessed the ceremony. Meg and Dennis pulled a reverend from a Rotary Club luncheon at the hotel. Said the bride, "I lost it so completely that every now and then I think we should maybe do it again so we have a clue of what we promised each other."

Dennis was getting his life back on track. Meg, who thought

herself the most practical and least romantic of the two, grabbed his hand. They jumped into the volcano.

* * *

The mercurial, mean-spirited director Herbert Ross, infamous for bullying actresses from Maggie Smith to Julia Roberts to *My Blue Heaven*'s Joan Cusack, called *Heaven* "a horrible experience, something I never should have done." Gene Siskel blamed Nora's "dull material" and Steve Martin "trying to skate by with just that spiky hairdo." Caryn James blamed Herb and Nora for wasting Steve Martin's talent. Nora blamed Herb for mangling her original vision.

"I realized that if you make movies with Rob Reiner and they're big hits, you don't necessarily want to direct, but when a script of yours that you liked is just destroyed in your opinion—of course, it's always your opinion—the writer always thinks he or she had nothing to do with it," she said. "I looked at *My Blue Heaven* and thought, 'Well, I could have screwed that up just as badly as Herbert Ross did and he got paid [$2.5 million], so I might as well think about directing.'"

Moreover, if Nora wanted to write movies about women, she might as well direct them herself. It seemed to her that the female experience intrigued only a handful of male directors, like Mike Nichols and James L. Brooks, thereby lowering her chances to make a film featuring strong (or simply existent) women characters. The gender imbalance was striking. For example, of the 1,794 studio movies issued between 1983 and 1992, just 4.5 percent were directed by women. Among the most visible woman directors of the time were Penny Marshall, Barbra Streisand, Jodie Foster, Amy Heckerling, and Kathryn Bigelow (whose action-adventure sensibility challenged presumptions that women could not get down and dirty with the boys).

It's sad, but true, that women got more breaks during the silent film era. Before the motion picture business became mainstreamed and moneymaking, with men pulling the studio strings, women gained influence as directors, writers, editors, producers, and actresses. Lois Weber broke gender barriers in 1914 when she became the first American woman to helm a full-length movie, *The Merchant of Venice*. She adapted the Shakespeare play for the screen and also acted as Portia. Her husband and collaborator, Phillips Smalley, played Shylock. Weber, who was Universal Studios' top-earning director in 1916, surpassed Smalley as the brightest star in their creative union. But by 1944, the only way a talented screenwriter like Phoebe Ephron could see her name in the credits was to partner with her husband, Henry. And while Henry nabbed a producer title on their adaptation of *Carousel*, Phoebe was left out.

When Harry Met Sally, a moneymaker at Columbia Pictures, positioned Nora as a potential director. Columbia president Dawn Steel, one of the first women to lead a major Hollywood studio, offered Nora the opportunity. Dawn enlisted producer Lynda Obst, a longtime friend of Nora's, to choose a project right up her alley: *This Is Your Life*, the Meg Wolitzer novel about two sisters coming of age while their single mother, a stand-up comedian, flourishes in her career. It had heart and meat and relevance to her own life; Nora wanted to make the movie. Who else would? She asked her sister Delia, the author of humor books *How to Eat Like a Child*, *Teenage Romance: Or, How to Die of Embarrassment*, and *Funny Sauce*, to collaborate on the script adaptation and join the production as full-time writer so that Nora could focus on the daily demands of directing.

Halves of the same comic brain, the siblings made each other laugh. Nora once called Delia "the funniest person I know." Delia was especially skilled at writing children, and of course she and Nora connected as few could to the bittersweet story of 16-year-old Erica and 10-year-old Opal Ingels (Engels in the book), daughters of a dominant showbiz matriarch. While Dottie Ingels is warmer than their real-life mom Phoebe had been, Dottie tends to use her girls as fodder for her traveling act. She's fulfilled by work and sees less and less of the kids. When they need her the most, she's not there. "Neither of us quite knew what we were doing," Delia wrote. "I was learning more and more about screenwriting, and she had never directed. Both being somewhat ignorant, we needed each other for skill as well as emotional support. Also, it was fun (not to mention easier) to collaborate. Nora and I would say to each other, I almost got this, please finish it, or we need a joke here, or why isn't this working?—send the scene off and back it came, done."

Their mission was to produce a ripple effect of directing opportunities, this film leading to a second. Nora groaned at the "woman director" thing, as if she were some exotic zoo animal set loose on a studio backlot. She wanted to be a *New York* director, like Woody Allen, for whom upper Manhattan was a stage. Nora's New York–based agent, Sam Cohn, who repped Woody and Sidney Lumet and despised LA, worked hard on Nora's behalf.

Under Dawn Steel's watch, they were protected. Then, in January 1990, the executive resigned her post after Sony acquired Columbia and installed *Batman* producers Peter Guber and Jon Peters. The project stagnated. Nora met with Peters in New York. He brought along his then-girlfriend Vendela, the Swedish model. He said he'd made some 68 movies without reading a script and basically requested Nora's CliffsNotes version. Rarely one to leave out a gossipy detail, she recounted: "He told me about his shrink who was trying to help him get in touch with his inner child, which I did not think was going to be much of a stretch." At the end of the meeting, Nora later joked, she was all but prepared to slit her throat.

Joe Roth was a guardian angel. The chairman of 20th Century Fox adopted and greenlit the movie (new name: *This Is My Life*) with a budget of about $9 million. Joe was wowed by Nora's confident—directorial—approach to ordering for their table at the Russian Tea Room. He supported her decision to hire a nonstar, Julie Kavner, the familiar (and very wealthy) voice of Marge Simpson, letting go his directive to get a *star*-star. At one point playing Dottie interested Bette Midler, a box-office draw, though Disney executive Jeffrey Katzenberg declined to break her studio contract. Nora pleaded, but "Jeffrey isn't really interested in women," she said. "His wife is a housewife. He just wasn't there, and it was heartbreaking to me."

Nora cast Samantha Mathis as Erica and Gaby Hoffmann as Opal. Dan Aykroyd agreed to play Dottie's talent agent, Arnold "The Moss" Moss, who eats paper—a trait inspired by Nora's real-life representative Sam Cohn. Carrie Fisher said yes to a small role as Arnold's assistant Claudia, without even seeing the script—very Jon Peters of her. "Several people turned it down and it really hurt my feelings...and I needed somebody with a little bit of a name to take the part." She called Carrie, and to her relief the actress said, "I'll be there."

Nora solicited advice from friends and luminaries like Sidney Lumet, Rob Reiner, Mike Nichols, and Alan J. Pakula. They warned her about sleep loss and suffering health. She was scared to death. "What they don't tell you," she remarked, "is that it's unquestionably the best job in the world." Nora's close friend Diane Sokolow, a TV producer who had a cameo in the movie, sent her a Mets baseball cap with the note, "This is what the guys wear. You're one of the guys now." Later, Diane was moved to see photos of Nora wearing the hat on set.

The first time she said "Action," a big smile materialized on her face. While Dottie and her daughters resided on the Upper West Side, the director filmed *This Is My Life* in Toronto. Nora was 50 years old. "She was hilarious and adorable and so much fun," remembers Lynda Obst, the tiny dynamo known for her toughness and intelligence. "And her first movie, that was a really big deal, because she needed the things that a director needs during a debut. She felt that the crew in Toronto was not taking her seriously. Back in those days you didn't see a lot of women directors. So the Toronto crew—which was, first of all, a mediocre crew; in those days you got a mediocre crew in Toronto—did not take her seriously. We fired our prop guy on the third day because when she said, 'I would like Dr. Brown's Cream Soda'...he brought generic cream soda. She said, 'Would you please tomorrow bring Dr. Brown's Cream Soda' and he continued to bring cream soda. We wrapped him. He just had no idea how important detail was in establishing New York. That's the kind of crappy prop man that Nora could not have when we were trying to establish New York."

A New Yorker in 1992 definitely recognized Dr. Brown's, a local soft drink brand, at the corner bodega. Nora, a stickler for specifics, wanted what was authentic. Details mattered greatly. Food. Design. Props. Costumes. Atmosphere. If you failed in these areas, didn't understand her taste, didn't care to listen, your job was on the line.

Nora, meanwhile, had tons to learn. She was inexperienced and eager to collaborate, a quick study. "I never saw Nora postulate that she was an expert at something she wasn't an expert at," says Caroline Aaron, who played Martha, wife of Dottie's ex. "She never had any shame at filling in her own blanks. She felt like that was completely legitimate. Everything is a team sport. Whether it's cooking or dressing, finding the best doctor or hairdresser or best way to make a loaf of bread. Everything was a team sport and you're just pulling all the 'A' people and you end up with the best of everything. It was such an interesting way to watch how power can be the sum of many parts; it doesn't have to come from one person."

Delia told me her sister loved collaborating and "if you had a good idea on one of her movie sets, she was always interested to hear it. It didn't matter who had the idea."

Nora knew the effect she wanted but not necessarily how to get there. There's a scene, for instance, when Erica and Opal run away to their absentee father's house and meet Martha, who invites them in. Nora said to cinematographer Bobby Byrne: "When you're sitting in the dark watching this, I want the audience to feel the way these little girls feel. When they're walking up the steps, even though it's four steps, it feels like they're climbing a mountain. How do I do that?"

Byrne—who replaced a director of photography whom Nora criticized for improperly lighting Julie Kavner so as to create shadows on both sides of her nose—suggested placing the camera underneath the steps to track their feet and give the illusion of a steeper ascent.

Nora drew lovely performances from her cast. Samantha Mathis was unforgettable as sullen, resentful Erica, who misses Dottie so much she puts up a wall between herself and the world. (Erica's loneliness and regret after losing her virginity is immensely affecting.) How unusual, how ahead of their time, for Nora and Delia to focus on a brooding female adolescent (not the Disney-fied *Little Mermaid* version), let alone the enduring hot topic of working mothers and work-life balance. "There is no answer to that question: that's what this movie is about," Nora explained. "You just have to make it up as you go along and hope you don't screw it up too horribly."

In a case of life imitating art, in the spring of 1991, Nora went away for 10 weeks on location. Jacob, 12, and Max, 11, accustomed to their mom working from home, making her own hours, making dinner, baking cookies, and attending school events, were "quite shocked" by the change, she said. "Looking back on it, I thought, 'Well, they're old enough to handle this,' and by the way, they did handle it," she recalled. "But the truth is, it was harder for them than I thought it was going to be. But I didn't care. I'm sorry, but I didn't. It was time for me to do this, and I thought, 'We have a good support system in place. They have a stepfather. They have a father. They have a great nanny, and they'll come visit me every other weekend. We'll all get through this.'" Nora, who tended to stick loved ones in the background of her movies, cast her boys and Lynda's son, Oly, as trees in the background of Opal's school play, a performance of T. S. Eliot's dark poem "The Hollow Men."

Nick was thrilled for his wife. While he got bored on the set of *Goodfellas*—indeed, much of moviemaking is "hurry up and wait"—the process, all that decision-making enlivened Nora. He said she was happier.

Back in the New York groove, Nora was adding the finishing touches to *This Is My Life* when a young producer guy out of LA requested her services on a project that had failed to tempt Meg Ryan. Could she help?

CHAPTER 5

Sleepless Nights

Jeff Arch was a 35-year-old martial arts instructor with a wife, two small children, and nothing to lose. He lived in Los Angeles during his 20s, working as a lighting designer and assistant to acclaimed cinematographer Conrad Hall (*Butch Cassidy and the Sundance Kid*), but he longed to make it as a screenwriter. At 30, he wrote an off-Broadway play that critics panned. After a series of setbacks, he found stability—normalcy—in small-town Virginia. He taught English at the high school. He taught tae kwon do at the local studio he owned. But he grew restless. Creatively, he had an itch that needed scratching. Personally, he wanted to prove it to himself, and his family, that he was more than what he was. He sold his business and picked up writing again. He completed a Cold War–themed buddy comedy that got some attention. But nothing came of it. "Russia wasn't our enemy anymore," he explains. "The day I finished it, the Berlin Wall came down."

At home on a frigid night in January 1990, he gazed up at the shining stars through a skylight window. "For every star in the sky there's a good idea," he told himself. Then, all of a sudden, he had one. One by one, the stars seemed to shoot right down into his lap. A title manifested.

Sleepless in Seattle.

At home on a Saturday afternoon in Los Angeles months later, Gary Foster choked up. He was sitting on the couch, burning through a script called *Sleepless in Seattle* by an obscure writer, Jeff Arch. The agent Dave Warden, who primarily represented screenwriters, Jeff included, sent Gary a copy. "Take a look at this," he said. "I think it's a precious little piece." The young father and producer of *Short Circuit 2* and *Loverboy*, a 1989 Patrick Dempsey comedy, put it down and said to his wife, "Whoa. This is a really good movie."

Jeff's *Sleepless in Seattle* was a romantic drama about star-crossed lovers who don't meet until the very last scene. His male protagonist, Tom Baldwin, was later renamed Sam. (I don't wish to confuse you, dear reader, so I'm going ahead and calling him Sam. Onward!) The story opens with Sam Baldwin attending his wife's funeral, 10-year-old son Jonah in tow. On Christmas Eve, Annie Reed drives to boyfriend Walter's family house and happens upon a radio conversation between "Sleepless in Seattle" and syndicated shrink Marcia Fieldstone. She gets sucked in. She stops by a diner and discovers she's not the only woman listening. She grows obsessed. She confides in friend Becky, who secretly mails Sleepless a letter inviting the widower to rendezvous atop the Empire State Building on Valentine's Day, as in the 1957 Cary Grant–Deborah Kerr melodrama *An Affair to Remember*.

Annie, a newspaper journalist, identifies the man behind the voice and travels to Seattle, meaning to introduce herself. There, she spots Sam and another woman she mistakes to be his new girlfriend. Annie catches Sam's eye. He remembers her as the beautiful woman he saw at the airport. Annie, embarrassed, is nearly run over by an oncoming taxi, an allusion to *Affair*; she avoids the tragic fate that befell Kerr's Terry McKay. Annie pledges allegiance to Walter, but when the two visit New York, she boldly dumps him—on Valentine's Day—and books it to the Empire State's observation deck before closing. Jonah, desperate to meet Annie, the woman from the letter, had flown solo (destination: the Empire State), with a distressed Sam on his tail. Father and son reunite and wait for Annie. Just in the nick of time, Annie races to the finish line and greets Sam, her fate, 86 floors up in the air.

Gary had a production deal at TriStar Pictures. He took the script to studio exec Richard Fischoff, who produced *Kramer vs. Kramer*, thinking he was the right set of eyes. "Richard, you need to read this personally," he said. "Do not have it covered. You need to experience it. Don't trust it to someone in the story department." Fischoff agreed. In entertainment industry lingo, script "coverage" is a written report, including analysis and comments for improvement. A time-strapped exec will generally assign reading and write-up duties to a less powerful staffer. The staffer's assessment helps the exec decide whether to place a script in the "yes" or "no" bin.

"The coverage on *Sleepless in Seattle* wasn't very good," said Fischoff, calling a week later. Gary fumed. "I asked you to read it personally," he told Fischoff. "I don't give a shit about the coverage. This is not going to cover well. You need to read it."

Jeff had broken a cardinal screenwriting rule that made people nervous: in a romance, the couple was supposed to meet early on—not in the last few minutes. *Would moviegoers stick around until the end?*

The next day, Fischoff—making good on his promise—told Gary he was right. He persuaded the brass to option *Sleepless in Seattle*, which TriStar bought around Memorial Day 1990. Gary, meanwhile, had never met Jeff Arch. They'd spoken on the phone once or twice. He flew to Virginia. The men formed a collegial relationship. Gary kept Jeff in the loop while writers more famous than he refashioned his characters and dialogue, keeping the bones of the plot intact. The heart, too. "It came from a place of passion and desperation and that's powerful," says Gary. "That's something that you can't re-create."

A disciple of self-help coach Tony Robbins, Jeff was introspective, disciplined, and determined to improve. His desire for fame fueled his youthful screenwriting fantasies. Older and more mindful, Jeff redirected his motivation outward. He learned that in order to fulfill his dreams, he needed to put the audience first. That fateful January night, he wondered: "How do I get two people in Finland to walk out of a movie theater holding hands?"

How about a love story? Love stories are timeless, Jeff had told Dave Warden. If you write one, said Warden, "I can sell it."

How about Sam and Annie get together at the Empire State? He remembered watching *An Affair to Remember* with a college girlfriend. "I thought it was the stupidest thing in the world and I couldn't believe it, how corny and hokey it was," he says. "I like love stories but this was just a gallon of syrup over everything."

How about Sam and Jonah live on a houseboat? He thought back to an episode of *This Old House* where a guy goes out to Seattle and builds a waterfront flat.

He poured his disappointment into Sam, the sad dad who's given up; his initiative into Annie, who steps outside her comfort zone to live a life less ordinary; and his yearning into Jonah, who believes that dreams can come true. "I was looking for a happy ending for me," says Jeff. "I was all three of those characters. I didn't know it."

He stepped out of the way and let the universe work its magic. He knew he'd created something huge. Bigger than himself. He said to his wife: "You are going to see Meg Ryan on the cover of *Premiere* magazine because of this movie."

Sleepless in Seattle reminded TriStar boss Mike Medavoy of the 1974 high-concept French drama *And Now My Love*. Written and directed by Claude Lelouch, it parallels the lives of two strangers, a man and a woman, who are meant for each other but haven't met. We *know* they're meant for each other because each orders coffee with three sugars. In the final moments, the soulmates are seated next to one another on a plane. The destination? New York City.

Medavoy liked *And Now My Love* so much, he was compelled to lock in *Sleepless's* stars right away. He sent the script to Dennis Quaid, whose production company had a deal with TriStar, and Meg Ryan, already a pro at the romance drama. "He knew they wanted to work together and they both liked the material," says Gary. "We then had to try to figure out the right director. There were a lot of people in the mix and we couldn't agree on somebody. At that point, we decided to go back and look at the script and make some adjustments."

Commonly in film development, another writer is brought on to polish a script and patch up issues. Jeff figured this might happen. Nora was at the top of Gary's list, but she was unavailable. He hired the playwright Larry Atlas but did not use his rewrite. According to Jeff, Atlas did a "terrible" job and "will forever go unmentioned." (Atlas, for his part, has never seen *Sleepless in Seattle*.) David S. Ward, an Oscar winner for *The Sting*, came on to rewrite Jeff in 1991. Ward added humor to diffuse the earnest tone of the original. He lightened up the father-son dynamic and, crucially, revamped the radio call-in scene so that Jonah—*not Sam*—reached out to Dr. Marcia Fieldstone. In Jeff's draft, Sam calls Dr. Marcia because he's worried about Jonah, declaring that every 10-year-old "oughta have a mom. So I'm gonna find him one." It was the first of several on-air therapy sessions.

That's the one big mistake, Ward thought. What woman is going to fall in love with a man so full of self-pity? "It's not the kind of thing that a guy's guy would do—especially as a guy's guy was defined back at that time," says Ward. "The definition of what a guy's guy *is* has morphed and changed over the years but [in the early 1990s], it was hard for me to see Annie developing a romantic sense about Sam from that kind of a conversation." And so Jonah's role became bigger, more active, as the engine setting events in motion. Sam, by contrast, grew stereotypically manlier. If the stars on the screen reflect who we are and whom we want to be and whom we want to *date*, then in 1991, that was Costner and Cruise and Swayze. None except Arnold were muscle-bound, neck-less droids. Rather, they exuded a quiet, strong masculinity. They were dreamers and doers, seekers and protectors. Sometimes they wore oversized sweaters. Never did they carry on about their dead wives to talk-radio psychiatrists and the wider world. That was for wimps.

"Hello."

"Gary, this is Nora Ephron."

It was January 1992 when Nora rang Gary for the first time. She'd suddenly become available to do a quick rewrite. Good thing, because *Sleepless* still required fine-tuning.

"Give me three weeks," she said. "I know exactly how to do this. I get it. I'm going to write you a movie for Meg Ryan and Tom Hanks. That's who should be in this movie."

"Yes, let's do it," Gary replied.

Nora, almost done sound-mixing *This Is My Life*, had a two-month gap before the film opened in February. She didn't make enough money directing the movie and needed cash to stay afloat. At the time, her screenwriting fee was in the "high six figures." She and Delia had written a Christmas comedy about misfits at a suicide-prevention hotline that was based on the wacky French movie *Santa Claus Is a Stinker.* Nora wanted to direct it. Until then, she'd be a gun for hire. "I'd made a horrible financial error years earlier when I refused to do the production rewrite on *Fatal Attraction* because I thought it was a disgusting, sexist movie," she said. "Then I saw it and realized that I was completely wrong, that it was basically a male nightmare and was quite a brilliant movie in its own disgusting, sexist, but brilliant way. I could surely have put my kids through college with the deal I could have made on that."

Flash-forward five years. Adrian Lyne was working on *Indecent Proposal*, and Nora was hungry to work with Lyne. She pictured dollar signs. "He's so weird and he's so serious—he's so hilariously serious," she said. The woman-for-barter premise was alarmingly antifeminist and appealingly controversial. A husband and wife gamble away their money in Vegas and a billionaire offers $1 million to sleep with the wife. Do they take the money? Would *you* take the money? *Would you accept the rewrite?* "I wanted to do it, but he was in a really grouchy mood about the project and didn't hire me." Lyne instead appointed William Goldman.

So, *Sleepless in Seattle*. During a 1993 talk at the American Film Institute, Nora recalled her immediate thoughts: "I looked at it and it was a very gloopy script. It was nothing like the movie that you saw—nothing like it. It was not a comedy at all. There were about two jokes in it—the kid had the jokes. One of them was 'Jed's got cable,' which gets a laugh, you know." She felt the Empire State Building scene was strong. But more could be done with the *Affair* theme. Or the concept that Sam and Annie, though separated by thousands of miles, could coexist within the same global community.

The night after reading *Sleepless*, Nora lay awake. She had an idea. An image. She bounded from the mattress to sketch a map of the United States and two people at opposite ends. She woke Nick to show him. *That's wonderful, darling.* He went right back to sleep.

Rita Wilson wanted to see Nora Ephron's *This Is My Life*. Tom Hanks, dutiful husband, came along. The actor—hardly the target viewer for what he deemed a "middle-aged chick flick"—fell in love. So did Rita. "We just thought it was so clever and funny," she says. "So intelligent and well-written and the performances were great." Tom dug the fact that Nora had pulled off the unthinkable: A "geographically correct moving montage in a movie." When Julie Kavner and the kids ditch Queens for the Upper West Side, the camera trails behind to capture the twists and turns of the actual route. As Tom put it, "real cars in real traffic in the actual order of transit required to get from point A (the ordinary life in not-Manhattan) to point B (Manhattan), a distance of miles physically but light-years culturally."

Though bunkered primarily in Toronto, Nora knew she had to go to New York to get that detail right. *This Is My Life* had its world premiere at the Sundance Film Festival on January 16, 1992, and did flimsy box office when it hit theaters two months later. "She told Sally Quinn that the Kavner character was too Jewish," Richard Cohen wrote of Nora's explanation for why her movie failed to resonate on a wider scale.

And yet, top critics heralded the arrival of an astute, clear-voiced filmmaker. Nora's long takes were engrossing, not tedious; she treated Dottie and her needy showbiz friends with winking empathy, not "these people are monsters" judgment; and she didn't wrap a tidy bow around the ending. "What I see is three women you don't fuck with trying to work out a truce," wrote *Rolling Stone*'s Peter Travers. "Ephron doesn't shy away from the bleak terrain ahead. Her gift, a rare one, is for being brutally honest and funny simultaneously. Her independent spirit validates the inclusion of *This Is My Life* at Sundance. It's one from the bruised heart."

Tall, white-haired, and intense, Bob Reitano, *This Is My Life*'s editor, could be Martin Landau's stand-in. The Upper West Sider got to know Nora while assisting editor Steve Rotter on *My Blue Heaven*. Rotter was "a great conversationalist and it's hard to talk to Nora," says Bob. "If you're not in her orbit, she gets bored. And when she gets bored, beware. She did not like boring people. But I didn't say anything." She admired Bob's work in the cutting room and later asked him to join *This Is My Life*. He jumped. "It could have been three armadillos in Pakistan; I would have done it to work with her. She was going to be the first film that I was going to do solo and not as an associate." While editing the scene in which Dottie and the girls have a blowout fight—"Don't I have a turn? Isn't it ever OK for me to have a life?"—Bob politely suggested to Nora that next time she should move the actors around a little. She appreciated the advice and was careful not to repeat the mistake.

Three or four months later, Nora phoned Bob. "I'm sending you something," he quotes her as saying. "Tell me why we should do this." It was *Sleepless in Seattle*. "She sent it to Nick, her husband. To Delia. To Sam Cohn, her agent. And me. I was that inner circle, which was incredibly gratifying....So I read it and I thought, This is *When Harry Met Sally* again. And Nora called and said, 'What do you think? Haven't I done this movie already?' I said, 'Kind of, but there are so few sweet films, so few nice films that I want to work on. Even though that's the case, you can make it different enough. It will be wonderful.' 'I'm not sure. I don't want to redo something I've done.' I said, 'Well, I'm looking for a job. That's part of it as well. That's 51 percent of it.'"

Nick Castle was to direct *Sleepless*. TriStar offered the picture as compensation for yanking Castle from *Hook* the year before.

117

The studio pushed aside the writer-director (*The Last Starfighter*, *The Boy Who Could Fly*, *Tap*) following disagreements with stars Robin Williams and Dustin Hoffman. Steven Spielberg replaced Castle on the fantastical Peter Pan update; TriStar wrote Castle a check for $500,000.

Sleepless was a second shot to repair relations and reputations. Says Castle, "I didn't have my choice of scripts. 'You want to do this, we'll make you the director.' I read it and really liked it." He boarded the project during Ward's rewrite, and he and Gary Foster scouted houseboats in Vancouver and Seattle. He met with legendary Swedish cinematographer Sven Nykvist about joining the crew. He met with an interested Kim Basinger about playing Annie. He lunched with an ambivalent Meg Ryan at the Ivy. At that moment, Meg wasn't sure she wanted to star—even though husband Dennis Quaid, with whom Nick did not meet, would remain in contention as a potential on-screen love match for Basinger. Dennis was lining up an assortment of leading roles after a two-year hiatus from the movies. His last film appearance was the 1990 bomb *Come See the Paradise*. His 1989 Jerry Lee Lewis biopic, *Great Balls of Fire!*, flopped hard. But things were looking up. He had quit cocaine, had married Meg, and was about to become a father for the first time. She was pregnant and due in the spring of 1992.

By the time Nora got involved, her talent agency, ICM, intended to "package" TriStar's *Sleepless in Seattle* with clients Dennis and Kim. But Nora—who didn't find those two all that funny—told Gary she had Tom and Meg in mind. Gary was eager to bring Meg back into the fold and loved that Nora and the actress were friendly. Allow me to translate Hollywood-ese: the practice of movie packaging is agents grouping together actors, writers, and high-level crew members in exchange for a commission. The purpose is to make more money while simultaneously unburdening the studios of hiring headaches. ICM also represented Meg Ryan. And David S. Ward. And Julia Roberts.

"They wanted her to come in and throw her brand of battery acid on it, and get it a little bit wide and a little bit snappy," Jeff Arch says of Nora. "The stuff that she's known for; the smart thing."

Castle met Nora in New York. She showed him *This Is My Life*, which he liked. They discussed approaches to the screenplay. She told him she'd write a draft, see if she was headed in the right direction. He told her about Meg's indecision.

"Oh, I'll get her to do it," she said.

When Nora's rewrite came in, Gary rushed a copy to Castle, then hunkered down to read. Nora relocated Annie from Lancaster, Pennsylvania, to Baltimore, a city that at least had a major league baseball team. (If she had been involved at the get-go, Sam and Annie would be living on opposing ends of Central Park.) She created her favorite character, Jessica, Jonah's bossypants friend and a younger version of Nora Ephron. She turned *An Affair to Remember* into a running joke that mocked the differences between men and women—her forte—and fleshed out the theme of global interconnectedness, with mass media the common denominator. Said Nora: "We all live in a place where we hear the same jokes within 24 hours of one another and watch the same television shows and see the same movies and turn against the President at the same exact moment or fall in love with the First Lady; that was the kind of stuff I didn't think the script had begun to do."

In Nora's hands, *Affair* became the avenue connecting the movie's women. Annie and Becky weep while watching it. Sam's friend Suzy weeps while describing it. Jessica weeps while saying, "This is the best movie I've ever seen in my life." The Empire State doorman grumbles that his wife loves *Affair*. The men? They

119

just don't get it. Sam dismisses the mushy Leo McCarey–directed confection as a "chick flick."

One of the great ironies, however, is that the attractive architect-superdad embodies *Affair*'s central allure: *Emotion*. Sam Baldwin likes baseball. Boats. Basic button-downs straight out of Larry David's closet. He's a quote-unquote guy's guy...who also happens to be America's most eligible bachelor. Female admirers send letters in droves. Why did that happen? He demonstrates to Dr. Marcia's listeners, including Annie, that he's man enough to express his emotions and capable of love—powerful, all-encompassing movie love. Walter's great, perfect on paper, but he can't compete.

```
ANNIE:  Time, distance, nothing could
        separate them. It was right. It was
        real. It was...
BECKY:  ...a movie. That's your problem.
        You don't want to be in love. You
        want to be in love in a movie.
```

Nora soaked out the sentiment, administering it in small but effective doses, so that in the final stretches, Sam and Annie's meet-cute felt extra meaningful. She wanted it both ways. Her *Sleepless* razzed tearful reactions to an overwrought movie like *An Affair to Remember*. At the same time, Nora aspired to re-create *Affair*'s lasting effect upon its tear-stained fan base. To peddle the fantasy. Brainwash young minds.

Gary was excited. The draft had edge and currency—it was going to be hot. According to the producer, Nick Castle thought otherwise. "He read it and called me up and said, 'Gary, this is a disaster.' I said, 'What?' He said, 'She took the heart out of it.' We had a real creative disagreement and he said, 'I want to have a meeting tomorrow at the studio. They need to hear my point of view.' So we had a meeting and he made his point of view clear, and they said, 'Thank you for sharing with us.' He left the room and they asked me to stay behind. They said, 'He's totally wrong. We've got to move on.'"

ICM heavies Jim Wiatt and Sam Cohn co-agented Nora's career from both coasts; Sam was bad at returning phone calls, but he'd pick up for Wiatt, the agency's LA-headquartered president.

"When she was [rewriting] it, she had the idea that she was going to be the director...that no one else was going to be the director except her," Wiatt tells me. "So she would subtly" pitch herself. "And the way she wrote—which was fantastic—her voice was so clear in the script that she said that she is the one who can execute it better than anybody else."

Suddenly, word got out and everyone started to realize that Nora's revision was something special. All manner of industry power players—actor, director, producer—angled for a piece. The Dennis-Kim package unraveled; Basinger, who switched agencies, left the picture. Later, she said she regretted turning down *Sleepless*, explaining that Nora "was not even attached" and she hadn't liked the script she read. Gary had included the *Batman* bombshell on an early shortlist. He says, "It was one of those moments of, yeah, we can get the movie made, but is she the perfect person?" (Other possibilities he listed were Andie MacDowell, Debra Winger, Jeff Bridges, and Basinger's then-partner, Alec Baldwin.) Nora called Gary every day to get the play-by-play. Gary called Jeff Arch with updates on the growing list of actresses who wanted the part.

Daryl Hannah. Demi Moore. Sharon Stone. *Madonna.*

Jeff couldn't believe it. And Nora? Nothing like this had ever happened to her.

"She had a very strong passion for it and she was the type who would do anything to get it," remembers Wiatt. "She wasn't going to let it go."

Concurrently, megashark Ray Stark was going in for the kill. A towering Hollywood figure, 76-year-old Stark had shepherded Streisand to stardom. He produced *Funny Girl, Annie,* and *Steel Magnolias.* His tactics were cutthroat, part of the legend. He had a long producing tenure at Columbia Pictures, corporate sibling of Sony-owned TriStar, and an option on Julia Roberts, Steel Magnolia–turned–supernova. For director he liked Garry Marshall, whose *Pretty Woman* minted Julia into a movie star, or Ron Howard, whose *Far and Away* starred supercouple Tom Cruise and Nicole Kidman. For Sam Baldwin, he liked Tom Hanks. "Ray liked the script and wanted to get involved in it," says Mike Medavoy. "We finally didn't get involved with him but he had already on his own taken the script to Tom, who said yes."

Gary Foster, who'd recently turned 30, a baby compared with Stark, was going to get eaten alive if he didn't protect himself. The young up-and-comer had this prized possession on his hands—one that *he* spotted and developed—and now Stark comes in swinging, trying to take charge. And Gary, a USC film school grad with far less prestige and much more to prove, worried that he would lose control of a movie that could potentially put him on the map. If Stark took over, that would make Gary the Jeff Arch in this situation—the guy who got the idea—and ultimately the shaft, as the A-listers swooped in to bench him.

"There he was, within inches of touching a green light, when suddenly this 900-pound behemoth, Ray Stark, came into the room and that was the end of everybody," remembered Nora. Where she spent a mere three weeks on *Sleepless*, Gary had been with it two years. The son of veteran producer David Foster, with whom he worked on the *Short Circuit* movies, Gary knew the business and how to massage egos and maneuver around strong personalities. He has kind brown eyes and an open heart. Back then, he had a mop of thick, brown hair. He was—is—unfailingly diplomatic, but when threatened, he would not hesitate to dive into the water and swim with the Starks. And he certainly wasn't going to turn away Julia Roberts. She'd make a great Annie, he thought. But if she said yes, then he'd have to accept Stark as a partner. "I will do that as long as she does the movie," Gary recalls telling the studio. "If she doesn't do the movie, Ray Stark goes away." And so "they gave the script to Julia and for about a minute she wanted to do it. And then a minute later she decided she didn't want to do it."

Before turning down the role, Julia Roberts had vocalized her wish that Nora direct—a vote of confidence that helped the writer gain leverage as a candidate to helm *Sleepless*. "When you have Julia's name on the marquee, you have the biggest female star in the world, one of less than 10 people in the world who can 'open' a picture simply because she's in it," Fox chairman Joe Roth told the *Los Angeles Times* in 1991. "And she's arguably the only actress on the list. That's what's so exciting about this phenomenon: At least at this moment, there's someone who broke the taboo about gender. Julia is up there with Costner, Gibson, Schwarzenegger. She can carry a picture regardless of genre, domestic or abroad."

And yet, in Gary's view, Julia was "a little young for this part and I think at the end of the day she realized that." *Variety* reported in its March 24 issue that she liked but did not love *Sleepless* and had decided to pass. Stark was livid. He reportedly vowed legal action for her reversal and blamed Julia's then-boyfriend Jason Patric for influencing her decision (a theory shared by Gary and others). Team Roberts brushed him off. "She thought indentured servitude was abolished years ago," a handler sniffed in print. According to the trade paper, TriStar dangled $3 million.

Julia went on to star in Warner Bros. Pictures' *The Pelican Brief*—collecting an $8 million salary.

Gary had grown increasingly frustrated with everybody throwing shit against the wall and using *Sleepless* to make themselves look important. He liked *This Is My Life* and called Nora to propose her as director. Was she interested? *Are you kidding?* With Nora's yes, Gary urged Medavoy to hire her. The TriStar chief consulted colleagues Stacey Snider and Marc Platt. Says Gary, "What came back to me was 'Look, we love Nora but it's a certain kind of point of view and sensibility.' And I said, 'Yeah, this is the woman who wrote *When Harry Met Sally*. This is the woman who understands the genre better than anyone else. This is the woman who took this script from being a solid B to an A. And she just had experience, so you should at least meet with her.' And I forced that first meeting and they flew her out."

Nora, always prepared and strong in an executive conference room, presented her ideas to Medavoy, Snider, and Platt. They said *great*. They said *thank you*. They made no decision. Nora flew back to New York.

Gary worried a Garry Marshall or a Ron Howard would gloss over Nora's sarcasm and oversweeten the movie. Marshall was threat numero uno.

But in a big leap of faith, Medavoy would stamp Nora's approval. He requested she hire Sven Nykvist, Ingmar Bergman's right-hand man, as her director of photography. Nora requested Delia, her right-hand woman, as her collaborator. There were two more sit-downs with Medavoy, and in the last, says Gary, "He went around the table and he said, 'OK, go make your movie.' And he greenlit the picture and she got the job."

Medavoy encountered people who thought he was crazy. *This Is My Life* was a disaster! Now he handed Nora a $25 million budget? Her pros outweighed the cons. "Smart, patient, organized, thoughtful, and a child of the industry," he says, checking off her positives. "On all accounts, she had everything going; I think she just made her first choice the wrong choice." And, of course, Nora knew Medavoy, whose track record as a studio exec included the Best Picture–winning trio of *Annie Hall*, *Rocky*, and *One Flew over the Cuckoo's Nest*. A talent agent during the 1970s, Medavoy proudly represented many in the new generation of hotshot auteurs rebelling against Old Hollywood, such as Steven Spielberg, George Lucas, and Francis Ford Coppola. Likewise, Nora, a New York intellectual, brought a singular artistic voice and sensibility to her work.

Nora and Medavoy were also co-godparents to CBS president Howard Stringer's son David. Despite their shared social connections, Medavoy sometimes found Nora a little distant; as a director, she was a huge risk. But Nora's professionalism and creativity swayed him: he believed in her.

Now in the driver's seat, Nora reconsidered Tom Hanks as Sam Baldwin. She "wasn't crazy about the idea of Tom in that part," says Medavoy, "because we knew then that Tom was not the traditional leading man. I guess you could have said that about Jimmy Stewart, too; he didn't look like Cary Grant."

Gary wanted Jimmy Stewart. A real *guy* whom men and women liked equally. He strongly believed that Tom should play Sam and told Nora so. They discussed other names (which Gary can't remember) and finally agreed that he was worth pursuing. Receiving word of Nora's involvement, Tom excitedly informed his agent: "She shot that geographically authentic move into Manhattan!"

What could his ex-Apthorp neighbor offer? How would they get along professionally? Was he Cary Grant enough?

They would size each other up at the Beverly Hills Hotel.

※ ※ ※

"Nora would just always think of me as the guardian of the screenplay," Delia said to me, explaining, "She knew she would be directing and she wanted someone who had her back and she wanted someone whose main priority was the script. Because she's juggling so many other things."

Nora said *Sleepless* wasn't ready to direct. She brought in Delia for an additional rewrite. An ideal setup, all around. Delia, who became obsessed with *Seven Brides for Seven Brothers* as a girl, innately understood the love-in-the-movies motif. *Seven Brides*, the backward plot of which involves the kidnapping of six women by backwoods bros, rocked tweenage Delia to the core, sparking a search for love that would entail a divorce—her first husband, an Ivy League professor, feared her writing career might bring fame—and a new relationship with Jerry Kass. She met the fellow writer, kindred spirit, and non-lumberjack in her New York apartment stairwell. (At their 1982 wedding, Delia's vows included a line you may recognize as Sam's tribute to his dead wife: "It was like coming home, but not to any home I'd ever known.")

Delia, a playful wordsmith, invented language. It was her idea to have Jessica use initials. MFEO, H and G ("Hi and Goodbye"), YOH ("Your Only Hope").

Stepmother to husband Jerry's son and daughter from a previous marriage, Delia was instrumental in giving Jonah an authentic, smart-alecky voice. ("Thanks for dinner," he deadpans to Sam's quasi-girlfriend Victoria. "I've never seen potatoes cooked like that before.") Delia had been skeptical that Jonah, who'd just lost his mother, would support Sam having a new wife so soon. But, ah, yes: The boy wanted a new wife for Sam because he wanted Sam not to be lonely.

"I guess it was the first thing I understood about myself as a writer," Delia says. "Writing tells you who you are." She wrote the 1978 best seller *How to Eat Like a Child* and "suddenly realized, Oh, I get kids. Being able to write them I believe comes from a powerful identification with children, empathy and memory of your own childhood."

Among Delia's contributions was a bit where Sam's colleague Jay declares single women are after "pecs and a cute butt." Then Jay offers Sam advice on what it's like to be a bachelor in the early 1990s. Dialogue by Nora:

JAY: Well. Things are different. First, you have to be friends. You have to like each other. Then you neck. This can go on for years. Then you have tests. Then you get to do it with a condom. The good news is, you split the check.

SAM: I don't think I could let a woman pay for dinner.

JAY: Great. They'll have a parade in your honor. You'll be Man of the Year in Seattle Magazine. Tiramisu.

SAM: What's tiramisu?

JAY: You'll find out.

SAM: What is it?

JAY: You'll see.

SAM: Some woman is going to want me to do it to her and I'm not going to know what it is.

Nora hoped the line about the trendy Italian dessert would get laughs from people in the know and confuse the rest.

And let's give credit where it's due: Three years before *Seinfeld*'s Soup Nazi episode, Nora name-dropped Manhattan soup vendor Al Yeganeh in her script. During a meeting at the *Baltimore Sun*, where Annie and Becky work, their co-worker pitches a story on Yeganeh: "This man sells the greatest soup you have ever eaten; there's a line around the block, and he is the meanest man in America."

Nora and Delia had ordered from Soup Kitchen International during post-production on *This Is My Life*. Says Delia, "We knew it was a terrifying place....I felt sorry for the person we sent from the editing room to buy lunch and never had the nerve to go there myself."

The sisters and Lynda Obst reunited on *Sleepless*. Lynda, named executive producer, had made *The Fisher King*, *Adventures in Babysitting*, and *Heartbreak Hotel*. She was divorced from David Obst, the literary agent who represented Carl Bernstein and Bob Woodward. Lynda, who was an editor at *New York Times Magazine*, first met Nora at a volleyball game in Washington. Later, the Obsts moved to LA, where Lynda began developing scripts for Peter Guber and David Geffen. She and producer Debra Hill formed a production company based at Paramount; in 1989, Lynda ventured out on her own to forge a deal with Columbia. Like Delia, Lynda had Nora's back. "The only note I ever gave her was basically a leftover from the Jeff Arch script that she had to run over more—which was that it was a little backlash-y for [Annie] to be chasing the guy," Lynda says. "So she loved that note."

In 1991, the prominent feminist Susan Faludi published *Backlash: The Undeclared War against American Women*, which argued that patriarchal institutions such as Hollywood had punished women in the 1980s for progress made during the 1970s. Faludi singled out *Fatal Attraction* as an egregious offender for portraying a single career woman as a deranged bunny-boiling stalker. Faludi's literary inspiration was a fear-mongering 1986 *Newsweek* cover story, "The Marriage Crunch," that reported a Harvard/Yale study on the husbandless futures of single white college-educated females. The scariest stat: a 40-year-old single woman, said *Newsweek*, was "more likely to be killed by a terrorist" than to marry. Ridiculous! Yet, for many, the "terrorist" nonsense stuck.

Critics and cynics would most certainly have a field day comparing *Sleepless*'s Annie Reed to *Fatal*'s Alex Forrest. Nora confronted the issue—girls chasing guys—by having Suzy lecture husband Greg when he invokes *Newsweek*'s incendiary statistic. Annie corrects co-worker Keith, with Becky acknowledging how the magazine had made her insecure:

```
KEITH:  It is easier to be killed by a
        terrorist after the age of 40 than
        it is to get married—
ANNIE:  That is not true. That statistic is
        not true.
BECKY:  It's not true, but it feels true.
```

Jeff Arch's draft places Annie in situations that are meant to remind her that she has no kids. On Christmas Eve, she's the only childless sibling in her family of four minivan-driving brothers. 'Fessing up to one brother, Dennis, she says of Sleepless: "All of a sudden I want to do things I never wanted to do before. Things I never thought were important before. I want to pick his kid up from school. I want to buy groceries.... I want to be like Mom."

The subtext: grow up, Annie. Without the husband, the kids, the minivan, you're not a functional adult.

Ward tones down the sappy mom talk, but includes desperate fan letters to Sam. One reads, "Dear Sleepless in Seattle. After listening to you the other night it was obvious to me that we were psychic soulmates. Do you like cats? I have 43."

The subtext: single women collect cats!

Nora and Delia have nothing to do with desperation. Annie is a grown-up. Her relatives are way weirder than she is. Yes, she's obsessed with a radio voice. Yes, she hires a private investigator to stalk him. Yes, she's making destiny happen. Isn't that more empowering than aspiring to buy groceries?

"She never hits issues on the nose," Lynda Obst says of Nora. "And so therefore because the scripts are never on the nose, because they're never treacly, because the devices are combed through to the point that you don't see them, she has much less work to do than an ordinary romantic comedy director has. She just has to be on her toes and light, and have fun with her directing. She just has to direct her actors. She has to cast well."

Tom Hanks met Nora at the fabled Beverly Hills Hotel on Sunset. The power-lunch landmark, showing wear and tear, was due for a two-year, $100 million renovation. She wanted to see it once more before the sultan of Brunei, its new owner, ripped the iconic banana-leaf wallpaper off the walls. Tom hadn't been there more than a handful of times. "I mean, it's that place you drive by," he says. "You remember it from that cover of the Eagles record [*Hotel California*]. And I had a couple of very intimidating business meetings at one point there. But it certainly was not a hang."

He thought of Nora as the "quintessential New Yorker" and hadn't realized she grew up in Beverly Hills or that her parents were screenwriters. "I saw her, she was coming down from some far hallway, surrounded by faded carpet and that kind of like very severe wallpaper with big, huge, massive floral patterns on it, that was all beginning to stain yellow," he says. "And we ended up sitting in the Polo Lounge," a shabby relic of "time gone by."

In another era you'd glimpse Rat Packers Frank Sinatra and Dean Martin having a drink, Marilyn Monroe nursing a milkshake.

At the Polo Lounge with Nora, Tom got the writer-director's "sense of permanence in history, as opposed to just meeting in an office at William Morris or CAA or something like that."

The all-powerful Creative Artists Agency wooed away the 36-year-old from rival William Morris in the spring of 1991. Tom had been frustrated following megaflop *Bonfire of the Vanities*, an adaptation of Tom Wolfe's best seller in which he was cast against type as Yale-chinned Wall Street bond salesman Sherman McCoy. Making movies back-to-back-to-back took a toll. "I made a particularly disappointing string of cheap comedies in which there was a goofy guy who does or does not get laid by the woman of his dreams," Tom said to the *New Yorker* in 1998. "My own rationale for taking them on wasn't what it should have been. I took whatever gig I got, whether I was tired, or whether I understood the material or not." As for *Bonfire*, McCoy "couldn't be anything other than a pussy. Therefore, there was no mystery to it. He was a pussy from the beginning, and he was a pussy all the way through."

After years of saying yes, Tom had "fuck-you money." He was making about $5 million per picture. He could afford to be choosy. So he told his new agent, Richard Lovett, that he no longer wanted to play pussies: "They're boring, they've got nothing to do with my life, and I don't want to have to waste time even considering them."

He aggressively pursued a character role as women's baseball team coach Jimmy Dugan in Penny Marshall's *A League of Their Own*. At first Penny thought Tom was too cute for Jimmy, originally written as a 52-year-old alcoholic. Tom put on 30 pounds and acquired a limp. His Jimmy sneered and heckled and peed in public. Still, you liked the guy. When he finally noticed the Rockford Peaches' work ethic and commitment to the game, Jimmy became their biggest supporter—a more decent guy, too. It was a critical juncture for Tom in terms of presenting a new side of himself to fans.

I distinctly remember sitting in the theater and thinking: *What happened to Tom Hanks?* But Jimmy Dugan set the actor free. The role sent the message *If Tom Hanks will play second fiddle to Geena Davis, looking like a trainwreck in the process, then he'll do anything.*

Like Jimmy, Sam Baldwin was a man dealing with some real-world shit, not a man-child resisting adulthood. According to Tom, his "motivation was immediately understandable. The guy is enmeshed in grieving, and no one has to work too hard in buying that attractive premise—as opposed to a guy who gets off the airline and picks up the wrong suitcase and it's full of uranium." He thought *Sleepless* wasn't so much about fate as the idea that "one person's second chance can be the other person's first."

During Tom and Nora's initial meeting, he spent a lot of time talking about Rita Wilson. "He said that he finally got the family he never had," Nora recalled. "That fact, I think, is the most important thing about him."

Tom felt Sam was underwritten.

"Without a doubt, I mean, the story was absolutely fantastic," Tom tells me, "and I was an extremely cranky actor at that time. Coming in and saying, 'Why does a kid have so many good lines?' I was always squawking about that, from this perspective. And I said this to her at that meeting. I said, 'You're a woman and you've had a kid and you have interactions with your son, exasperating interactions, that are in the screenplay. I'm a *dad*. And I'm gonna tell you right now, dads and their sons do not have these conversations. You have moments in which the dad is flummoxed by this eight-year-old kid's reasoning, and doesn't know what to do or say, and I got news to tell you: A dad would say, 'Hey, shut up you little brat! You're going to have to deal with it.'

"So, I was very defensive in that way," he continues. "At that time, I had made enough movies to get smoked on a couple of occasions as well as thinking that I was a big shot and 'My voice must be heard' and things like that. Not knowing then that Nora was that fantastic a collaborator...listening to everything I said, utilizing it later on. I knew that she and Delia were going to be doing a rewrite of the screenplay. Which was fine. I just had to go in and squawk a bunch about [how] I didn't want to go off and be the pussy dad in a thing in which a precocious kid was going to bring together the two stars. I probably said, 'Why don't we just cast Shirley Temple in here and call it quits?'"

Nora was charmed. Her reservations apparently dissolved in the Beverly Hills Hotel. Afterward, she called Gary and said he was perfect.

✳ ✳ ✳

When Nora asked if she believed in destiny, Meg Ryan replied, "Absolutely." Everyone yearns to stumble across someone special, and the universe works in odd and mysterious ways. Meg and Dennis had, after all, nearly bumped into one another on Amsterdam Avenue while they were living just blocks away in New York a decade earlier. ("I imagined I'd be with a Madison Avenue type, or at least an East Coast type. But instead I'm out riding horses and chasing bears," she said of their Montana getaways.) On April 24, 1992, Meg gave birth to their son, Jack, via emergency C-section. She hadn't always felt the maternal urge—"the baby bell wasn't ringing"—but her instincts swiftly kicked in. En route from the hospital, she fretted for Jack's safety, worrying the speedy cars on the road would blow stop signs.

As is natural, Meg did have a moment of "Wait, what about *me*?" She worried about her future as an actress. Given the travel required, was movie-stardom antithetical to motherhood? Was she on the right track?

Meg had read *Sleepless's* revisions and decided this one was worth doing. Nora had called her personally and said: "We've got to do this together." And once sold on Tom Hanks post–Polo Lounge, the director then convened with Meg to have the difficult conversation about casting Tom, not Dennis, as Sam Baldwin. Nora "basically had to say, 'I think the best way forward is you and Tom,'" says Gary. "I know for certain that after the meeting was complete, we had our cast and everybody was ready to move forward."

Nora and Gary worked around Meg's due date and maternity leave. The actress, helped by a nanny, would take Jack on location in Seattle while Dennis filmed the Herb Ross spy comedy *Undercover Blues* in New Orleans. The shoot would begin July 12, with Nora filming Tom's scenes first.

A Tom-Meg pairing engendered wide support, although Mike Medavoy, who had been disappointed by Julia's exit, wasn't so sure about Meg. "She convinced me that she was the right person for the part. No big thing," he says, adding that had Julia stayed in, "I don't know if [the movie] would have done better or worse."

As Nora pointed out, "Tom Hanks wasn't quite Tom Hanks at that moment. Tom and Meg had already done a movie together, and it had been a big flop, *Joe Versus the Volcano*." In other words, landing those two in 1992 proved a lucky bargain. She looked on the bright side: *Well, this is great.*

You would think, given how much I've gone on, that Tom and Meg were the only actors in this movie. But Nora had many other roles to fill. She hired casting agent Juliet Taylor and held auditions at the Four Seasons in LA and the Apthorp in New York. On April 24, Juliet issued a "breakdown" to notify agencies they were looking for Jonahs, Jessicas, Walters, Beckys, and Suzys in addition to family members and co-workers and kooky babysitters and ghosts of deceased wives. An internal memo in Juliet's office broke down the star paychecks: the studio earmarked $5 million for Tom, $3 million for Meg, and $100,000 toward the actor playing Jonah; the voice of Marcia Fieldstone would pocket $10,000.

For Becky, Annie's quippy and sympathetic best friend, they considered Mercedes Ruehl (a no), Laurie Metcalf (another no), Marisa Tomei (busy), Emma Thompson (unavailable), and Kirstie Alley ("technically available," according to casting notes). Rosie O'Donnell was technically available—and keenly interested in playing sidekick to Meg Ryan. The 30-year-old comedian and Madonna bestie was about to break out big-time as mouthy Rockford Peach Doris Murphy in *A League of Their Own*, her first feature film. Rosie came in April 29 and killed. Nora would describe Rosie's reading as electrifying. She knew, right there and then, that she had her Becky.

Rosie connected deeply to the story of Sam and Jonah. Her mother, Roseann, died of breast cancer when Rosie was just 10 years old. Rosie's dad, Edward, an Irish immigrant and electrical engineer raising Rosie and four siblings alone in Commack, Long Island, coped with the loss through emotional detachment. Said Rosie, "As I told Nora when I auditioned, this is a real movie-fantasy version of what happens when a mother dies and leaves young children behind: that the father is together and talks about the feelings of it....*Hello? Reality 101?*"

In early May, Barbara Garrick showed up to read for two characters: Sam's love interest Victoria and ghost wife Maggie. Barbara had appeared in Broadway's *Eastern Standard* and in the movies *Working Girl, Days of Thunder,* and *Postcards from the Edge*. Big-eyed, square-jawed, and Juilliard-pedigreed, Barbara had long, straight brown hair down to her butt. (She had been growing it out since age 12.) Her distinctive, high-pitched laugh made an impression upon Nora and Gary, who was there that day and laughed a lot. "I kept flipping [my hair]," she says. "That's how they got that thing that my character Victoria flips her hair all the time. I guess I laughed a lot because then suddenly in the script it says she laughs like a hyena."

Later that month, Nora successfully tested Carey Lowell as Maggie (the ghost wife) and Parker Posey as Lulu, Sam's flirtatious, spandex-sporting neighbor who makes a brief appearance at Sam's doorstep to invite him to a party on her houseboat. Gwyneth Paltrow, Jennifer Aniston, and Anne Heche were also seen for Lulu. Parker, not yet the indie queen of the '90s, was the funniest.

"It was a one-day part," Parker says. "I met [Nora] and she just laughed at me. She got me. My little scene was cut but she sent me a real beautiful card. Said, 'I'm very sorry to tell you, your scene is cut from the film. It happens in films if it doesn't move the story forward quickly enough...you're a gifted comedian and would love to work with you again.' It was so classy. I was so touched by it."

As described in Juliet's casting breakdown, "Walter is Annie's fiancé, a successful publisher, a cultured and cultivated man with a patrician background. There is really nothing wrong with Walter, allergies aside, and although Annie cares for him, there is no 'magic' when they touch."

Any takers?

Early possibilities included Griffin Dunne, Peter MacNicol, Kyle MacLachlan, and—no joke—Jim Carrey, pre–*Ace Ventura*.

Nora and Meg wanted Bill Pullman.

"It was a real interesting journey," Pullman says. "My feelings about it have swung one side to the other over the years. When I first heard about it and I read it, I had no business thinking about turning it down because I wasn't that well established. It was a second male lead and good people. But for some reason I thought there was a lot of baggage on it. I was not feeling it. I was working on another movie at the time and I told my agent, 'I think I'm going to pass. Just pass.' But Meg Ryan and Nora didn't want to hear that. So they said, 'Look at it again. Think about *The Philadelphia Story* and how that Jimmy Stewart character was. *The Philadelphia Story*, that's what we want it to be. There are a lot of ways she could have gone for him, but she decided in the end to go for Cary Grant.'

"So I read it again and I really appreciated the movie. So this is hard for me to confess, that I was just selfishly thinking, 'Am I up for this?' Because there's a little more than the allergies. He's given a little bit of a bag of cement. But overall in the playing of it, Nora was interested in developing the humanity of it, so it didn't turn out that way. I was really skeptical but then I said, 'All right, I'll do it.'"

Rita Wilson set her sights on Becky. What a great, fun role, one Carrie Fisher might do, she thought. "So, Lynda Obst had a party at her house and Nora was there," she recalls, "and I went up to her and started talking. I said to her, 'Look, I read the script, and if you don't cast Carrie Fisher in that role of the best friend, I would love to audition for it.' So I did. I auditioned for it, and I didn't get the part. Rosie got the part. But Nora offered me the role of Suzy.... I remember having to think, 'What is that role again? I better go look at the script.' So I went back and looked at the script again and thought, 'Oh, well this is kind of fun. This is a monologue. This'll be cool.'"

When Sam mentions Annie's loony Empire State Building plan, his sister-in-law Suzy is reminded of *An Affair to Remember*. She spends roughly two minutes blubbering over the emotional wallop of reformed playboy Nickie Ferrante (Cary Grant) discovering why teacher Terry McKay (Deborah Kerr) failed to keep their date, booked six months in advance, on the 86th floor. Tragically, she had been struck by a car while crossing the street and lost the ability to walk.

At this point, Leo McCarey cranks Harry Warren's vibrant, violin-heavy theme at full volume.

> **NICKIE:** If it had to happen to one of us, why did it have to be you?
>
> **TERRY:** Oh. It was nobody's fault but my own. I was looking up. It was the nearest thing to heaven. You were there. Oh darling, don't—don't worry, darling. If you can paint, I can walk! Anything can happen, don't you think?

Rita watched the movie a couple times to prepare. Tom, who calls *Affair* a dated "museum piece," made himself scarce. "I asked Tom to watch it with me," she said. "He looked at me like, 'Yeah, I'll be right in—*not*.' He came in at the end when I was wiping my eyes. I tried to be pretty objective about the movie, but it's manipulative. I cried, yeah. Anyway, I wasn't sobbing profusely."

Rob Reiner accepted the role of Jay, Sam's work buddy, without reading the script. *This Is My Life*'s Gaby Hoffmann signed on to play Jessica. Nora was starting to collect a stable of regular players.

That stable included her own discoveries. Nora lived to source the best chili, the best cookie, the best *anything*. She knew how to spot talent. A good actor, like an idea, could be found in the place you least expect—a Seattle health food restaurant, for example.

Amanda Maher was working the lunch shift as a waitress at the Gravity Bar when Nora, Gary, and Jane Bartelme, *Sleepless* associate producer, sat down in her section. Nora was in town seeing local actors for minor roles, and Gary had contacted Seattle casting director Jodi Rothfield to find Jonah's teenage babysitter, Clarise, among other inconsequential parts. Nora OK'd one young woman, but she was still looking for someone who had that Shelley Duvall quality she wanted.

Taking one look at Amanda, Nora told Jane: "She has to be in the movie."

"They were just kind of sitting there, and they kind of like flagged me down and said, 'We're ready to order,'" says Amanda, now a government administrator living in Santa Fe.

"And I said, 'Oh, I'm sorry, I didn't realize you were ready because you're all still looking at your menus,' and took their order and then Nora just said, 'You know, we're filming a movie and we'd like it if you'd come audition.'"

Jane handed Amanda her card.

Oh yeah, aren't we all just filming a movie?

The next day, the 23-year-old liberal arts school graduate went to her other job as an assistant at a law firm. She had been working on a class-action lawsuit and told colleagues she was asked to be in a film. "I think it's called *Topless in Seattle* or something." She pulled out Jane's card. It said *Sleepless in Seattle* and included a time, date, and address—no details about which part they had in mind. A woman in the office—who worked as a stringer at an area newspaper—corrected Amanda: "No, that's a real movie. That's for real." "Really?" "Yeah, Tom Hanks is gonna be in that."

* * *

Nora searched far and wide for Jonah—well, mainly the New York tristate area. Juliet and her associate, Laura Rosenthal, held an open call in New York and posted notices in dozens of Long Island and Westchester papers, as well as Manhattan and Brooklyn schools.

They reached out to Little League. They spotted one 10-year-old boy in line at Planet Hollywood. They hit up the top child-actor agents, like Judy Savage and Iris Burton, both based in LA. At least 73 non-professional and 59 professional kids were seen, including Elijah Wood, Jason Schwartzman, Joseph Gordon-Levitt, and future *Boy Meets World* stars Ben Savage and Rider Strong.

According to a casting memo, Al Franken's son Joe and Sam Waterston's son Graham were considered. Leaf Phoenix (now known as Joaquín) was judged too old.

Nora auditioned about 10 potential Jonahs. Clever beyond his years, Nathan Watt—the umpteenth eight-year-old in contention—walked into his audition, looked around, and asked, "Do you think this place was named after Vivaldi's 'Four Seasons'?"

Gary had witnessed the precocious remark. Nathan's mother, Linda Watt, recalls the producer relaying the room's reaction: "We all looked at each other and said, 'Damn, he's cute and he's smart.'" Or something to that effect. Linda laughed. Her son was quirkier than most.

Nathan, an only child, and Linda, a single parent scraping by, moved to LA from Phoenix after meeting Iris Burton, who discovered River Phoenix, Henry Thomas, and Kirsten Dunst. Nathan was six and had done two local commercials back home. Under Iris's wing, he effortlessly booked five-figure national TV spots for Dial soap and Colgate toothpaste, and landed the role of Randy Quaid's youngest son in the short-lived CBS sitcom *Davis Rules*, which ran from 1991 to 1992. Like *Sleepless*, the plot hinged on the relationship between a widowed father and his offspring. The show's producers, Danny Jacobson and Norma Safford Vela, told Linda: "Don't ever let him take an acting class because he's so natural, and we would kill to have kids be like this."

Nathan saw acting as "hanging out with people," observes

Linda. He got excited when other kids guest-starred on *Davis*. He and co-star Jonathan Winters would banter and improvise. Otherwise, he had his lines down pat. Once, an actor on set had trouble remembering a line. Nathan leaned in and fed it to him. *Oh no*, Linda thought. "That was very kind for you to do that," she said to Nathan, "but in the future, let's not do that, OK?"

Physically, he was the opposite of generic. The boy had laughing brown eyes, a sweet smile, and a ski-slope nose. Beanpole-thin.

Nathan was "just frickin' adorable," recalls Laura Rosenthal, and "had a certain kind of a natural, odd, very appealing, not typical cutesy, Disney look. Somebody that you would care about."

He was Nora's first choice, Laura says. He got the part.

A month before filming, Tom got cold feet.

He was disappointed because some of the issues he discussed that day at the Polo Lounge weren't addressed to his satisfaction. He had also been wary about shooting the majority of his scenes with a kid. He and Nora were just not communicating.

Richard Lovett called Gary and the two decided the actor and director should huddle together and talk it out. In mid-June they took up a space at the Four Seasons, joined by a few members of Nora's crisis management team: Gary, Delia, and Lynda. The fear was Tom didn't like what the movie *was*. "No amount of script work will change that," says Gary. Nora had steeled herself to solve the problem. Over the course of two days, as Tom read scenes and rewrote dialogue to make it edgier and more real, from his brutally honest masculine perspective, Nora the journalist wrote down verbatim what he was saying. He was her interview subject—a source—expounding on the male mind, much as Rob Reiner and Andy Scheinman had done seven years before.

Tom had balked at a scene where Jonah melts down because Sam is going to spend the weekend with Not-Annie. In the screenplay, Sam stays home, placating Jonah. "That is such horse-shit," said Tom. "Let me get this straight, a man has not gotten laid in four years, and he's got a shot to get laid this weekend, and he's not going to go because his son doesn't like the girl? I got news for you, that kid's going to the sitter, and I'm going off to get laid."

He was walking around the room going, "Here's how I'd say it." And she'd go, "That's great. I like that."

But still, the tensions between the director and her lead actor simmered—at least on his side. Weeks would go by without Nora contacting Tom. She had been actor scouting, location scouting, and otherwise mired in pre-production obligations. But the radio silence irked the star, who felt he was out of the loop.

"At one point, she did call me up because I had squawked to, I guess, my agent about some of the kids she had to meet with," he said. "And I probably said something like, 'I don't want that kid in the movie!' or something like that. And she called me up and laid down the law...." Hanks was about to see the steely Nora, whom her stars didn't often have cause to witness.

"She says, 'Look, there are some things I have to do as the director to please the studio. And these things I have to do are *meet-ings*. That's all they *are*.'" Hanks was abashed. "I had to say, 'OK, I completely get it. I'm sorry.'...First of all, it was very charitable for her to do that. It was very wise of her to tell me to shut the fuck up and let her jump over the hoops that she had to."

Nora, relatively new to the job, did not have the final say in "her" movie. And if Nora wanted to cast a particular actor in a particular role—the role of young Jonah, for example—TriStar reserved approval power. The studio saw auditions and readings. It. Was. A. Process.

As Gary sees it, that Four Seasons come-to-Jesus confrontation bonded Nora and Tom for good. "If he had walked away, it would have changed a lot of his life," says the producer. "He trusted her. She allowed herself to be vulnerable and open. She made him a partner. Actors want to believe the directors consider what they're feeling or thinking. She showed him that she would."

Everything made sense when Tom got to Seattle. There, he watched Nora—under massive pressure and a six-hour flight away from her New York comfort zone—get gritty. Her guts would astonish him.

CHAPTER 6

Nearest Thing to Heaven

The helicopter flew around the Empire State Building. Nora Ephron, terrified of helicopters, was inside the thing, holding on for dear life, along with her cinematographer, Sven Nykvist. She probably should not have listened when her handsome assistant director, Jim Skotchdopole, suggested the idea of booking a helicopter to whisk them from JFK airport to the skies above Manhattan. The mission: to scout the Empire State before filming aerial footage of Jonah tapping strangers and asking, "Are you Annie?"

Though she mentioned her fear to Skotchdopole on the walk to the copter, Nora remained calm so the crew wouldn't think she was a "hopeless female." After they landed, Sven climbed out, looked at Nora, and said, "That was terrible."

Oh, good. She wasn't the only one.

Tall and quiet, understated and unflappable, Sven Nykvist was a beloved figure on the set of *Sleepless in Seattle*. The 69-year-old had a weathered face and shock of white hair. Cast and crew looked at Sven as some kind of Norse god. "It was Sven's 102nd movie and he is the kindest, nicest, gentlest, sweetest, most brilliant, fastest cinematographer in the West," gushed Nora in 1993. "He can light in 20 minutes. It was unbelievable for the actors because you didn't lose your performance waiting for the close-up to be lit."

Nora had been in on every production detail—costumes, hair, sets, props—but Sven was the only department head to whom she bowed, according to Barbara Garrick. "She just completely trusted him and he did his thing," says the actress. "She never came in and said, 'Can you put more light on Tom?' or anything like that."

And Tom was starstruck. "I was anticipating meeting someone akin to Picasso by way of Stanley Kubrick," he says. "Sven was just a little bit of an older guy, little bit of an accent.... I remember he used a lot of soft bounce cards that would illuminate things. Make all of us look better."

Back in Sweden, Sven cut his teeth on a slew of moody Ingmar Bergman movies, such as 1972's *Cries and Whispers* and 1982's *Fanny and Alexander*, for which he won Oscars. He was groundbreaking in his devotion to naturalism and indirect, shadowless lighting; he thought himself a painter and would light up his compositions with a single source, like a candle or kerosene lamp. He wasn't afraid of the dark. He was experimental. For Bergman's *Winter Light*, he and the director sat for hours in a church watching the light shift; the transformation of the interior inspired the visual texture of that film. Sven loved photographing women and would get emotionally involved in their performances; he was known to shed a few tears while training his lens on Bibi Andersson and Liv Ullmann. American directors clamored to work with him. American actresses swooned for him. Sven romanced Mia Farrow and Jane Fonda. Nora once joked that she was "the only woman in Hollywood who had not slept with Sven Nykvist."

He obeyed the director's vision but let his opinions be known when it came to cosmetics. In pre-production he told Nora: "In American movies people like to put on too much makeup and it covers the skin. I cannot allow that. Let it be natural. It will be beautiful and it will be alive."

Sven was alarmed to view the dailies at the beginning of the shoot. Everybody had a tan! "What is with all the tomato faces?" he said, to which Nora responded: "That's the way they look, Sven."

He called the lab in New York that printed the raw material, demanding: "Take the red out." And so Tom and Meg—Southern Californians—looked like pale Swedes.

The *Sleepless in Seattle* production was to wind its way through four cities: Seattle, then Chicago, then Baltimore, and finally New York. A group including Nora, Gary, executive producer Pat Crowley, and production designer Jeffrey Townsend spent the month of June searching for places to shoot. They ate. A lot.

In the Windy City, Nora steered the gang toward Jim's Original polish sausage and pork chop stand.

"It was in the South Side of Chicago and I was like, 'OK, this is kind of scary looking,'" says Crowley. "And she goes, 'This place is the place to go.' It was like a little open grill. They made pork chop sandwiches, in which they cooked whole pork chops and a huge pile of caramelized onions that you put on top of the pork chops and make a sandwich out of it. And Nora was like, 'This is the best.' Because this was so authentic. And she went one step better: across the street was a place that sold used shoes. We went up with Nora and it was all people's shoes. All these cars were lined up and down the street and people were selling stolen car radios for people to put them into their cars. And she said, 'This is it. This is as good as it gets.'"

In Baltimore, Nora nibbled on crab legs at Faidley Seafood.

Previewing Annie's uncluttered workspace at the *Baltimore Sun*, she remarked, "A reporter's desk is not clean." More clutter, please.

"She's from Baltimore; what matters to her?"

"She'd certainly be a Baltimore Orioles fan," said Gary. "They're rabid baseball fans."

"Who do you think she would like?"

"Brooks Robinson, greatest third baseman ever."

Nora dressed the desk in Orioles paraphernalia and added Gary's Brooks Robinson line to the script. (That's how Robinson became Annie and Sam's favorite baseball player.)

In Seattle, Nora and Gary split the meatloaf sandwich at Pike Place Market's Three Girls Bakery. When she decamped to the Pacific Northwestern seaport in the summer of 1992, she brought Nick and rented an apartment a block away. Outdoorsy and insular, Seattle had been on the map in recent years as the birthplace of grunge. (Think buffalo plaid. Angst. Kurt Cobain. Nothing Nora would wear or listen to.) Starbucks, founded there in the early 1970s, was about to go public on the stock market. (Nora invested.)

Nora insisted that *Sleepless* be headquartered in Seattle for the bulk of shooting. But there weren't many facilities for visiting filmmakers. While the crew sourced wonderful spots—Alki Beach, the Athenian Inn, and the Dahlia Lounge—they required a home base to construct the interiors of Sam's houseboat and Annie's apartment. Otherwise they couldn't stay long.

"We had all these sets to build and Seattle just doesn't go there," says Townsend. "They don't have big soundstages, let alone construction crews and painting crews and rigging crews that you need to build big sets. But that was what she wanted. We had this exhausting process of finding, scouting, then ultimately ruling out all these warehouses and other kinds of non-soundstage spaces.

Then somehow we got permission to at least look at these decommissioned hangars at Sand Point Naval Station. And they were perfect. These big open spaces with no posts or columns. Just gorgeous places sitting empty. So we began the process of trying to secure permission to essentially lease them to build our sets. And we kept getting declined. We didn't know what was wrong.

"Nora got wind that there was still a backstage struggle and in a moment that I would have characterized as empty bravado, because I wasn't buying it, she says, 'Do you want me to handle this?' And I thought, 'Yeah.' She called somebody in Washington, DC, that she knew through Carl Bernstein and the weeks and weeks of no turned into a yes. And it turns out to have been a radical precedent. It was finally revealed to us why we were getting a no. Which is that no division of the military had ever made a landlord arrangement with a movie that wasn't about the military. And Nora got the yes. She was very discreet. She didn't tell anybody about the phone call or who it was with. I snickered privately and I couldn't have been more wrong; she completely handled it."

Nora had contacted John Warner, a Republican U.S. senator from Virginia and the former secretary of the Navy. He was Elizabeth Taylor's sixth husband. Nora said he owed her one.

The houseboat. Ugh. What a headache. They needed the real thing for exterior scenes and some offstage interiors but couldn't find one. They were going to build a set when opportunity knocked: a location manager had been in touch with an attorney named Don Mohlman. Mohlman and his wife were getting divorced, which meant their Lake Union houseboat was up for grabs. It was beyond charming. Roughly 2,200 square feet, 2460 Westlake Avenue North had four bedrooms, greige-painted siding, and a wraparound porch begging for Tom Hanks to lean on it. Mohlman agreed to rent the cozy jewel to the production, pissing off the neighbors.

Everyone was excited and relieved. Yay for divorce?

Here's the dirty secret about *Sleepless in Seattle*'s last scene: it was filmed on a replica of the Empire State observation deck at Sand Point's Hangar 27. Even Nora, with her vast network and powers of persuasion, had trouble wrangling access to the skyscraper. It didn't help that its manager, Leona Helmsley, was in prison.

Helmsley, nicknamed the Queen of Mean, was a very successful hotelier and real estate developer joined in marriage and business to self-made billionaire Harry Helmsley, her third husband. Leona and Harry were part owners of the Empire State, which Harry could not resist acquiring because "every morning you would look out of the window and the building is staring you in the face. So, you'd say, 'Well, I gotta have it.'"

When Leona met Harry in 1968, she was a twice-divorced condo broker and he a tycoon married 30 years. He divorced his first wife to take Leona as his second, and the two lived large and lavishly, cavorting from gala to gala. Leona threw "I'm Just Wild about Harry"—themed birthday parties at their Manhattan duplex, which had been decorated with Camille Pissarro paintings and pink jade objets d'art. She earned notoriety as the public face of the Helmsley Palace Hotel on 50th and Madison. The Palace "queen," Leona starred in a batch of brazenly effective ads touting the luxury brand and her unyielding high standards: "I won't settle for skimpy towels. Why should you?"

That haute Trumpian persona came back to bite Leona amid scrutiny over unethical finances and boorish behavior toward underlings. In 1987, Harry and Leona were indicted on charges that they'd avoided more than $4 million in income taxes by listing pricey personal purchases as company expenditures. Harry, in poor health, was off the hook during the two-month tabloid trial during which witnesses testified to Leona's greed, arrogance, and hot temper. A housekeeper quoted her as saying, "Only the little people pay taxes."

Seventy-one-year-old Leona reported to a Connecticut minimum-security facility and served 18 months for federal tax evasion. While Leona did time, Nora pursued her blessing to film on top and inside the Empire State. Management, dependent on tourism dollars, was loath to relinquish precious hours to some movie crew. Been there, done that, take a number. Rising up 1,454 feet, the Art Deco wonder had been in high demand since its 1931 ribbon cutting. The world's tallest building until the North Tower of the World Trade Center beat the record in 1972, it had been cast in *King Kong*, *On the Town*, *The Producers*, and Leo McCarey's *Love Affair* with Charles Boyer and Irene Dunne. McCarey remade his 1939 romance with *An Affair to Remember*, changing up the storyline, casting, and music. But the Empire State, captured in exteriors, maintained top billing. McCarey re-created the observatory at Fox Studios, though it more resembled a train station in Kansas City.

Any filming requests had to fly by Leona in addition to real estate investor Peter Malkin, who shared ownership with the Helmsleys. "Mrs. Helmsley was notoriously difficult," says Peter's son Tony Malkin, the CEO of Empire State Realty Trust, formed when the Malkins took the building public in 2013. "While she is notoriously difficult, she's also a savvy businessperson.... Even if they pay for the lost revenue, what about the tourists down on the street who want to come up the whole day while they're filming?"

The *Sleepless* crew snapped photos from every vantage point and set off to duplicate the view in Seattle. Sven being Sven, he wasn't used to working with translights, which are photorealistic backdrops used instead of shooting on location. Rather than hang a single translight of the glittering New York horizon, Sven and Jeffrey Townsend mounted miniature models of distant buildings,

Nora Ephron as swashbuckling journalist in 1960s and '70s New York City. *(The Everett Collection)*

As her career blossomed, tensions with husband Carl Bernstein grew—culminating in divorce and the sweet revenge of *Heartburn*. *(Ron Galella/Ron Galella Collection/ Getty Images)*

Billy Crystal, Rob Reiner, and Meg Ryan on the set of *When Harry Met Sally.* *(The Everett Collection)*

Neither Crystal nor Ryan were the studio's first choices for Harry and Sally, but onscreen their chemistry just *worked. (Hulton Archive/Moviepix/ Getty Images)*

Bruno Kirby and Carrie Fisher—the heart and soul of the movie. *(The Everett Collection)*

Ryan was so nervous about the famous Katz's deli scene that it took all of director Reiner's persuasive powers to convince her to go through with it. *(The Everett Collection)*

Reiner oversees crooner Harry Connick Jr.'s iconic score. *(Hulton Archive/Moviepix/ Getty Images)*

Ryan and Dennis Quaid at the *When Harry Met Sally* premiere in London. *(Georges De Keerle/ Hulton Archive/ Getty Images)*

Janice and Billy Crystal; Rob Reiner and his wife, Michele, who "met cute" during the shoot and married just weeks before the movie's July 1989 Hollywood premiere. *(Kevin Winter/The LIFE Picture Collection/ Getty Images)*

Tom Hanks and Ephron had several heart-to-heart talks before filming. He had to be talked into the role of Sam Baldwin. *(The Everett Collection)*

Sleepless was the second movie Ephron helmed...and she knew everything was riding on its success. *(top: Barbara Garrick* and bottom: *The Everett Collection)*

Hanks wasn't thrilled about acting opposite a kid, but once Nora fired the first Jonah and hired Ross Malinger, things went much more smoothly. (top and bottom: *The Everett Collection*)

Dave Chappelle...in a turtleneck? *(The Everett Collection)*

Ephron hitting her stride in *You've Got Mail.* (top and bottom: *The Everett Collection*)

Ryan had become much more comfortable on the set, and her ease with Hanks was palpable. *(top and bottom: The Everett Collection)*

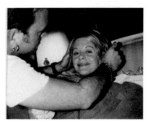

The iconic Kathleen Kelly shag. *(Matthew Shields)*

Ephron with her love, Nick
Pileggi. *(The Everett Collection)*

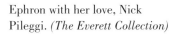

Ephron and her sister, Delia Ephron.
(The Everett Collection)

She would go on to make other
beloved films (like *Julie & Julia*
with Meryl Streep), but her
New York Trilogy reimagined
the city and the romcom for an
entire generation of moviegoers.
(The Everett Collection)

such as the Chrysler, and arranged them for spatial accuracy. In a trick of the eye, the Chrysler appears three-dimensional instead of flat and phony.

"We all kind of thought it was crazy," recalls Jim Skotchdopole. "We all thought, 'This looks like crap; it's never going to look good.'"

Sven lighted the sky—painted pitch-black and misty-grayish at the bottom—like an urban aurora borealis. There was no trace of blue, a color Nora fiercely opposed on film.

The romantic climax was to occur on the north end of the observation deck, which is a narrow walkway. The art department, led by Jeffrey, embellished the area to match the grandeur of the scene. They stretched 3 feet into 25 feet, pushing back the elevators even farther. As Jeffrey tells it, "every production designer's nail-biting, white-knuckle nightmare is that you will take a liberty that is too much and the audience says WHAT." The plan could backfire: Why mess with the parameters of an icon? "We invented a completely different architecture for the north side and thought, 'If we just build it convincingly enough, if we just sell it, people will somehow say, 'Yeah, I sort of remember that part. I think I was there once.' Which is crazy."

Nora held the first read-through in LA on July 1, giving each actor a book that related to their character. Tom received a volume about the Brooklyn Bridge, a nod to Sam's profession. Bill Pullman got David McCullough's Teddy Roosevelt biography *Mornings on Horse-back*. "Because [Walter] had allergies," says Bill. "She wanted me to know that great men have allergies. Right away she was looking to ennoble all the things about him and what she liked about him."

As another gift for select cast, wrote Lynda Obst, Nora "bought beautiful replicas of the Empire State Building encased in glass snowballs."

The primary cast converged at Sand Point for several days' rehearsal before filming. They practiced like a play. The furnished sets had tape on the floor to mark actors' spots; the crew arranged temporary tables and chairs for scenes that were shot outside the hangar. "We just did it and did it," says Barbara Garrick, who played Victoria. "Got familiar with the lines and that was it." Nora gave no notes. Barbara had not worked that way since Mike Nichols. And Tom hasn't worked that way since Nora. Her scenes were long and involved lots of movement and leeway to improvise. Delia would observe on the sidelines, making script changes. "You went from room to room to room," Tom explains, "and in doing that, you start playing around with the dialogue, and then everybody's just saying, 'Well, how about this? And how about that?'"

Out of that process came Nora's idea to reference *Fatal Attraction* during Sam and Jonah's blowout fight.

> **SAM:** There is no way that we are going on a plane to meet some woman who could be a crazy, sick lunatic! Didn't you see *Fatal Attraction*?
> **JONAH:** You wouldn't let me!
> **SAM:** Well I saw it. And it scared the shit out of me. It scared the shit out of every man in America!

While practicing the part where Sam numbers the women he slept with in college (six, maybe seven), Tom ad-libbed an eighth: "Mary Kelly!" Meanwhile, *Sleepless*'s script supervisor—Mary Kelly—fell to her knees in stitches. She had been in a low mood and Tom cheered her up. Typical Tom Hanks. "I think he feels a responsibility to make people happier," says Delia.

Some situations Tom couldn't smooth over. He and movie son Nathan Watt had rehearsed quite a bit together. It felt unnatural.

Anticipating the worst, Jim Skotchdopole strategized in pre-production to roll the camera on Nathan, get him used to it, and see how he played. Gary reached out to casting director and acting coach Robin Joy Allan via the producer's agent, who delivered an urgent message: "You have to come up here. We're having trouble. Tom is being driven crazy and this boy keeps repeating dialogue off-camera when Tom's trying to film a scene and he's not adding to the film right now."

The next thing she knew, Robin was in a limo with Nora and Lynda Obst en route to the set. Robin tried to work with the child, but to no avail. He was "really talented and very funny" but undisciplined, she says. "He just wasn't willing to work. He was very obstinate.... It was kind of a terrible situation. You don't want to fire a child."

Tom and Nathan filmed several days in a row. Father-son stuff, not key scenes. There was one scene in a rowboat. It did not go well. Seemingly shell-shocked, Nathan cracked under pressure. His mother had made him memorize the entire script, observers say, and it was all he could do to get out the dialogue.

"The kid wasn't much of an actor, but most importantly he couldn't remember his lines," says Bob Reitano, on-site editor. "They were feeding him lines and he was reading it without any intelligence and understanding. He was a stick."

Barbara, who became friends with Nathan during rehearsals, says: "He was impish, but far too fragile to stand up to Tom."

Despite his background in the fast-paced world of TV sitcoms, Nathan was green. Untrained. Apparently overcoached. This had been his first time on a film set. He showed none of the charisma that wowed Nora at the Four Seasons. His natural instincts evaporated. And Nora wasn't totally equipped to handle Nathan when he choked. It's difficult for a director to put a child actor at ease, and production designer Jeffrey Townsend observed Nora at her wit's end.

"It was horrible," he says. "It's like, how do you not know how to talk to a child? Don't you have a couple? Let alone an *actor* child. . . . She just began to berate him and he just kept shutting down further and further until he was just a basket case. You can't shame a child into being a better actor. I've never known that to work. That was horrible. And that was, I think, part of the crew going, 'Oh, gosh. What did we sign on for?'"

Nora blamed herself. Says Jim, "She felt responsible for casting him. She felt responsible for the days of filming that we had with him. . . . And I didn't need to tell her this, but I reminded her of the fact that people will only remember what the finished product is. Not how we got here. Not that it took another two days. We got too much riding on the movie not to have this kid be perfect."

Gary and Lynda said the same. Nora had to let Nathan go, and once she made the decision, she never second-guessed. It was done. Time to move on.

"The saddest thing was wrapping the young child," says Lynda. "But then we started realizing it wasn't the young child who wanted to do this; it was his mother. . . . After his first bad day, his mother was hysterical for him to stay in the show. So we gave him another day. We started seeing that this was not his intention, his drive. This is not uncommon with child actors. When we wrapped him, it was the mother who was so upset. I think the child was afraid of disappointing the mother. But I felt relief. It's a very different thing to read lines in an audition than it is to suddenly be sitting across—in a boat, on a bay, with 100 cameras rolling—with a movie star."

Gary called Linda Watt at the Sheraton Hotel, where she and

Nathan were staying. "It's just not working out," he said. Although present on set, she says she hadn't watched Nathan film and, frankly, didn't know there was a problem. She didn't know why they cut Nathan loose.

Had she been savvier, Linda would have pushed back and said to Gary, *What do you mean it's not working out?* It was over, and that was all she knew. Later, she heard from a crew member that Nora scarcely directed Nathan. As for memorizing the script, "He's very bright and has a photographic memory," Linda says. On *Davis Rules*, "he would just know the whole script. . . . I think he just read it like it was a book and he just knew it."

Nathan's agent, Iris Burton, was apoplectic. Screaming and crying and dropping the F-bomb. "It's like, 'Iris, for God's sake, he's got a pay-or-play contract. He's gonna get paid, you're gonna get paid, what's the deal?'" says Linda.

Linda understood that filmmaking is a tough business. Nobody's there to ruffle your feathers. Still. Where was Nora's bedside manner? Wasn't she a mother, too?

Nathan Watt, grown and living near Atlanta, is today director of sales operations for a global telecommunications company you might've heard of. He remembers little of *Sleepless*. Not Tom Hanks. Not that boat scene. He remembers Nora being "abrasive" but has no memory of her berating him. Leaving Seattle, filled with confusion. Rosie O'Donnell rapping in the van on the way from the Sheraton to the set and incorporating his name into her raps. He would sit next to her and giggle. She was really funny and really kind. When *Sleepless* wrapped in Seattle, Barbara Garrick and her boyfriend met the Watts at California Pizza Kitchen in LA. "I think Nora was pissed that I was still friends with this kid," Barbara says. "You're supposed to hop on the new boat, right? And I just was empathetic to somebody being fired."

A couple years later, Diane Keaton picked Nathan to star in her 1995 comedy-drama *Unstrung Heroes*, about a boy whose wacky uncles (Michael Richards, Maury Chaykin) help him deal with the impending loss of his cancer-stricken mother (Andie MacDowell). *Unstrung Heroes* premiered in New York on September 12, 1995.

"I remember it being outside, and I look up and here comes Nora with her coat flowing behind her and her entourage around her," says Linda. She leaned down to give 10-year-old Nathan the heads-up: "Nora Ephron is headed across the plaza."

She hoped Nora would at least acknowledge Nathan's talent and how good he'd been in the role. Lots of celebrities congratulated him that evening. But Nora walked right past, as if Nathan didn't even exist.

Nathan stopped acting in his early teens and continued his education at Kansas State University. He graduated in 2006. He's humble, almost bemused, about his past life, admitting the only thing he'd take now is the money.

"It was fun when I was a kid," he says. "I was basically playing pretend and make-believe for cash and got to go to a lot of cool places, see a lot of cool things, and meet a lot of great people."

After a while, though, he lost interest. He's a bit disappointed by what happened on *Sleepless in Seattle*. But it doesn't define him. As Nathan sensibly points out, "I was eight."

"I thought it was the bravest thing I'd ever heard," Tom says. "There was no doubt that it was not working....That's all you can say about it. It was not going to be natural.

"And for Nora, on the first weekend of shooting to have to make that sort of change...well, then you're into the reason why most people don't want to direct movies. Or end up directing movies that have big, fat, gaping holes in the middle of them—because they don't want to fire somebody like that. They don't want to be the mercenary who has to do a very, very extreme and devilish deed in order to make the movie live the way they see it in their head."

A Nora Ephron set, muses Tom, was choreographed like one of her famous dinner parties. "It's very comfortable but at the same time, it's no-nonsense. So for someone to be making their second movie like that, to have that power to be no-nonsense, to make the incredibly tough calls, well, that's the sign of somebody who probably should have been making films 10 years prior."

If she failed to pull the trigger, he'd make do—"I've worked with dogs, you know"—but Nora wasn't messing around. She was under tremendous pressure to deliver TriStar a hit; otherwise she could kiss her directing dreams goodbye.

She called Tom and said she was bringing in another Jonah. They would have to rehearse all over again.

Meg Ryan, who had given birth three months before, agreed to flip schedules with Tom and start working sooner. On a tight, two-week deadline, the producers and casting directors relaunched the Jonah expedition. They reviewed audition tapes and flew pint-sized hopeful Ross Malinger to Seattle for a screen test alongside Tom. Nora Eckstein, who co-managed the eight-year-old Ross with partner Diane Hardin, accompanied him first class on Alaska Airlines, which served cold poached salmon as the meal.

"Oh, gosh, maybe we can get you something else," Eckstein said to her charge. "I don't know if you're going to like this."

"Oh no," he replied, "salmon is one of my best fish!"

Eckstein was impressed. Ross had quite the sophisticated palate—a necessity on a Nora Ephron movie—plus a vivid imagination, a prerequisite for playing Tom's son. "He'd be, like, alone in the other room and he'd be singing and talking to pretend people all the time," she says. "He had a good sense of humor. He was very bright."

What was supposed to be a day trip turned into three days while everyone waited for TriStar to approve footage of Tom and Ross. The two had tested the scene where Sam calms Jonah after a nightmare. Ross's mother, Laura, had presciently packed Ross a change of clothes, but Eckstein brought nothing. She picked up a nightgown at a Victoria's Secret near the hotel. It was crazy. Exciting. They got to hang out on the set. Nora and Delia were warm and welcoming. Ross goofed off with Tom; he wasn't intimidated. "At that age they don't really understand what's at stake," says Eckstein. "He obviously knew who Tom Hanks was, but I don't think he knew too much more than that. . . . If people around him don't get too excited, or put the pressure on too much, they just take it in hand."

Spotting Eckstein, Tom asked Ross, "Who's that?"

"Oh, that's my manager," he replied.

"Hey, she give you like a rub-down before each scene?"

While she loved Ross, and would praise him as "brilliantly talented," Nora had at first been troubled by his appearance.

"I got a call one day to come down to the trailer to take a look at some of the screen tests," says Reitano. "They put up the kid who is Jonah in the film. I saw him and said, 'He's perfect. He even looks like Hanks.' And Nora said, 'You're another one.' Because everyone else said the same thing. Nora said, 'Doesn't it bother you that he's got this chipmunk chin and he's got this fat around his neck?' I said, 'He's eight years old. They have those things, Nora.'"

Alas, Ross was at first unavailable. CBS had picked up his sitcom pilot, *Good Advice*, which just so happened to be a TriStar production. It was to air in early 1993. Lynda accessed her problem-solving powers and coordinated an arrangement that allowed Ross out of the TV show so he could do *Sleepless*.

Delia thinks they got it right the second time around. Ross was natural and real and "had a soundness," she says. "It was important that you felt that Jonah was a solid kid, not neurotic, not about to skid off the rails."

You've got to make Tom happy....

"He was innately an actor," says Tom. "He was an eight-year-old who understood that there's a difference between saying the lines and playing around. And he got it done.... I don't know what it was, but as soon as we started work with Ross, it was the movie. Inexplicable. But some people can, some people can't. He could."

CHAPTER 7

Sleepless, Stressed, and Addicted to Starbucks

With all eyes monitoring Nora to succeed, and Tom still settling into his role, Meg proved to be a steady, constant force on set—despite the fact that her life was in very real danger.

Janey Bergam picked up Meg every day and drove her to work in a Ford Explorer. She would fetch the actress lunch and take her back to her sweet rental home in town when the day was over. Every night, Janey ran into the front post in the driveway. The Seattleite, who received a credit as Meg's assistant, had never driven a celebrity before this job. "Don't ever worry about making a mistake," Meg told the rookie movie-crew driver. "Because everybody is human."

One time Janey kept missing the ramp to Seattle-Tacoma International Airport, where Meg was to film Annie's landing. The late arrival frustrated crew members. Covering for Janey, Meg got out of the car and explained they had to do recon. Couldn't stop until the area had been scanned.

Meg's excuse, by the way, made complete sense: she had a stalker and a bodyguard to protect her from him. The bodyguard manned Meg in Seattle and rode with her to work. The stalker, according to Jeffrey Townsend, "used to get ahold of call sheets and shooting schedules—no one knows how—and so she'd gotten used to having a bodyguard who was just out of frame (the fewest number of steps to be able to reach her) for every shot."

An agent at the bodyguard's security firm pulled Janey into a room and recommended she take special driving courses and maybe pack a gun. "If anything goes down," he told Janey, "you're last man on the totem pole. But we will send someone back for you." Afterward, Janey informed her passenger-target.

"Meg, they want me to get a gun."

"*What?* No!"

It was terrifying. Meg kept calm and carried on. Jack and his nanny mostly stayed at the house. (Fans around the world would mail baby clothes to production; Meg donated them to charity.) The stalker later surfaced on the East Coast, but the vibe in Washington was low-key. Like Meg.

The woman Janey knew was wise, cool, and funny. A girl's girl like Sandra Bullock. To her horror, Janey accidentally slept in one morning and rushed to Meg's trailer, assuming she'd been fired. Meg shrugged off the gaffe: it happens.

Meg told Janey she had majored in journalism, acted to pay for college, and "never looked back." When a local newspaper journalist asked to interview Janey about driving Meg, the actress advised her not to. "It can be misconstrued so easily," she said. "Don't do it."

When approached by autograph seekers, she griped: "It's not about me. The experience is about *them*."

When musing on fame, she pointed to the sky and said, "Janey, you know, the only stars are up there. The minute that somebody thinks otherwise, trouble begins."

Colin Hanks seemed as if he was bored hanging around the

set. So Maggie Murphy, second second assistant director, gave the 14-year-old a walkie-talkie and told him to go get Tom from his silver Airstream trailer. Colin, on location with Tom, Rita, and two-year-old brother Chester, seemed to enjoy the assignment.

"Later, Colin was like, 'Yeah, my dad said, "Don't become a production weenie,"'" says Maggie, laughing.

As the second second "production weenie," Maggie handled the actors. She learned some rules: don't interrupt when they're rehearsing lines. Don't knock five times if they're crying. Give them a moment before a hard scene. Be sensitive to their needs.

That requires finesse. First assistant director Jim Skotchdopole (who managed *Sleepless*'s schedule) and second assistant Don Lee (who managed the daily call sheet) were tough and competent. Maggie had to be on her A game.

"Usually they give the girl the hardest job," she says. "Because the girl has to work hardest to get ahead in the business. So the girl will not be lazy."

Maggie Murphy was good at her job. *Production weenie.* She sensed Tom wasn't totally happy to be there at the beginning. She knew him on screen as a comedian, but rather than being all ha-ha-ha, in person he'd been slightly cranky. Mean? Never. Diva-ish? Not his style. But definitely not warm, not at first. Later, Maggie saw that his mood lifted and "he was awesome."

What changed? It might have been Tom's discovery of Seattle's finest export: great espresso. As production continued, Tom became hooked on the stuff.

"We lived in a house out on Mercer Island and a former Kodak Fotomat booth had been turned into a drive-thru coffee thing," he says excitedly. "And I thought, 'This is just the coolest thing on the planet Earth.' And I drank *way* too much coffee. I drank so much coffee that they started sneaking me decaf without me knowing it.

Because I was coming home amped up because the stuff was just so delicious. This was the first time that I had been exposed—and anybody really had been exposed—to something other than drip coffee from a Bunn coffee maker or something like that. With the hot milk in it? It was sensational. I drank it like hot chocolate. And I was coming home, wired on six or seven lattes in the course of the day. My wife will tell you that I got very cranky at some point. And I did. Because I was just jagged out on coffee."

He wasn't the only one. Starbucks flowed liberally on set.

One day, Nora looked at Gary and said, "We should just all invest in this. It will be a memory of Seattle." Nora and Gary bought stock. Nora asked Mike Badalucco if he planned on investing. "Nah." He laughed. "I'm a prop guy!"

Tom did not invest. Ross Malinger might have joined in, had he been old enough. Ross would "demand coffee" following Starbucks runs, recalls movie-babysitter Amanda Maher. While the big kids sipped lattes, he wondered: *Where's mine?*

Prop guy Badalucco's first impression of Nora: aristocrat. "She's always well dressed," says the stocky, boisterous Brooklyn native, one of many New Yorkers the director enticed to Seattle. "She presents herself in a nice way. I remember she'd wear these scarves. I thought, 'This one might be a little snooty.'"

While Badalucco appreciated the finer things—opera, foreign films, a nice glass of prosecco—other guys in the crew lacked Nora's sophistication. But Nora, who clearly liked big personalities and characters, valued their company and humor. Just don't make a mess: keep it neat and organized. When some of the sloppier technicians crowded her set with gear, she'd say, "The quality of life, right now, is not very good." To a gaffer or electrician, she'd go, "Do all these wires have to be here?"

Nora was civilized. Only the best craft service would do. Stale, generic-brand cheese cubes? Pass. How about hearty fried chicken, luscious Washington cherries, and double-chocolate brownies? Now we're talking.

If something on the table fell short of her standards, it was gone in five minutes; and if service sucked two or three days in a row, the caterer was on probation.

"She loved to have a good time," says Betsy Sokolow-Sherman, *Sleepless*'s in-house publicist. "Like every day, the highlight is what we were going to eat, what was on the craft service table, what restaurants were around whatever location—and she was very inclusive, I think, sitting with different crew members during lunch. Unless there was a crucial studio note that had to be addressed, she was really part of the crew.... I've been on so many movie sets where the directors eat in their trailers and are not intermingling like that."

For *Sleepless* she threw on a shiny olive-green parka over a casual shirt and blue jeans, accessorizing with owl-shaped glasses and a blue-and-white scarf wrapped around her neck. (The blue was robin's egg, not royal, from which Nora recoiled.)

A production assistant making $100 per day found it hard to keep up. Not that Nora expected her team to go broke splurging on expensive outerwear and the like. But she did, through sheer presence, foster an unofficial dress code: a budget-minded PA merely tried looking *nice*. Presentable. Leave the sweatpants at home. In other words, says Maggie Murphy, "Don't be a slob."

Running the show with a gimlet eye for elevating the experience of cast and crew—thus ensuring a smoother ride in a high-stakes production—Nora compelled a sort of best-behavior atmosphere: people mostly treated each other nicely. She mostly liked people, unless they got on her nerves. Or belonged to a "different food group," as she'd dub someone who didn't necessarily fit in. "There were times when she ran much too loose and friendly a set," says Reitano. "She wanted to control the social situations and she wanted everybody to be happy. She wanted to please everyone and be pleased by them. If you did that, you became an obvious part of the making of the movie."

Both Nora and Delia loved loyal, dry-humored second assistant director Don Lee, who I'm told would prank younger staff by toting around a copy of *The Art of War*. Don, whose pre-*Sleepless* credits included *Bull Durham* and *Born on the Fourth of July*, worked hard and knew exactly what he was doing; Nora trusted him. He was a family man and serious foodie. He belonged in Nora's food group.

Jim Skotchdopole, in his late 20s, earned the nickname the Big Youth because he had so much experience for his age. He had been assistant director on *Days of Thunder, The Last Boy Scout,* and *What about Bob?* He was tall, fair-haired, and widely acknowledged as good-looking. "She liked having handsome men on the crew," says Reitano. "She liked being surrounded by handsome men.... I could understand that Nora liked being around [Jim]." Nora was viewed by some as manipulative—wielding cleverness to get what she wanted— but, as one witness swears, Jim flipped the tables on the master. "He was working her, he had her number so down, he flirted with *her*," says the witness. "She just loved it and lapped it up."

If she harbored a workplace crush on Jim, it was extremely benign. They got along famously. He made sure she angled the camera to grab certain shots and slipped her notes the night before the daily production meeting so she was extra prepared.

Here are three Nora bon mots relayed to me that sum up the above:

1.   "When you're making a movie, it's the one
     time you can control the experience."

2.   "I don't want to work with anyone that I
     wouldn't be willing to have dinner with."

3.   "Never walk barefoot on a hotel rug."
     (Badalucco abides by this rule. Whether at
     the Four Seasons or a Holiday Inn, he'll pay
     attention to quality of life. This means sporting
     flip-flops to ward off toe fungus.)

Nora required her actors have the perfect coif. "I didn't want to have as big of hair in *Sleepless in Seattle* as she wanted me to have," says Tom. "She won. It's a realm of aesthetics, costumes as well. Nora had to completely OK every single look, down to the cut of the shoes."

Nora kept Meg's mane healthy and full, twisting it into a meticulous bridal updo. She forced Barbara Garrick to chop her brown, butt-length tresses.

"Nora said, 'We have to make her look like Rita Wilson' and Rita had short hair," she says. "And they were going to make us both redheads but then one day they decided to cut my hair. They sat me in this chair and it went from butt to chin in one cutting. Delia was there and Nora was there. They just talked to me and read to me from [a] book to try to make it a less traumatic event."

Barbara wound up with a triangle-shaped, curly bob: "At the time I was totally traumatized. I didn't realize they could do that. I didn't realize that you have to get it in your contract that they can't change your hair."

Supervising the wardrobe, Nora distilled her vision into a single word: *timeless*. She was obsessed. If *Sleepless* was going to last, then it couldn't look dated in 20 years. And so it followed that Meg Ryan must be clean-cut, conservative, and American classic.

"I told Meg when we did this movie that she was playing a Republican who had never had an orgasm," said Nora. "And as she and I have often noted, [that] was approximately the only guidance I gave her toward finding the part. But not a whole lot more was necessary."

Costume designer Judy Ruskin dressed Meg in mid-length skirts, shawl-collar coats, and a festive red velvet dress from a La Brea boutique. She procured a gray TSE cashmere sweater set and add-a-pearl necklace that made Meg Ryan appear simultaneously out of time and retrograde. In *An Affair to Remember*, Deborah Kerr's cinch-waisted, formal day dresses shouted 1957; in *Sleepless*, Meg transmitted 1950s innocence without the glamour and formality. On Meg, though, that stuffy cardigan seemed fresh and coming-soon-to-a-Gap-near-you. You couldn't pin the year.

"Meg and I spent days going through clothes until we found two or three things we absolutely agreed on," said Nora. The actress "started out with all sorts of things that I wasn't crazy about, but when we began to find the one or two things that were touchstones, then we could say, 'No, this doesn't work; it's too stylish.'"

She gave Meg a virginal nightgown.

"She would wear that to bed?"

"Do you know who you are?" Nora remarked. "You're the Breck girl."

Meg had been in a new-mother haze during *Sleepless* and "didn't remember a lot of it," she told *Premiere*. Including the unhip footwear. "I look at it and say, 'Why was I wearing that?' Like, I don't understand why I wore the white shoes in the film. It took me right out."

As it happened, the Sandra Dee–ification of Meg Ryan held a mirror to sexually anxious times. The tumultuous 1960s and 1970s gave rise to Ronald Reagan and a new climate of political and social conservatism during the 1980s. The Cold War ended and the Soviet Union collapsed, boosting Americans' national pride. In 1988, Rush Limbaugh exploded on right-wing talk radio, trumpeting the Gulf War, demeaning feminists as "feminazis," and targeting progressive values and policies. The "pro-family" movement, which seeped into the GOP, protested threats to its churchgoing, traditional-gender-roles, white-picket-fence view of Americana: Gays. Pornography. Abortion. Working women. Meanwhile, a steady drop in the divorce rate accompanied declining marriage rates. The trauma of HIV/ AIDS, which predominantly affected the gay community, claiming thousands of lives, heightened public awareness of safe-sex practices. On November 7, 1991, Magic Johnson announced his HIV-positive diagnosis, stunning the sports world and the nation writ large.

Peter William Evans, a film studies professor at the University of London, labeled Meg the post-AIDS "safe-sex alternative" to edgier actresses in romantic comedy. "Above all, Meg Ryan does not toy with men's feelings," he wrote. "The very essence of loyalty, trustworthiness and all things natural, she is the approachable safe harbour for all those negotiating the Scylla and Charybdis of modern sexuality. For every siren lying in wait 'out there,' as Sam puts it in *Sleepless in Seattle*, there is a Meg Ryan character offering wholesome relief with a friendly grin."

Sleepless, which shot Meg to superstardom, firmly cemented her reassuringly sunny image as the ideal wife, mother, sister, and friend. She came along at just the right moment. In the mid-1980s, romantic comedies started to reaffirm traditional romantic love and renew focus on the courtship phase rather than the ups, downs, and unhappy endings of a relationship in progress. These were the flip side to reality-rooted romances (*Annie Hall, An Unmarried Woman, Broadcast News*) that explored messy gender relations in the wake of the second-wave women's movement and the sexual revolution. Nora knew that battlefield well but glided blithely across it post-*Heartburn*. On the front lines stood squads of single, professional women who longed to get married someday; she would not deny them the happy ending she found in Nick.

When Harry Met Sally, which nearly ended unhappily, is heralded as the leader in a love-affirming trend that restored the balance of yesteryear's MFEO screen couples while maintaining a modern sensibility playing to women's fantasies about what love should look like. (In the 1990s, Mr. Right was Mr. Sensitive.)

Left to her own devices, Nora out-schmaltzed Rob Reiner by light-years. *Sleepless* always had a happy ending. While promoting *When Harry Met Sally*, Nora, an atheist, explained how "Christian" and "Jewish" romantic comedies differ: external forces separate lovers in the former, while characters' neuroses obstruct happiness in the latter. Though Sam Baldwin questions the afterlife, he experiences a sort of muted spiritual rebirth at the Empire State's pearly gate. *Sleepless* is "born again." But heaven is a place on earth.

The films shared genetic material: rat-a-tat-tat wordplay, musical standards, Meg Ryan. Wildly optimistic, Annie and Sally nonetheless exist on different wavelengths: one has sex (Sally, with Harry offscreen) and the other doesn't (Annie, with nobody because Walter fell asleep to the whir of his humidifier). "Annie is much more square than Sally," said Nora. "These two people in this movie are very old-fashioned people. I mean, these are people that love is more important to than work. These are not the fabulous, driven *Broadcast News* people...."

When *Rolling Stone* asked whether Nora had been concerned about alienating '90s-generation workaholics, she answered: "The younger persons that I know, especially the ones in California, I don't even think they have sex. They have business dinners and business breakfasts, sometimes two business breakfasts. But I believe very strongly that underneath all of that is just a bunch of romantic stuff. Everybody's got it."

In the same interview, she dismissed a prediction that she would be remembered more for her romantic comedies than her acid writing. "What a hilarious notion that it would be me!" she said. "But I don't really think it's a risk."

Nora drew a parallel between sexless *Sleepless*, rated PG, and the screwball comedies that skirted anti-sex Production Code rules through wit and innuendo. "You couldn't have sex in a movie in the '30s and '40s, so how did people have sex with one another? They talked to each other. That was sex," she said in a 1993 press conference for the movie. "One of the things I'm very fond of in this kind of movie that we've made here is that it's a return to words.... I actually think that now that we're in this age where it's more problematical to have sex in life, where people are becoming more cautious about sex, I actually think people are getting a little more romantic with one another because you can't just tumble into a casual sexual thing as much."

Joining the sex-kills-the-romcom discussion, Meg said: "It's a very easy way for a woman to be empowered sexually by men. It's not such an easy thing to be empowered because you're intelligent or that you're funny or that you nurture well or that you are a listener or any of those other things. I think that, you know, uncrossing your legs...in a movie is a very easy way to get people's attention."

Hear that shade, Sharon Stone?

Tom played yin to Meg's yang. He gives you *stable* and *decent* and *good dad*. Sex scenes in male-nightmare Michael Douglas movies weren't his cup of tea. "I don't actively avoid roles that are robustly sexualized," he told the *New Yorker*. "It's just that the stories I have been drawn to have not had sex as one of the motors that drove the narrative. There are so many other things to explore."

* * *

"Standby on milk mustache! Rolling milk mustache! Action milk mustache!"

So shouted Ross Malinger before at least six takes that required him to drink a glass of milk and scowl at Barbara Garrick, his *Sleepless* nemesis. In the scene, Victoria cooks Sam and Jonah dinner, dissolving into extended giggle fits at Sam's jokes. She cranked out that hilarious hyena cackle—equivalent to nails on a chalkboard—with astonishing consistency. "It was believable every time," says Amanda Maher (Clarise the babysitter). "I'm in awe of that." At her hotel room, Barbara had watched a National Geographic special on hyenas. "I just started imitating them, and I thought it was so funny that it made me laugh," she says. "To kick off any jag of laughing that Nora wanted, I would laugh like a hyena and it would come tumbling out."

Afterward, Ross complimented Barbara: "That's the biggest laugh I ever heard onstage in five years of working."

The crew heard that and snickered. Nora helped Ross save face.

"Is that true?" she said flatly. "You have a lot of experience."

During setups, Nora and Ross played the puzzle game Tangoes. When playtime was over and acting time began, she coached the boy to fake smile.

"I guess you couldn't smile that time," she said.

"I'll smile."

"You don't have to."

"I'd like to."

"What happens when you smile? Let me see."

He flashed his tiny teeth.

"OK," she said, "let's try it."

With Barbara, Ross didn't have to feign irritation. "You could see how she annoyed Ross," says Gary. Her hyena-giggle "wasn't authentic to him."

Barbara stepped out of the costume trailer into the night. She wore a boxy bubble-gum pink suit and gold brooch. "Oh God," said Nora, "is that the only thing you have for her to wear?" They were on the clock to film Sam and Victoria's date at the future James Beard Award–winning restaurant Dahlia Lounge, so pink suit approved. Garrick, self-conscious about her body after gaining 20 pounds, was happy that her costumes were on the baggy side.

The first thing she had to do was stroll into the restaurant and gently bump the table where Sam, awaiting Victoria's arrival, had stacked sugar cubes into a pyramid. She intended to knock over the sugar stack, but instead she spilled beer all over Tom's lap, four or five times in a row. Barbara says, "Wardrobe and makeup get a blow dryer and start blowing his crotch, trying to get his pants dry. And he never said anything."

Barbara never saw Nora give Tom a note. The director had just one gripe with Barbara: her lips. "You see me smiling the same way the whole movie because Nora kept saying, 'Keep the sides of your mouth going up,'" she recalls. "She'd come and do it on my face. That's why I'm smiling the whole movie because I was petrified that I was going to make that face that she hated."

When Nora needed Barbara to loosen up for her kiss scene with Tom, the actor stepped in to calm her stage fright.

"It was incredibly tense on my part and didn't look natural and Nora hated it," she says. "It was late at night and it was very cold out on the water. Tom, in all his generosity, just started talking to me very intimately about his first marriage and his time in New York and his time as a Christian. Very intimate things." He spoke at a low volume. "Nora gave him the cue and he pulled me in and I kissed him. So that it was very natural, very coming-out-of-a-conversation, very relaxed.... He was telling me the most personal things and touching my heart. I mean, you want to kiss him anyway, but I was nervous about kissing him."

Nora had hit another wall while filming the scene where Jessica (Gaby Hoffmann) refuses to give up Jonah's location under interrogation from Sam and her parents (Hannah Cox and Rich Hawkins). She went outside and dialed Delia, out of town that day, on her mobile phone. As written, Gaby was to end the standoff and start talking, stating simply, "He's on his way to New York."

This just isn't working, Nora told her sister. How to punch it up? As Delia explained, "I had always wanted that character to say NY for *no way* . . . just because it isn't of course. It's NW. So I said, 'Well, she should just say NY,' and Nora heard it as New York. I didn't even realize that NY stood for New York."

Thanks to miscommunication, the writers improvised this:

JESSICA'S DAD: Tell us where he is. Right
this minute.
JESSICA: NY.
SAM: What is that?
JESSICA'S DAD: No Way.
SAM: *That's NW.*
JESSICA: New York. He's on his way to
New York.

Delia called it collaboration; Nora called it a miracle. Colleagues noticed the director brighten when Delia was around. Viewed by many as the sweetest of the sisters, Delia became a liaison between Nora and those afraid to challenge her. "Working with Nora in Hollywood was like traveling in an armored vehicle," she wrote. "Once she left a studio meeting for a few minutes and everyone fell on me, giving me all the script notes they didn't have the nerve to tell her. This happened as well on our movie sets all the time. And I, blessed (or doomed) to be the middle child—always understanding everyone else's point of view—would tell Nora their notes/concerns/complaints, which she sometimes listened to and as frequently dismissed with a face. From seeing it so often, I can make the face, too. It's just scrunching up a bit, nothing too extreme."

When Reitano couldn't convince Nora of something in the cutting room, he occasionally used Delia to get through to her: "If Delia agreed she'd say, 'I'll take care of it.' And the next day Nora would be more open to the idea."

Delia, no fool, would only approach Nora with ideas she supported herself. Bringing others' alterations and that of her own, "I often drove her crazy because I was certain she wasn't going to do what I wanted even when she promised she would," wrote Delia, noting: "I was right, she didn't always listen. Sometimes she would boss me around, and then I would go home and try to boss my husband around. This did not go over well."

When in Seattle, Delia was joined by her other half, Jerry, whom she's called her destiny. She believed *Sleepless* was about *love*, not just love in the movies; perhaps she coined MFEO because she lived it. Said Delia, "I don't think there's a million people that you can fall in love with.... I actually think to make a great match is a very lucky thing."

Though Delia's romanticism rang loud and clear, the question of whether Nora drank her own Kool-Aid was up for debate. The question transfixed journalists who continued to see her as Nora Ephron, media scourge and woman scorned. When *Rolling Stone* asked circa 1993 how she managed to believe in romance after three marriages, she replied: "If I weren't a romantic, why would I keep doing it? There's no one who's more romantic than a cynic." The question eluded even those close to her, with Delia telling *Premiere* that same year, "the reason why she has such a wonderful marriage now is that even after being so terribly hurt, she kept believing in love. But romantic—I just don't know about romantic." Among those who knew her, she freely dispensed practical love advice. While *Sleepless* costumer Judy Ruskin complained about a no-good lover and a lamp on her nightstand that broke, Nora turned on a dime and said, "Get rid of the boyfriend and get rid of the lamp." (She did.) Then, no-nonsense Nora would turn back around and weigh down a sailboat with a trillion strings of Christmas lights, an impractical—unabashedly romantic—flight of fancy.

Scouting Seattle, Nora learned that locals strung twinkle lights on their boats and sailed around Lake Union at Christmastime. She conceived a scene with that image in mind and chartered a sailboat to execute her plan. Suspended from bosun's chairs, crew members laced tiny white lights around the mast. They flicked the switch to show Nora, but she wasn't satisfied. "What, are there five twinkle lights on this boat?" Gary quotes her as saying. "No, I want lots of twinkle lights. Ten times this, 20 times this." Panic broke out as crew ran to hardware stores and bought up seemingly every last strand left in the city.

"I'm not going to get stressed about this," said Nora, leaning over the dock of Sam's houseboat. "I want what I want."

A group including Jeffrey Townsend extravagantly wrapped the mast and sail as though they were twinkling trees at the Central Park restaurant Tavern on the Green, Nora's inspiration. They added generators to sustain electricity. After some eight hours, including a second thumbs-down from Nora, they were finally in the clear. In the wee small hours of the morning, the twinkle-boat sailed low across the dark water and past the houseboat, casting golden reflections. Perfection. Nora was happy.

While Seattle is famous for rain, there had been a terrible drought that summer, the driest on record in 90 years. The snow on the Cascades had melted. The city imposed mandatory water restrictions. This posed a problem, as rainfall jokes peppered the script. "In the greenest city in America we couldn't waste water without risking the ire of the entire population," wrote Lynda Obst.

Jeff Arch visited during one unseasonably hot 95-degree day when special effects was making rain for a scene on the houseboat dock. Nora looked "adorable" in a yellow rain slicker. "She could have cut me to shreds and she didn't cut me to shreds," says the screenwriter. Though she did seem to crouch into the defensive position whenever he approached with a kind word. "I was never on the other end of her venting," he adds. "I know that the production designer got fired, got replaced. To this day, he's got PTSD about her."

"We're shooting the tiramisu scene in the little diner in Pike's Place with Rob," recalls Jeffrey Townsend. "I'm basically in my nightmare. I'm fully realizing that I've entered into an irreconcilable relationship with my director that I'm so embarrassed by and humiliated about. And I can't seem to fix it and every day is difficult. I've gotten a few approvals on things and I've got my whole folder of things that need to get done."

Rapport between Jeffrey and Nora disintegrated amid the Seattle shoot. It was a personality conflict. Gary Foster had recommended Jeffrey, whose production design credits included Martin Scorsese's *After Hours* and John Sayles's *Baby It's You*; Nora's first choice, *Heartburn* designer Tony Walton, was unavailable for the job. Jeffrey felt that Nora had made him a scapegoat, deflecting untoward criticism in the form of quotable put-downs, because she needed time to respond to issues, including actors' questions. She would approve something only to denounce it later. And rather than saying, "Is this the table that's supposed to be here?" she would phrase it as "Could somebody tell me what kind of production designer lets a table like this occur in a set?" Often, she'd point at something and say, "Wouldn't it be possible to have something pretty instead of this?" He had begun to resent the word *pretty.*

"If an actor approaches you while you're already shooting, they usually want a change made to a set," says Jeffrey, thinking back to the Athenian Inn. "I'm sitting there and Tom suddenly appears at the table and says, 'Can I sit down?' I braced myself and thought, 'What does he want now?' That's how dark I'd become.

"And he said, 'Now that we've been shooting on the houseboat set, I feel like I never had a chance to tell you how much you helped me.' I said, 'How do you mean?' He said, 'I'm busy with the day in and day out of the dialogue and things with my son. As soon as I walked in there, you reminded me that I'm an architect. All these little touches, everywhere I looked, pulled me back into my former life. It's not quite the life I'm in now; I'm doing remodels, not really the architect I was planning on being. I'm doing something a little different. But you gave me that tension; you gave me that history all around me. I just wanted to thank you.' And he gets up and walks away.

"Now, here's what I know—I would swear on a gigantic stack of Bibles. That maybe sort of is true for him, but not necessarily something he needed to say. But rather—and this is the Tom Hanks part—he saw me across the room and saw the mood I was in. What makes him completely different than any other actor on the planet, almost, is he thought, 'I've got five minutes. Let me see if I can fix that. Let me see if I can change that guy's mood.' And that's what he did."

❋ ❋ ❋

Always on time, always prepared, Meg had been quiet on *Sleepless*. "She just had a child," says Maggie Murphy, second second AD. "That's hard to be the star." Maggie viewed Meg as personable and shy instead of standoffish. To Jim Skotchdopole, she seemed a bit reserved and thus temperamentally different from Tom. To Rosie O'Donnell, she was a kindred spirit.

Rosie, the life of the party, befriended the actress and complemented her goofy side. The two fell into hysterics filming Annie and Becky's *Affair* sob session. They often ganged up to tease Sven's hunky camera intern, Lucas Bielan, causing him to blush. "He was a beautiful man, he really was. Flowing blond hair," Meg told *Premiere* in a joint interview with Rosie, who joked: "I sexually harassed him the entire time." When Rosie couldn't remember her lines for a page-long scene, she taped dialogue to Lucas's leg. "At the end of the movie, Rosie's last shot, she had a tattoo on her chest that said LUCAS, with a big heart on it!" giggled Meg. (Rosie, who came out as gay in 2002, has said of her *Sleepless* confidante, "As a best friend, you feel that you could be intimate with her and she wouldn't betray you. And that's the truth.")

Not that Meg needed Rosie to let loose.

Script supervisor Mary Kelly names Meg among the culprits who tried to make her break character during her *Sleepless* cameo as an airplane passenger. Gary Foster characterizes Meg as having a vivacious personality: "Kooky in a really attractive way. She gets excited about things." On *Sleepless*, "Completely outgoing and just wanting to be part of the group. There's moments when she's pre-paring and she's going to go sit in a corner and do what she needs to do, but I found her really accessible and fun."

This description seems to differ from how Meg was perceived on the *When Harry Met Sally* set, suggesting that she felt more comfortable on *Sleepless*.

"It's part of the feeling that Nora creates on the set, which is, 'We're working hard and spending all this time together,'" Gary says. "'Let's also be a family. Let's also talk about things and chal-lenge each other intellectually and gossip.' There was a lot of gossip."

The news cycle in the summer of 1992 provided much of the fodder. Newspapers—notably the *New York Times* and the *New York Post*—were primary sources for what became Hollywood (and the rest of America's) tabloid obsession for months to come: Woody Allen's affair with Soon-Yi Previn, the 21-year-old adopted daughter of his longtime partner Mia Farrow. "It was almost like we had to shut down the film," says Caroline Aaron (Dr. Marsha Fieldstone), recalling that Nora and Lynda had their offices and assistants fax over fresh updates about the scandal. "They wanted every single piece of print on it. When there would be a break, they would go get everything and we'd have out-loud readings about Woody and Mia. It was one of the most hilarious things. They loved it so much."

Around that time, Nora told *Rolling Stone*, "He's not a close friend, but I do know him and her. I found *Husbands and Wives* very painful to watch and not in the way it was intended. I couldn't separate it from what was happening in real life. I saw a whole other level of cruelty on his part. One watches it thinking, 'Did she say that line knowing what was going on?'"

Bob Reitano never heard Nora say a negative word about Tom or Meg in dailies. She adored Rosie and loved listening to her stories about *A League of Their Own* co-star and friend Madonna. "She spoke to actors sometimes in a way that some people perceived as hostile, but I didn't," said Rosie. "I knew her and I loved her and I was never afraid of her. I always wanted to please her, but that's very different than being afraid." Echoed Jacob Bernstein: "My mom was kind and she was generous. Really generous. She was also stern and unfailingly honest. And the combination of those things made people seek her approval. It is very powerful to be someone who's both loved and feared."

It's tempting to compare Nora with Meg's character, Annie Reed. Each was a cosmopolitan go-getter. Annie, though, lacked Nora's self-possession. She freely expressed emotions. "Nora was very chatty and social, but Nora drew the line," says Pat Crowley, executive producer on *Sleepless*. "It was hard to really get to know Nora because she was very aware all the time of the various boundaries between people. Much more so than the character that Meg played."

✳ ✳ ✳

Nora and Jeffrey Townsend were having a heated argument over wall color in Annie's living room and kitchen. As Gary tells it, she had gone to preview the set, and to her dismay, it was painted a hue she expressly forbade: "mustard yellow." But in Jeffrey's version of the story, he had chosen a soft, faded rose because Nora insisted on pink from the very beginning. The issue, he recalls, was the *brightness* of the shade. When she asked for a brighter pink, he flatly refused: "Over my dead body I'm going to paint this pink," set decorator Clay Griffith recalls him saying.

It was almost their last week in Seattle, and Jeffrey had broken. He took personally Nora's last-minute edict to repaint the walls an unflattering "Pepto-Bismol," which, in his opinion, would clash against Meg's golden skin tone and make her look green. "I don't think there was any part of her that wanted that set to be that color," he says. "I think she was picking a fight. I went to Gary over the phone and said, 'I think she's actually starting to mess with the movie over how much she hates me and I don't know how to fix it.'"

Parting ways was the only solution. He begged Gary to fire him. "I stayed in Seattle," Jeffrey says. "Kept the pager on. Ran interference for the art department. Made sure everything got handled the way it needed to for that last week and a half. But that's how badly it ended for me, with a step I've never taken before. And so, the amount of soul-searching for years afterward was monumental. 'Did I do that? What was that about? What happened?'"

Gary gives full credit to Jeffrey for the movie's set design: "There's nothing he did not do." At the same time, "He was a little passive-aggressive. Or she would say things and he'd say, 'No, I'm going to do it this way.' He got a little arrogant in that way too. He just didn't know who he was dealing with, because that doesn't work for her. I think she would acknowledge it was more personality than anything."

Planning the houseboat interior, Jeffrey had pictured an unruly single-dad life: Piles of unopened mail. Toys on the floor. A bike with no front tire. Nora always made the set dressers remove the clutter.

"Nora, it's starting to look like a catalogue."

"Yes, that's the whole idea," she said. "It's like a fantasy."

She was right and he was wrong. He's happy to say he lost that battle. Alas, Jeffrey would not be the last crew member to get on Nora's bad side. Her unapologetic, sometimes maddening quest for excellence—and perfect chemistry between director and those tasked with pleasing her—soon became part of the legend.

CHAPTER 8

Make Nora Happy

When the props department handed Meg a red apple, she asked for a green Granny Smith: easier to peel. Onstage at Sand Point, in Annie's (dusty pink) kitchen, she prepared to listen to Dr. Marcia's *You and Your Emotions* while peeling the fruit in a single stroke. In a single take.

Meg and Nora developed a shorthand both verbal and nonverbal: the director would explain the point of a scene, or the significance of a pause, in clear and precise terms. Meg described her vernacular thusly: "a little less, a little more, faster, funnier, maybe emphasize this." During the making of the movie, she told a reporter, "I don't have to interpret Nora's direction with that extra beat that I have to give it with a man. In fact, she's so specific in everything she does that I almost feel like I can read her mind."

Camera rolling. Meg flipped on the radio, grabbed the apple, and began peeling. Off to the side, Mary Kelly read a line from Disappointed in Denver (Nora would loop in her own voice in post): "Every time I come close to orgasm, he stops and goes to make himself a sandwich." Then her face crumpled as the radio show replayed Sam's Christmas Eve appearance, notably his Mag-gie meet-cute: "It was like coming home, only to no home I'd ever known. I was just taking her hand to help her out of a car. And I knew it. It was like...magic."

In under two minutes, Meg effortlessly peeled that Granny Smith into one long curly strip.

"Boy," said Nora, "was that a dream!"

A dream indeed. That scene played to a Nora strength: trans-forming a mundane activity, the peeling of an apple, into some-thing meaningful and unexpectedly romantic, like a bag of subway coins from Nick Pileggi. It connected to a later scene where Jonah awakens from a bad dream in a cold sweat, anguished over los-ing his mother—"I'm starting to forget her"—and Sam conjures a small, specific character quirk that helps him remember: "She could peel an apple in one long curly strip. The whole apple."

When directing the light and the comic, Nora had the touch. She sought feedback on the dark and the dramatic—Jonah's night-mare, for example.

"I'm a much more sentimental person than she is," says Gary. "We had numerous conversations throughout the process, where she would look at me and say, 'What do you think? Is this too much or not enough?'...The first time we shot that scene, we looked at it in dailies and I didn't feel it had the emotional heft it needed to have. I had a discussion with Nora and she wasn't sure. I explained to her what I thought, how it should feel." He refer-enced Dustin Hoffman and Justin Henry in *Kramer vs. Kramer*.

"Tom didn't want to overplay it; he wanted to keep it real," he continues. "She heard me and she came to me later and goes, 'OK let's reshoot it.' And we did, and the version that's in the movie is the second version because she trusted that my instincts were on."

Could Nora Ephron get away with this?

It was the day to shoot the big payoff at the Empire Fake Building, and pressure was on. But first, hurry up and wait.

Technically, the ending—filmed out of sequence, like much of the movie—had been tricky to light because of the reflective glass in the background. "It was the only day this movie felt like all the other movies everybody's ever worked on," she said, referring to the technical tedium. One stage, two whammies: Sam and Jonah's emotionally charged reunion and fateful Annie introduction upon returning to the deck for the boy's backpack and teddy bear, Howard.

First, Sam must retrieve Jonah, who's run away to keep his appointment with Annie, whoever she may be. Sam squeezes an answer to Jonah's whereabouts from Jessica, troublemaking junior travel agent, and can barely sit still on the plane to New York. Jonah, looking everywhere for Annie, leans against the wall, a dream dashed. Sam is relieved to find his son safe and sound in the big city; Jonah is relieved to see his father again. "Tom knew a kid having an emotional reaction like that is not easy," says Gary. "He really hugged that kid. He told Nora to keep the camera going and he really tried to make him feel the desperation of how much he loved him and how much it hurt."

Then, magic-time: a wind machine blew air through Meg's hair, ever so gently. Though her lines consisted of polite small talk, her eyes glowed with passion and life. She looked at Tom as if he were indeed the nearest thing to heaven. Tom's reactions—a gentlemanly stance, a knowing smile, a sly squint—recalled Cary Grant's understated performance. Working on a micro level, Tom conveyed the magnitude of emotions from shock to excitement to deep connection in the bat of an eye. An understated performance is often more powerful than the over-the-top posturing you'll see in many contemporary romances.

Less enthused, Gary says, "He's just staring, and there's not a lot going on in his face. I guess you could put into it what you want to. And then he goes, 'Shall we?' and it's not a real sympathetic reading. But he puts his hand out. Was it too restrained? Do you get a sense of 'Oh my God, my life's changed'? You do from her. You do from Jonah. I'm not sure you get it from Tom. My feeling is he was afraid of it. I mean that respectfully. He was afraid of the sentiment and was restrained."

Hindsight blurry, Tom says, "The nature of the scene was just so loaded. I recall just kind of doing it. I think the only real direction that sort of went down was trying to figure out the spacing for the various shots. . . . I think Nora trusted Meg and me to get to where we needed to be by way of the shorthand certainly that she developed with the two of us. I think the bigger task at hand for that day was for the son. How do you shoot him?"

Nora grabbed a tight shot of Ross grinning cutely at Meg, his new movie mom. Ross led the way as Meg and Tom walked hand in hand toward the elevator, and when the elevator door closed on the trio, his happy face hogged the frame. The camera photographed the door, on which a silvery silhouette of the Empire State gleamed with hope and promise. In the final cut, that image morphed into a cool effect: a computerized likeness revolving in swift motion to the gravelly tune of Jimmy Durante and "Make Someone Happy."

Nora was readying to wrap up when Jim Skotchdopole suggested she get a close-up of Tom's and Meg's hands. Later, Nora called from the cutting room and said, "You made the scene."

But the show wasn't over. They were still wrangling the Empire

State—that magnificent diva—to star in additional scenes, and that would require Nora work her Leona Helmsley connections.

Shortly before moving production eastward in September, Nora arranged a Seattle meeting with Jeffrey's replacement, Charley Beal. The amiable art director assisted Tony Walton on *Heartburn* and other Mike Nichols productions, including the Harrison Ford drama *Regarding Henry* and a Lincoln Center revival of *Waiting for Godot*. Nora felt safe knowing he was a Walton protégé; he would skip Chicago and join *Sleepless* in Baltimore.

"Charley, whatever you do, don't use blue. I don't want any blue," she said, listing prior crimes against design: the mustard yellow. The sailboat with only four twinkle lights. The Christmas dinner table for which she flew out her own decorator to handle the cozy-classic display of food, cutlery, and holiday cheer.

Charley got the message. *Romantic and pretty.*

Before flying to Baltimore, Charley joined location manager Jane Raab in New York for an important meeting at the Empire State Building. They had only a few weeks to obtain a reasonable window of time to film Jonah approaching not-Annies on the observatory and Annie running into the lobby and sweet-talking the security guard. Negotiations included getting the building (which houses various businesses) to dim office lights while a second unit shot it from the Rainbow Room, 15 blocks uptown. That way, the red heart Nora digitally imposed on the side of the 'scraper would appear sharper.

"Nobody had shot at the Empire State Building for decades I believe," says Charley. "I remember they were having a horrible time securing the location." The Empire State negotiators included the head of public relations; they didn't want to hear about a film shoot that would disrupt tourism.

"We made a proposal and we were turned down," says Gary. "That didn't sit well with Nora or me." Nora knew Leona Helmsley's publicist, Howard Rubenstein. She made a phone call and Rubenstein agreed to bring it up to his imprisoned client. "He made an impassioned plea on our behalf and she said, 'Fine, but they have to get it done in one day.'"

When Charley touched down in Baltimore, he told an assistant: *We need a lot of lights.* He twinkle-lit every door, window, and tree within two blocks of Annie's apartment in historic Fell's Point, the city's cobblestoned shopping district. Only the exterior of her quaint row house would be shown, since the interiors had been filmed on a Seattle stage. "You better believe I didn't use a drop of blue," he says.

Charley was right to be on guard.

"She could cut you with a knife if you made a mistake," Jim Skotchdopole says of Nora. "It's not that she wouldn't forgive you. But there were times: you knew about it from the look. Not the word. . . . I would say to Don Lee that something was going on. I would take him and say, 'Check channel two. Check the travel memos.' Because somebody would be traveling out. It was a little code that someone was going to get fired. She wasn't firing for firing sake. Her neck was on the line to make whatever film we were doing perfect. She had a responsibility to the studio. And she looked at it as her responsibility. 'I'm doing my best and I want to be surrounded by the best.' If I'm identifying someone that shouldn't be in the same orchestra as the rest of my musicians, then it's time for me to find a new musician."

Gary joined Meg on a bench overlooking the harbor in Fell's Point as crew set up the scene in which she meditates on her love crossroads, torn between the familiar (Walter) and the unknown

(Sam, or someone like Sam). They chatted about life and learned they were both 30 years old, pretty young to produce a movie let alone carry one. "There was nobody else in the world," he says wistfully. "Just the two of us sitting there on the bench."

The Baltimore leg of the tour ended triumphantly. Nora ordered dozens of mouthwatering crab cakes and soft-shell crabs and thought, *I could have shot this movie forever.*

"They knew within the first few weeks of shooting that they had something special," says Beal of Team Nora. "They were already using the term 'sleeper hit,' well before they got to Baltimore.... When they showed up from Seattle, they really had a head of steam. It was great. It was really clicking. And, *oh my God*, Tom's last night [in Baltimore], and his final shot, it was very emotional."

Tom filmed a pensive close-up on the waterfront, something he could have done in Seattle but they didn't get what they needed. When he wrapped, they clapped. Though Tom had been cynical toward "destiny," an aura of fate formed around his relationship with Nora. Had the writer-director and her romantic comedy scared him off, he'd have missed so much, including his front-row view to Rita's tour de force retelling of *An Affair to Remember*. And based on his early performance, TriStar approved Tom's leading role as AIDS-stricken lawyer-hero Andrew Beckett in the drama *Philadelphia*, to be directed by Jonathan Demme. A formal offer was made in mid-August.

Tom would get a remarkable second act, thanks in part to his decision to play Sam Baldwin and put trust in Nora.

Usually couples got married or engaged at 30 Rockefeller Center's Rainbow Room—that's where Nora and first husband Dan Greenburg had their wedding celebration—but she chose the 65th-floor event space as the site of the most amicable (and controversial) breakup in romantic-comedy history.

Her conscience guilty, Annie divulges her one-sided emotional affair to Walter while sitting in the bar area. His response is impossibly mature, agreeable, and unrealistic. "Look, Annie, I love you, but let's leave that out of this," he says. "I don't want to be someone that you're settling for. I don't want to be someone that anyone settles for. Marriage is hard enough without bringing such low expectations into it. Isn't it?"

A red heart flickers upon the Empire State Building, in full view to the south.

"It's a sign," says Annie, to which Walter responds: "Who needed a sign?"

With some trepidation, Bill Pullman as Walter filmed a juicy, funny monologue that refers to HBO as "Home Rox Office" in an early draft:

I have a life insurance policy, I'm fully invested in growth stocks, I have a paid subscription to Home Rox Office, I have no sexual diseases, I have been steadily employed in a part of the economy that isn't soft, I have expectation in the way of inherited wealth, I dress nicely, I am a member of the private sector, an independent voter, I don't watch Monday Night Football, the only thing wrong with me is that I am allergic to wheat, strawberries, penicillin, pollen, nuts and wool. There are plenty of women who see me as the brass ring. If you don't—marriage is hard enough without bringing such low expectations into it, isn't it?

Oh, snap.

Bill thought that was brilliant. But he had doubts about its placement at the end of the movie. He asked Nora: "Are you willing to take the time to have this great speech? Isn't there some kind of momentum going?' 'No. No, Bill.' Sure enough it was cut," he says. (Bill was right. It was too long.)

* * *

Getting dumped for Tom Hanks did bother Bill, but who better than Meg Ryan to bring the pain? "Meg is such a brilliant soul to be hearing this from," he testifies. "She dances around all those emotions and the humanity of not wanting to hurt. It was so alive with her. I always loved that. We did a lot of those scenes at the beginning where we're carrying luggage into her apartment and stuff like that; we shot it in Baltimore. I remember thinking, she is really dazzling in an effortless way."

At one point, Nora heard that Liza Minnelli was rehearsing her act in a separate corner of the Rainbow Room, complete with a full orchestra. "She said, 'Wouldn't it be fun to go down there and see if we can listen to her do her sound check?'" recalls Bill. "So we did. That's the kind of thing you wouldn't normally get on a film. 'Oh, at lunch let's go down and see Liza Minnelli.'"

While Liza jazz-handed in preparation to perform at a bar mitzvah (that was the word), 30 Rock catered to the movie stars in its midst. An elevator was reserved. Going up and down, "everybody's watching you on every floor that you stop. They're all trying to see what's going on," says Bill. "So you feel like you're right at the epicenter of New York City culture and it's culminating into a movie."

Down on the street, however, the vibe was dirtier and surlier than it appeared through Nora's rose-colored lens. In 1990, the city's murder rate spiked to a record 2,245 homicides, and that year *Ghost*, the Patrick Swayze–Demi Moore love story, captured a wild feeling of rampant crime and urban decay. A mugger shoots

Swayze and runs off with his wallet. The subway is a crazy train. And Whoopi Goldberg, as Oda Mae Brown, one of the greatest sidekicks in romcom history, warns Demi's character: "Molly, you in danger, girl."

Two years later, murders dropped by 250 and would slide downward throughout the decade as New York underwent a sanitizing that put more cops on the ground and shuttered strip clubs and peep shows near Port Authority, replacing them with Starbucks and Dunkin' Donuts. An influx of Harrys and Sallys— young, single, and upwardly mobile—had embraced city life, which was more exciting than in the 'burbs. On television, *Seinfeld* and *Friends*—which continued the Harry-Sally dynamic with Jerry and Elaine, and Ross and Rachel—presented Manhattan as a safe, small village where serendipitous encounters often lead to romance.

But *Sleepless in Seattle*, pointing Cupid's arrow toward the Empire State Building, led the revival of New York as America's love capital in the popular imagination.

The same day Meg dropped Bill, a second unit shot the skyscraper from the Rainbow Room. The locations people and the Empire State people were on the phone to make sure this light in this office and that light in that office were turned off.

The next day's schedule, on September 24, called for the Empire State to shut down half the observation deck, permitting the Hollywood interlopers a few hours to film the kid. At around 10 in the morning, hundreds of pounds of equipment were loaded into the elevator and crowded into tight quarters on floor 86.

Betsy Sokolow-Sherman played the not-Annie who shakes her head no when Jonah asks if she's, *you know*. "I think people were stressed in case they didn't get the shot that they needed but it seemed to go very smoothly."

Hovering overhead, a helicopter camera captured the scene below—just barely—since radio waves from the building's antenna scrambled most of the footage. "We have every frame of what was usable," says Gary. "It was just one take, one pass by."

That evening, *Sleepless* took over the lobby to film Annie and the elevator operator, Jonah skipping through, and Jonah leaving with Sam, the last shot.

Charley made a failed cameo as a street vendor attempting to sell father and son flowers on their way out of the building. The scenery guy could not act. After one tepid try, Nora said to him, "For the next take, why don't you sort of hold the flowers out toward them?" And when that tanked, she advised: "You know, it's not really working. Why don't you just *stand* there?"

At the wrap party around the corner from Fifth Avenue and 34th Street, Nora made cheeky comments that Charley survived. "Well," she teased, "at least you made it to the end, kid."

Several years later, Charley was production-designing another movie, and where did they want to shoot but the Empire State observatory? Bracing for another round of tough negotiations, he found himself in a meeting with the same PR woman who pushed back at *Sleepless*'s requests until Leona OK'd them. Her tone was quite different.

"Oh, Charley! You couldn't have been more right!" she said. "A week after that movie opened, our receipts went up $10,000 a day."

They had gone up and they stayed up, she said.

CHAPTER 9

Stardust

Back at her post-production office in the Brill Building near Times Square, Nora Ephron brought in a desk from the houseboat set—a little present to herself. Bob Reitano plunged into editing. "A lot of [it] goes on in your head but it's not something you can verbalize," he says. "Nora wasn't about that. She wasn't visual and she required another kind of stimulation. Fortunately, there was the telephone that she was on all the time talking with friends. She was ideal to work for because like other writer-directors, you never had to tussle with them over the technical aspects of the cut. I would say to her, 'That's wrong. I need to fix that. That's really clumsy.' And she would say, 'Go do it.' And she would give me the time to do it."

Though Nora had a rich social life to which she tended, "She was always giving you something," he adds. "She was always contributing. She never sat back and let you do the work."

Reitano defied star cinematographer Sven Nykvist and restored color to the actors' complexions. He didn't like the way Nykvist had printed the film—with that pallid white skin—and he knew Nora didn't, either.

"We got back to New York and I said, 'Reprint the dailies,'" Reitano recalls. "It cost a lot of money. And we got the dailies printed the way they're supposed to look. Sven was working in Chicago and he said, 'I'd like to see the film.' So I flew out to Chicago and he and the crew who had been on *Sleepless* came to the screening room and I showed him the film. With tomato faces. And he was apoplectic. He called the lab and said, 'You have to take the red out.'

"I got into a taxi to go back to the airport and I said, 'Don't do anything.' I'm thinking, 'This is an editor overriding Sven Nykvist.' I knew it's what Nora would have done. Nora was very disturbed at this ghostly image we had, but there was no need for a confrontation because in the end, we controlled the finishing of the film. And it should be warm and it should be American and not Swedish."

Nora did *not* want Céline Dion in her movie.

TriStar pushed back *Sleepless*'s release from April to June when Peter Guber, chairman of parent company Sony Pictures Entertainment, demanded the inclusion of a sappy contemporary duet in place of the bombastic vocal standards Nora preferred for the soundtrack. Guber was very hot for a radio-friendly remake of Nat King Cole's "When I Fall in Love" featuring Dion and Clive Griffin (never to be heard of again after 1993).

"'Someday My Prince Will Come' or whatever the hell song it was," says Lynda Obst. "He thought Nora knew nothing about music. . . . And he was horrified that she was like a Frank Sinatra old fart who didn't understand rock and roll the way he did, and didn't understand the market. He charged me with A) making sure the Céline Dion song was the last song of the movie and B) making sure Nora stayed hip and cool. I found it hilarious. Nora really understood a soundtrack from a completely different point of view than Peter, who ran a record company, sort of. . . . He thought of himself as a person who clearly understood the record business. Yet Nora looked at the soundtrack as part of a narrative. She loved music, but she loved the kind of music that she loved, and she felt that the lyrics were as important as the tune."

Lynda continues: "We were both laughing the whole movie about the Céline Dion song. Peter kept calling me the whole movie. 'Have you heard it? How is it?' I was always putting it 'on the roof' as I call it. I was waiting until the movie could be tested with Nora's choice. Ultimately the studio head doesn't decide; the audience decides. So we were sitting in the mix and Nora's like, 'I can't wait for you to hear the song for the scene at the end of the movie.' So it came up and it was Jimmy Durante. And it was the most perfect choice for the end of the movie that I've ever heard."

The song: "Make Someone Happy." Lynda cried.

"The voice, when it came on, was so gravelly and so emotional and so happy, it perfectly encapsulated the whole movie," she says. "At the moment I heard it, I knew that it was perfect. I knew that I was going to have the most astonishing conversation with Peter Guber of my career. So he called me because he knew I was seeing Nora's cut for the first time and he said, 'How's the movie?' And I said, 'It's a gigantic hit.' He said, 'Does it end with a Céline Dion song?' And I said, 'No.' He said, 'What does it end with?' And I said, 'It's perfect. Just wait. Wait until you hear it. I'm not even going to tell you. I just want you to hear it with an audience.' Because I knew if I said, 'Jimmy Durante' he would have a full-on heart attack."

Meg packed into the jet with the Hankses and Nora. Landing in Phoenix for a sneak preview, she was stunned to see a throng of white limos awaiting their arrival. "I have never felt so much like a celebrity," she said. Rosie asked to view the movie in LA, though Nick Pileggi apparently blanked on passing along her telephone request to Nora. She recalled: "I was waiting by the phone feeling like, oh my God, they don't want me to see it! Maybe I'm not in it!" Lynda celebrated with Nora. "I remember we walked around looking at everybody—I always do—saying, 'You're the most important person in my life,'" she says. "And wondering if people were the right audience for us. We had the same anxieties that we always do, but they loved it. This was the preview in which it was clear that no songs would be changed."

Around this time, a cast and crew screening was held at LA's Mann National Theatre. A gracious Nora approached a cautious Jeffrey Townsend and told him a story: Warren Beatty, set to produce and star in 1994's *Love Affair*, his remake of *An Affair to Remember*, asked to view *Sleepless* in the not-quite-ready-for-prime-time stages. He phoned Nora afterward with a technical camera question: "What kind of lenses were you using at night on the Empire State Building where you hold the foreground and still see the city?" Warren Beatty—*the Warren Beatty*—actually believed the Sand Point set was the real observatory! "She was thrilled to share that with me and it was a truly thrilling thing to hear as a production designer," says Jeffrey. "We fooled a filmmaker."

On June 21, *Sleepless in Seattle*'s Plaza premiere party was, hands down, the hottest ticket in town. Tom and Rita arrived in their Old New York best, he in a shiny black suit and she in an elegant black number and... *wait, was that Madonna?* The Queen of Pop, sporting cheeky pigtails like the club kid that she was, crashed the event to hang with Rosie. Also on the guest list: New York Knicks coach Pat Riley and Stevie Wonder.

Two nights later, the red-carpet Hollywood screening beckoned an unshaven Dennis and casual-cool Meg, who wore a slate-gray tank dress, flat sandals, and a black cross necklace, her wheat-colored hair just past chin-length. Grasping son Jacob's hand, Nora smiled brightly in a sharp black Katharine Hepburn suit (probably Armani); Nick, snazzy in pinstripes, looked proud as can be. A tuxedoed Ross Malinger mugged for the camera, revealing missing teeth. Céline Dion, bane of Nora's existence, performed "When I Fall in Love."

Barbara Garrick was crushed.

"Everybody was saying how obnoxious Victoria was," Barbara says. "That was the key word they used to describe her. And I was in shock because I had not meant to be obnoxious in any way, shape or form. I remember George C. Wolfe, at that time head of the Public Theater, saying to me, 'Well, you did your job; you were completely obnoxious.' And me just sitting there and Tom overhearing it and coming over and saying, 'Victoria and Sam were just too much alike. That's the only reason they never got together.' Wasn't that kind of him?"

Then "I had an agent say to me after the movie came out, 'Well, the verdict is not out yet in Hollywood whether you're the best actress in Hollywood or the worst,'" says Barbara. "People were saying things like that to me because Victoria...who knows why. I don't know why. Maybe they don't like aggressive women. Maybe she reminds them of somebody in their lives, but the response was kind of negative toward her, which surprised me."

Bill Pullman also nursed his wounds. He had fallen victim to Ralph Bellamy syndrome, an unclassified condition that afflicts actors pigeonholed as chumps doomed to lose the leading lady to the handsome rake. Patient zero: Ralph Bellamy, serial dumpee tossed aside for Cary Grant in *His Girl Friday* and *The Awful Truth*.

"I had done three very different roles and I never put them together," says Bill, "but somehow, the zeitgeist and the press pick up on each other. They're saying, 'The guy who never gets the girl is Pullman.' And I thought, 'Oh, no.'"

The pro-Walter threads on IMDb.com would get heated and remain so several years after the movie's release; one user went so far as to say that Bill has "better hair" than Tom Hanks and "can handle aliens" because of his presidential turn in *Independence Day*. "I find this all terribly troubling," wrote another. "I do believe in magic in relationships, even experienced it a time or two. But Annie's abandonment of this fine, righteous man, who lets her go, is tragic."

Screenwriter David Ward jumps to her defense, saying, "There was just another man who was better for her. And she had this sense that even though Walter was a great guy and she loved a lot of things about him, that for her there was something missing. The idea that there is someone out there that maybe no one else can touch, for you. It's a great romantic idea. As we get older in life we may not necessarily believe that."

Even so, we, as a society, are conditioned by movies, music, and literature to believe that romantic love conquers all—with romantic love being the primary reason people get married these days. In 1993, TriStar's ingenious marketing message (*What if someone you never knew was the only someone for you?*) capitalized on a soulmate fixation that would bloom in intensity as entire industries, online dating for one, flourished around it. But that was in the future. *Sleepless* opened Friday, June 25, finishing second behind *Jurassic Park* with weekend earnings of $17 million. It had done better than *Pretty Woman*.

When the last tickets were tallied, *Sleepless* grossed $127 million domestically and $228 million worldwide. The "sleeper" in blockbuster's clothing ranked fifth among the best-performing movies that year. The top four were *Jurassic Park*, unbeatable with $900 million in global ticket sales, followed by *Mrs. Doubtfire*, *The Fugitive*, and *The Firm*. Then, Nora Ephron, besting *Indecent*

Proposal (for which she wasn't hired), *The Pelican Brief* (to which she lost Julia Roberts), and *Dennis the Menace* (which Nick Castle directed after disputing Nora's script).

"She went from a total disaster, to a movie that basically reopened her career," says Mike Medavoy. "If the Fox movie [*This Is My Life*] had been the last movie that she had done, I don't think she'd have a career. Certainly not as a director."

Certainly not as a *woman* director. *This Is My Life*, made on a shoestring budget, wasn't an unmitigated *disaster*. Surely a male director of Nora's promise would have been allowed second and third chances following a disastrous outing, but as any female filmmaker will tell you, it's harder for women than men to regain footing after a failed directorial effort. So often they've got one shot to prove themselves, and if they blow it, or don't add to the bottom line off the jump, their time is up. Considering the odds stacked against Nora, it is remarkable that Medavoy gave her a second chance at the helm of a $25 million movie that happened to net 10 times that.

Despite her success, reviews for *Sleepless* were good but not great. The movie transcended negative write-ups. The exposure led to sales of two million VHS copies of *An Affair to Remember*, and, silencing naysayers, the standard-heavy *Sleepless in Seattle* soundtrack went multiplatinum, reaching number one on Billboard's top albums chart in August of 1993 without producing a top-10 radio hit. (Dion's "When I Fall in Love" capped at number 23.)

In Hollywood, if something works, the instinct is to make more of it and right away. That summer, Gary called Nora two to three times per week with a sequel idea, but she wasn't hooked. Assuming Sam and Annie lived happily ever after, would their blissful—uneventful—relationship sustain audience attention over an hour and a half? Doubtful. Now if they broke up, even temporarily, *that* would be drama. But a breakup would negate the movie's uplifting kicker: *Once you find The One, your troubles melt away.* Depicting the couple as anything less than perfect would feel like a betrayal to their fans.

Anyway, Nora was preparing to direct *Mixed Nuts*, her third project with co-writer Delia and a remake of the absurdist French comedy *Santa Claus Is a Stinker.* She eventually signed an all-star cast including Rita, Steve Martin, Madeline Kahn, Liev Schreiber, Adam Sandler, Parker Posey, and Jon Stewart, with Rob Reiner slated to appear briefly alongside wife Michele Singer in her film debut.

While the sisters Ephron flexed the funny bone, Meg and Dennis reteamed for the bleak drama *Flesh and Bone*, in which she portrayed a woman who survived the brutal murder of her entire family and Dennis the love interest whose father (James Caan) committed the crime when she was a baby. The film, helmed by Steve Kloves, was pulled from theaters in mid-November after just two weeks, marking it a bust.

The publicity-shy pair took the extra step of promoting *Flesh and Bone* in *Vogue* magazine, which featured photos of bare-chested Dennis giving Meg a piggyback. In another shot, the grinning rascal threw the demure actress over his shoulder. In the accompanying interview, Dennis (filming the Western *Wyatt Earp* at the time) called Meg his best friend and fatherhood the best thing that ever happened to him. They presented their lives as perfectly imperfect. Rustic-aspirational. Answering for past career blunders, Dennis said, "I find most movies today are really well-made television shows. I'm not putting them down, but sometimes they disappoint me in that they don't take enough chances. I like working with filmmakers and stories that are on the edge."

One of those stories was *Wilder Napalm*, a romantic comedy

from *Breaking Bad* writer Vince Gilligan that starred Dennis and Arliss Howard as pyrokinetic brothers vying for Debra Winger. Distributed by TriStar, it flamed out upon release in August. A month prior, the studio set off romcom stink bomb *So I Married an Axe Murderer*, with Mike Myers as the San Francisco beat poet dating a beautiful butcher (Nancy Travis) he fears is a serial killer. *Sleepless in Seattle*, a tough act to follow, was proof that sweetness can sizzle. Although Tom and Meg shared barely five minutes of screen time, they were chemically tuned through impeccable comic timing and mastery of the Ephron dialect. They were equally openhearted in taking seriously material others might deem unserious. They inspired their word-obsessed director, and in turn, she inspired them. They became Nora's boy and girl muses, the living incarnations of her voice in romantic comedy.

"I think she loved working with Meg because Meg sort of embodied someone that people wanted to be around and be with and was lovable," says Betsy Sokolow-Sherman. "She was very attractive, smart, could be quirky, and maybe that's how Nora did see herself."

Lynda described Meg as the "girl-next-door version of Nora— sophisticated and urban without being New Yorky."

And Meg? As Jeff Arch predicted to his wife the night *Sleepless in Seattle* came to him, the actress had made the cover of *Premiere* magazine, gracing the July 1993 issue in a seductive power suit with the jacket unbuttoned and no shirt underneath. A few weeks later, *People* ran portraits by photographer and hairstylist Sally Hershberger that displayed Meg braless underneath her white tank top and flashing her toned torso. Whether it came from Meg, the shutterbugs, or a combination of both, the decision to pose in a playfully sexy manner delivered the memo: *I am not Annie Reed.*

"I guess I've been thinking a lot about dysfunction," she

told *Vogue* of *Flesh and Bone* and 1994's *When a Man Loves a Woman*, for which she earned strong reviews and a Screen Actors Guild nomination as Andy Garcia's alcoholic wife. "Both movies are about managing your past in your present." She was gravitating to roles that dealt with "bigger, spiritual questions" and "get at something I don't understand—then I'm highly interested," she said. "I'm feeling really lucky lately. There are some very interesting things coming my way. Maybe it's that I'm 31. Now I can *play* parts like that." Furthermore, she'd "played enough journalists in my life. But they're always sort of weak journalists. They're always people who write about cheese or something."

Highly in demand in the months surrounding *Sleepless*, Meg rejected a slew of major movies like the black comedy *To Die For*, which the actress's agent, Steve Dontanville, explained as "a scary piece for her." (Nicole Kidman accepted the juicy part of a diabolical housewife who schemes to kill her husband.) She also turned down Nicolas Cage–Bridget Fonda romcom *It Could Happen to You*, about a New York cop who wins the lottery and gives half his money to his favorite waitress. A heartwarming premise, though Meg had her pick of the genre: she chose *I.Q.*, wherein Albert Einstein (Walter Matthau) helps a handsome mechanic (Tim Robbins) woo a winsome academic (Meg, obviously) by pretending he's a physicist. It opened to so-so box office in December 1994.

The next two years, Meg doubled down on drama (and death scenes) as a hero Army captain in *Courage under Fire* and Robert Downey Jr.'s 17th-century baby mama in *Restoration*. Though she tried to switch things up, she continued to be viewed as a romantic comedy princess. As an actress equated with "adorable," Meg would have to work harder to break the mold and get taken seriously, with varying degrees of success.

Tom Hanks, however, was not pigeonholed by romantic comedy

and easily transitioned to the heights of his dramatic career. Starting with *Philadelphia*, the first big-league Hollywood film to address AIDS, Tom channeled everyday heroes in a spectacular run of well-curated non-coms exploring social issues and significant historical and cultural moments. He often played hero opposite other male actors, or carried a movie on his own. He shed 30 pounds to play gifted gay lawyer Andrew Beckett, who gets fired for having AIDS. Beckett sues his firm and recruits homophobic lawyer Joe Miller (Denzel Washington) to defend him in court. "Reading the script, I saw how I could play either role, but the one I was most attracted to was Andy," said Tom. "In a lot of ways, even though he's gay, he's in fact closer to who I am than any role I've played before. He's at home in his skin, and he isn't yearning."

Philadelphia became one of the most successful dramatic films of 1993, earning $125 million globally and an Oscar for Tom. In his heartfelt (almost *presidential*) acceptance speech, he paid tribute to Rita, his high-school drama teacher, and all those who died of AIDS. "I know that my work in this case is magnified by the fact that the streets of heaven are too crowded with angels," he said shakily. "We know their names. They number a thousand for each one of the red ribbons that we wear here tonight. They finally rest in the warm embrace of the gracious Creator of us all....God bless you all. God have mercy on us all. And God bless America."

That night in March, Nora celebrated her best original screenplay nomination with *Sleepless* co-writers Jeff Arch and David Ward. (Unfortunately, Delia didn't get credit because Writer's Guild rules prevented recognizing more than three writers. Nora named Delia an associate producer.) The trio were dark horse contenders up against *Philadelphia*'s Ron Nyswaner and *The Piano*'s Jane Campion, who snagged the golden statuette for her acclaimed drama.

Jeff loathed *The Piano*. Ward kept him company at the Governor's Ball afterward. "Boy, was he upset that we didn't win," says Ward. "I tried to explain to him before it was ever announced. I said, 'Jeff, we're not going to win. And here's why: the Academy likes to give the writing award to one writer. A single writer. Or if they give it to two writers, it's because they're a team and write as a team. They don't like to give the award to a movie that was written by three different people who are not a team. They feel like they're giving to someone who wasn't the single vision.' They want to give it to someone who has the single vision, and that year they gave it to *The Piano*. They never really give it to comedies and romantic comedies. I'm stunned we got nominated. Romantic comedies are not serious enough.... I also felt it was particularly a 'tip of the cap' to Nora that she directed the film so well that a film by three people can be nominated."

And speaking of, "Nora was fine," says Ward. "She knows, too. She knew. She's a veteran of the Academy. Romantic comedies just don't usually win."

As she rose through the ranks of in-demand directors, Nora used a one-liner to deflate the importance of her rarified role as a woman filmmaker to be reckoned with.

Once, after a successful screening of *Sleepless*, someone walked up to her, asking, "Hey, Nora, how does it feel to be one of the most powerful women in Hollywood?"

She replied, "I still can't get my sound editor to take out a boat horn."

When Jim Healy took girlfriend Loretta to see the movie, she pinched him and said, "I'm going to live in that house." Within a matter of months, the Princeton, New Jersey, couple, both divorced, became engaged and transferred to Seattle for Jim's mobile communications job, snatching up Tom Hanks's houseboat for $560,000. All moved in by February 1994, they strung white twinkle lights and flipped them on each night. "I wanted the same look as in the movie," says Jim. They waved at passing kayakers and tourist boats, which had grown in number, and when curious strangers came knocking, they greeted them with a prank. "People would come by and ask for Tom Hanks," says Loretta. "And Jim would act like he was Tom Hanks. We had a cutout once."

"Is this the house in the movie?" tourists often inquired.

"You mean *Splash* or some other one?" Jim would retort.

Each of the 95 invitees RSVPed yes to Jim and Loretta's wedding there in September. Among the guests was Don Mohlman, the lawyer and previous owner who sold the floating home to the Healys following his divorce. In a delicious irony Nora would have appreciated, Mohlman sparked a love affair with a fellow guest and divorcée named Melissa who had flown in from Jersey for the occasion. They wed a year later, holding the reception at Jim and Loretta's.

The bride, I've learned, graduated from Wellesley College in 1962, the same year as Nora.

CHAPTER 10

"A Bouquet of Newly Sharpened Pencils" (Also Known as IM-ing with the Enemy)

Tom Hanks had mail.

In 1997, Kevin Feige, assistant to producer Lauren Shuler Donner, dropped off a script on the actor's doorstep. It was a romantic comedy Nora and Delia Ephron wrote with the actor in mind.

"Nora sent it along saying, 'I have a thing. It might be right for you and Meg. I know that might be a problem. No one wants to make a sequel. Here's the thing, just read it,'" Tom recalls. "By then, Nora had read a bunch of stuff that I had been considering. We developed a real—as she did with a great number of people— willingness to read material and weigh in on it. Nora was on the list. I would read anything she sent along. She didn't send along everything. Just the stuff she thought was special."

The part, should he choose to accept it, was a trip: Joe Fox, who runs mega-chain Fox & Sons Books, falls for a witty and charming woman he meets across a crowded internet chatroom. The email pals, both dating other people, make a pact not to reveal their identities. When they finally do make blind-date plans, Joe peeks inside a café window and realizes his sweetheart is none other than professional rival Kathleen Kelly, owner of the Shop around the Corner, the beloved independent children's bookstore he's putting out of business on the Upper West Side.

The good news: she's beautiful.

The bad: *she's Kathleen Kelly.*

A shaken Joe (screen name: NY152) bolts the scene but returns moments later, squashing the urge to reveal himself. While Kathleen (Shopgirl) sits alone, eagerly anticipating NY152's arrival, Joe takes the seat across from her. Smirking, he mocks *Pride and Prejudice*, the book she intends to give this perfect stranger, but Kathleen—waging a bitter public campaign against neighborhood interloper Fox Books— one-ups Joe as neither could have imagined. "You," she snipes, "are nothing but a suit." Joe, defeated, takes that as his cue to leave. NY152 gives Shopgirl the silent treatment until she alludes to her uncharacteristically blunt takedown of an enemy, expressing remorse, and wonders why he stood her up. When the Shop around the Corner shutters, Joe swoops in to pick up the pieces—and make a play for Kathleen.

"I knew it when I was done reading the screenplay," Tom says of his decision to star in what would later be titled *You've Got Mail*. "I called her immediately. I said, 'Hey, this is so great and, yeah, this should be me and Meg. It was kind of a sequel to *Sleepless in Seattle*.' She said, 'Well, yes, but let's keep that in our pocket. I'm saying something that's obvious, but we're not going to call it *Sleepless in Seattle II*; we'll call it something else.' Then I said, 'If Meg wants to do it, I'm in.' And she said, 'Great, let's make the movie, but we need to do it in the next five minutes before email is no longer part of the vernacular.'"

It all started three years earlier, when writer-producer Julie Durk, then working at Lauren Shuler Donner's production company in Los Angeles, got the bright idea to remake the 1940 classic *The Shop around the Corner* starring Jimmy Stewart and Margaret Sullavan as anonymous correspondents who fall in love over letters but despise one another in real life. And in real life, they're co-workers competing to sell the most pocketbooks at Matuschek and Company, a leather goods shop based, amazingly, *in Budapest*. If it seems odd that Stewart, with his unmistakable American speech ("letter"), and Sullavan, with her faux mid-Atlantic accent ("lett-ah"), were filmed on a Hollywood soundstage crafted to resemble the Hungarian capital rather than, say, Main Street, USA, then consider the romantic comedy's source material: the Miklós László–penned, Budapest-set play *Parfumerie*. László debuted the show at the Pest Theatre in 1937, one year before fleeing his homeland for New York City amid the rising menace of Nazi Germany. Settling in Manhattan, László staged plays that captivated a niche fan base of immigrants homesick for the Old World. His most popular, *Parfumerie*, was adapted by screenwriter Samson Raphaelson and turned into the motion picture from director Ernst Lubitsch, keeping Budapest as the site of the action.

"Lubitsch had come to Hollywood from Germany, and so the Central European setting of this movie had a real personal resonance for him," A. O. Scott, the film critic, said. "When *Shop around the Corner* was made, the society it represented was on the brink of total destruction. This threat is never acknowledged by any of the characters but rather it fills the film with a bittersweet sense of nostalgia."

The supporting cast includes mustachioed Frank Morgan (the

Wizard in *The Wizard of Oz*) as type-A shopkeeper Hugo Matuschek and bespectacled Felix Bressart as kindhearted employee
Pirovitch, who accompanies Alfred Kralik (Stewart) to the café
where he is to meet the angel-correspondent (Sullavan's Klara
Novak) at the other end of his love letters. It's Pirovitch who peers
into the window and gently breaks it to his smitten friend:

> **ALFRED:** Is she pretty?
>
> **PIROVITCH:** Very pretty. . . . I should say she
> looks—she has a little of the
> coloring of Klara.
>
> **ALFRED:** Klara? What, Miss Novak of the
> shop?
>
> **PIROVITCH:** Oh, Kralik, you must admit
> Klara's a very good-looking girl
> and personally, I always found
> her a very likable girl.
>
> **ALFRED:** Well, this is a fine time to
> talk about Miss Novak.
>
> **PIROVITCH:** Well, if you don't like Miss
> Novak, I can tell you right
> now, you won't like that girl.
>
> **ALFRED:** Why?
>
> **PIROVITCH:** Because it is Miss Novak.

The blood drains from Alfred's face, though he crosses the
threshold to engage Klara. Thus begins a testy war of words:

> **ALFRED:** There are many things you don't
> know about me, Miss Novak. As a
> matter of fact, there might be

> a lot we don't know about each
> other. You know, people seldom go
> through the trouble of scratching
> the surface of things to find the
> inner truth.
>
> **KLARA:** Well I wouldn't really care to
> scratch your surface, Mr. Kralik,
> because I know exactly what I'd
> find. Instead of heart, a handbag,
> instead of a soul, a suitcase,
> and instead of an intellect, a
> cigarette lighter.

Klara, distraught over the no-show, calls in sick the following day, and Alfred, in love despite himself, visits his foe's apartment and squanders the opportunity to bare his soul. He'll correct his mistake on a snowy Christmas Eve, when the two close the store for the night. Alfred, with newly acquired backbone (and sex appeal), purposely blows his cover by taking Klara into his arms and spilling details that only her "Dear Friend" could ever know. Klara is shocked, then ecstatic. They kiss. *End scene.*

Nine years later, *The Shop around the Corner* was remade into a movie musical, *In the Good Old Summertime*, with Judy Garland and Van Johnson. (The frenemies worked at a Chicago music boutique, selling harps and spontaneously bursting into song.) In 1963, a second musical remake, *She Loves Me*, premiered on Broadway, running for 302 performances. It was revived in 1993, with Judy Kuhn (the voice of Disney's *Pocahontas*) and Boyd Gaines (whom Nora considered for *Sleepless*'s Walter).

Those remakes aside, "most romantic comedies obey the logic set down in *The Shop around the Corner*: the path to true love must pass through conflict, hostility, and misunderstanding," said A. O. Scott, pondering: *"But is this how love really is?* Well, yes and no. It is true that hard feelings are part of the experience of love and that intimacy and estrangement often go hand in hand. What may not be true is that we move so simply and smoothly from one state to the other. And perhaps because of that, the romantic ideal that the movie celebrates feels like a gift."

To Julie Durk, the executive who got the bright idea, it felt like high time for an update. The question was *how*. She brought the film to her boss, Lauren Shuler Donner, producer of such hits as *Pretty in Pink*, *St. Elmo's Fire*, and *Dave*. Lauren felt the letter-writing conceit was too retro. Another bright idea: *Rather than pen and paper, how about email?* "This is [1994], and I had just gotten online, and I was on AOL, and I said, 'Oh my God, I know how to do this,'" she says. "And that was it, actually. So we went to Turner [Pictures], which Amy Pascal ran at the time, and she said, 'Great, yes, let's do it.' And Amy said, 'I have an idea who could do this: Nora. Nora Ephron.'"

The setup could not be better: Turner controlled the rights to *The Shop around the Corner*, and studio president Pascal, a Nora cheerleader, had been the one to greenlight the director's bland, off-brand heavenly fable, *Michael*, in which Archangel Michael (John Travolta, in *Pulp Fiction* comback mode) visits earth and changes the lives of those around him. He teaches a cynical tabloid reporter (William Hurt) how to love and be loved in return, pushing him toward a comely "angel expert" (Andie MacDowell); he resurrects a Jack Russell terrier from the dead; he smokes, drinks, and flirts with unsaintly abandon, though he also smells like cookies. Nora and Delia co-produced the project and rewrote a script by Pete Dexter; while critical reception was mixed, *Michael* proved a box-office blessing, collectively earning $95 million. It premiered on

Christmas Day 1996, two years after the biggest flop of the sisters' collaborative career and arguably the worst picture Nora ever made.

Mixed Nuts.

"It's really, really bad," Ebert told Siskel on *At the Movies.* "Why would you have Madeline Kahn in a movie and have her spend the whole movie stuck in an elevator screaming? I mean, what did she think when she was looking at the script? 'Oh, great, I have 17 screams.'"

"If she thought it was her masterpiece, that would have been sad, but she didn't think it was any good either," says Caroline Aaron, who voiced a hotline caller. "I don't think she knew when she was off the tracks. If she knew what went wrong she would have steered it back on course." Heading into the Beverly Hills premiere on December 8, 1994, Nora looked to be in jovial spirits. "She really could turn the faucet a certain way," adds Caroline, remembering what Nora told her right before the movie started: "OK, this one's going to stink."

Delia wrote, "Of course. What were we thinking? Many of life's flops, like marriages, are obvious in retrospect. If you knew it, you wouldn't do it, but you didn't, so you did. Probably Nora and I should never have tried to adapt something French. We are so not French. French comedies are French in the most peculiarly French way, largely because they're played by French people."

Mixed Nuts grossed a meager $7 million to rank 131st among 1994's movie releases; number one at the box office was Tom Hanks's *Forrest Gump,* which pulled in a quarter of a billion dollars and spanned the evolving romance between an extremely nice, slow-witted man and his childhood crush.

Her friendships with powerful industry people like Tom helped her during professional setbacks. Following *Sleepless,* her directing fee went up substantially—into the millions. A big step for Nora, a giant leap for women filmmakers. Even though women held prominent production jobs at several major studios, they were vastly outnumbered by men as writers, producers, cinematographers, editors, and, yes, directors. In 1998, women were more likely to be hired on romantic comedies, romantic dramas, and animated pictures over action-adventure and science fiction, according to a survey by Martha Lauzen, the executive director of the Center for the Study of Women in Television and Film.

That year marked the lowest employment level for women directors in eight years, and the trend was pointing downward. In 1997, only 5 out of the top 100 moneymaking movies were directed by women.

"If you're drawn to subjects that are about women, they are not as compelling to the men who run studios as movies about men," Nora said at the time. "Action movies have an incredible insurance policy of an illiterate third-world population who will see them."

On the shortlist of romcom directors, Nora sat down with Lauren Shuler Donner about *You've Got Mail* before embarking on *Michael.* The producer, married to *Lethal Weapon* director Richard Donner, admits she "was a little intimidated to meet her because she had a reputation for being very tough."

Busy Nora was interested, tapping playwright Wendy Wasserstein to do a draft, but when Wasserstein sent in her version, it skewed in a different direction than she would've liked. The *Heidi Chronicles* playwright, according to Delia, "didn't really change [the story] that much." At that point, Nora and Delia decided they would write it themselves.

After *Sleepless*, Delia moved into the Apthorp (as did Rosie O'Donnell, coincidentally), and so Delia and Nora "had only to cross a courtyard" to work together. Neither wanted to update *The Shop around the Corner* without a good reason in the culture—after all, says Delia, the original "was perfect to begin with." But technology provided the compelling hook to differentiate it from *Shop* and place the chatroom couple in the here and now. How, then, to solve the other big problem? *Shop* existed within Matuschek's, making it more a *play* than a movie, an insularity that could test a late-1990s filmgoer's patience. "I said to Delia, 'I have no idea how to do this,'" Nora recalled, "and Delia said, 'Oh, it's very simple. The Upper West Side, bookstores, and they each live with other people.'"

Too many romantic comedies contained warring duos, low stakes, and predictable endings. Immersing the love-hate narrative inside the New York book world, however, had authentically high stakes in that it reflected a David-and-Goliath drama playing out on upper Broadway. Since opening in 1993, the 82nd Street branch of bookseller Barnes & Noble threatened the indie bookstores surrounding it, fueling residential uproar and gloomy newspaper headlines. By 1996, the superstore, which sold cheap books and strong coffee, had witnessed the death of Eeyore's Books for Children at Broadway and 79th, where Jacob Bernstein once worked, and Shakespeare & Company, where Harry and Sally reconnected in self-help. "After 15 years on West 81st Street, it is with great sadness we find that we can no longer serve you at this location," read a notice on Shakespeare's window. "Our store has been a home for great literature and a sense of community that is getting harder and harder to find in New York City."

To go up against Goliath, owners and brothers Steve and Bill Kurland had cleared room for a used-book section and considered opening a café. When a second Barnes & Noble location claimed 66th and Broadway, the Kurlands—backed into a corner—shut down the shop to focus on their two downtown locations. "That extra bit of lost market share just put us over that line," Steve

Kurland told the *New York Times*. "It is a strategy that the super-stores use. They call it 'clustering': open a store north and south of the smaller store, and then just squeeze them out."

Counters Steve Riggio, former Barnes & Noble CEO: "We were the first bookseller to offer such massive selection within four walls. That began at our store (now closed) on 18th Street and Fifth in the early '70s. The store on 82nd and Broadway was the first to combine the massive selection with comfortable surround-ings, author events, and high levels of service from knowledgeable booksellers."

Though locals publicly supported the indies in the bookstore wars, there were traitors among them. Many of the guilty would venture into a Barnes & Noble and walk out converted by the vast inventory, 30 percent discounts, and caffeinated beverages. It was a hangout away from home, with comfy chairs on which to sit, sip a latte, and catch the eye of that attractive spy fiction enthusiast who lingered there Sunday afternoons. And unlike Shakespeare & Company, known for snooty service, nobody at Barnes & Noble was going to judge your purchase of *The Firm*. (If you dared read a Grisham on the subway, though, you might have hid the paper-back inside the latest *New Yorker* in order to stave off judgy stares.)

"The truth is I love my local Barnes & Noble," Nora said of the 82nd Street locale. "I find it sad that no one who works in it can answer a question, but the theme-parking of the American bookstore is not entirely a bad thing. When you go to the chil-dren's section of Barnes & Noble and you can't find a patch of floor space that doesn't have a kid on it, there's no way you can say those bookstores are bad for the book business."

Like Starbucks, Barnes & Noble (as well as rival bookseller Borders) was cornering the "third place" market. "One of the things that I think is so interesting is this thing that the Barnes &

Noble bookstores are a part of, these kind of gigantic 'third places,' as they're called by the sociologists, these sort of multifunctional things, like the gym where you can exercise, fall in love, have dinner, and get your dry cleaning done," observed Nora. "At Barnes & Noble you have coffee, fall in love, buy books, and do your homework." How could the Davids compete?

And what might happen if an indie bookseller fell for a bookplex baron?

Where *Sleepless* asked whether there was one perfect person out there for you, *You've Got Mail* posed a different question: "Can you fall in love with the person who isn't the perfect person for you?" As Nora and Delia would put it, "Can you fall in love with a Republican?"

While Nora's screenplays were less autobiographical than her other writing, she and Delia could not resist weaving in personal references: they named the male protagonist after Nora's ex-boyfriend, Joe Fox, a beloved book editor who died of cardiac arrest in 1995. "Mr. Fox, a tall man with a bearlike shamble, was known as a gentlemanly raconteur and passionate backgammon player," the *Times* said of the 69-year-old, who edited Truman Capote, Philip Roth, and Ralph Ellison. At Random House, "Mr. Fox, whose appearance was rumpled and professorial and whose voice was warm and gruff, developed a reputation as daring, eccentric and independent in spirit. Twenty-four hours after the Italian liner *Andrea Doria* sank in 1956, Mr. Fox liked to tell friends, he and another friend put on scuba gear to inspect the submerged ship."

For their female heroine, Nora and Delia initially chose the name Betsy, an allusion to *Pride and Prejudice*'s Elizabeth Bennet, invoked repeatedly over the course of the movie. In 1980, Nora wrote an essay, "A Few Words about Elizabeth Bennet," in which she fangirled over Jane Austen's "world of manners and domestic arrangements, a world where nothing—not politics nor war, which are simply not mentioned—is as important as the right match.... And when it becomes clear that things will work out, the lovers will triumph—when Elizabeth unexpectedly meets Mr. Darcy while walking through Pemberley and realizes his feelings for her are unchanged—I cry. All this may say more about me and my rather dippy capacity for romance than it does about the book, but I doubt it: *Pride and Prejudice* is one of the greatest romantic comedies ever written, a novel about the possibility of love between equals, and in many ways it is the forerunner of a genre it was undoubtedly instrumental in creating."

Austen omitted specific details about Elizabeth's physical appearance, allowing Nora to picture herself as the character. It wasn't completely a stretch: like Elizabeth, Nora was feisty and fearless in challenging the status quo of social gatekeepers who would prefer she stayed in her place, mouth zipped shut. "It is the dream of any woman who has ever wanted to believe that what really matters is not beauty but brains, not flirtation but wit; it is the dream of every young woman who has ever been a wallflower," she wrote.

However, Nora's identification with Elizabeth Bennet could only go so far: while Elizabeth's only flaw is her habit of making snap judgments, like writing off Darcy as an arrogant snob, Nora boasted "at least a dozen as serious as that and a few far worse." She saw shades of her personality in Emma Woodhouse, the meddlesome and manipulative antiheroine of the Austen novel *Emma*. "I prefer my literary heroines to be perfect, unlike me; and Lizzy is as close to perfect as she can be and still be interesting," Nora wrote. Elizabeth was on a pedestal nobody could touch; not even her literary heirs, Anne Shirley and Jo March, both of whom were wonderfully flawed. "It means that those of us who would love to be like her can never feel too bad that we aren't; no one is," she observed. "That's what makes Lizzy so lovable: she doesn't exist."

The name Betsy would persist throughout these early drafts, but eventually Meg Ryan's distaste for the name meant the character became Kathleen in the final movie.

For Kathleen's boyfriend, Frank Navasky, an anticomputer, anticapitalist columnist for the *New York Observer*, they combined the journalists and public intellectuals Victor Navasky and Ron Rosenbaum. Nora used to date Navasky. In the early 1960s, he operated *Monocle*, a satirical start-up magazine, from his apartment on West 69th Street—on the same block as Maya Schaper Cheese and Antiques, the exterior of the Shop around the Corner. In 1995, Navasky became publisher of *The Nation*, a weekly title with a left-wing skew on the news. When asked for his opinion on Barnes & Noble, he stated that "one lives in terror that, once the competition is eliminated, these chains are going to revert to a per-cubic-foot, maximum-profit philosophy."

Ron Rosenbaum wrote "The Edgy Enthusiast," a weekly column at the *New York Observer*. "We both knew him," Delia told me, "and he was totally esoteric and insane and brilliant and kind of crazy, so we based it on that." Rosenbaum campaigned to rescue independently run Books & Co. on the Upper East Side, but that one bit the dust in 1997. Like Frank, the writer had a technophobic streak and raved about his Olympia Report Deluxe electric typewriter. Like Frank, he was drawn to historical subjects. In 1998, he published *Explaining Hitler: The Search for the Origins of His Evil*—an ambitious, exhaustively researched book that Frank might have read, if not written.

Rosenbaum met Nora when both worked at *Esquire*. The two crossed paths while covering the Watergate impeachment hearings in Washington, and he interviewed her for his *New York Times Magazine* profile on Jack Nicholson when Jack was starring in *Heartburn*. She had him over for dinner, and he dug into Nora's pear and lima bean casserole, a *Heartburn* recipe he "otherwise wouldn't have imagined liking." Nora and humorist Roy Blount Jr. once attempted to turn Rosenbaum's 1978 novel *Murder at Elaine's* into a musical, but nothing came of it. "A crazy old right-wing rich guy, the father of the male lead, was going to sing 'The Big Nuts Rise to the Top,' the *Times'* science section having recently reported that in a can of mixed nuts the largest ones actually do make their way to the surface, for scientific reasons," Blount said in the book *Everyone Comes to Elaine's.* Then, in the late 1990s, Nora asked Rosenbaum if he was interested in writing a screenplay about nuclear terrorism detection teams. He did one draft, but nothing came of that, either. The last time Rosenbaum saw Nora, they played the party game Mafia with a witty group that included Navasky.

Joe Fox's high-strung girlfriend Patricia Eden—"Patricia makes COFFEE nervous"—was said to be inspired by New York publishing doyenne Judith Regan, who ran a namesake imprint at HarperCollins and lived large on the Upper West Side, in a four-bedroom apartment near Central Park. Delia gave Patricia the funny line describing Frank as "the greatest living expert on Julius and Ethel Rosenberg," a nod, perhaps, to Navasky, who authored a definitive book on Hollywood's Communist witch hunt, or even Carl Bernstein, who released a memoir revealing his parents' Communist affiliation. The sisters added a blink-and-you-miss-it speaking part for Bruce Jay Friedman, author and Elaine's patron. They made references to love letters between George Bernard Shaw and Mrs. Patrick Campbell; to writer Anthony Powell, subject of an article Frank wrote in the *Observer*; and to Generalissimo Francisco Franco, a past love of Kathleen's co-worker Birdie and unredeemable Mr. Wrong. They razzed novelist and Upper West Sider Thomas Pynchon—a literary recluse whom urban legend once labeled the Unabomber—as a character called William Spungeon, who emerges from seclusion to join the crusade against Fox Books;

Spungeon would get cut later on, along with a host of other sub-plots that slowed down the central love story.

The Ephrons expertly shuffled between affection and animosity in writing those love/hate scenes, with Joe's thoughtful emails the fantasy edition of what every woman hopes to find, and rarely does, on Tinder (where grammar goes to die). My all-time favorite Nora observation, delivered through Joe: "Don't you love New York in the fall? It makes me want to buy school supplies. *I would send you a bouquet of newly sharpened pencils if I knew your name and address.*"

Hesitant to mess with a good thing, they preserved *The Shop around the Corner*'s famous café scene, slightly changing the dialogue. "It's just so perfect in design," Delia told me. "There's some stories that have such enchantment connected to them that they are redone and redone and reloved over time and we just got lucky and got to make that ours as well."

Nora knew the minute they finished that it would get made. Ten pages to the happy ending, she said to Delia: "We are going to get Tom Hanks and Meg Ryan." Then she called Tom's agent, Richard Lovett, to get the scoop on Tom's schedule after *Saving Private Ryan*. Lovett, according to Nora, smoothly replied: "He's doing a romantic comedy with you, Nora."

The script took about three months, and when Lauren received it, she was overjoyed: "I remember I came to New York and I remember being there with my husband and getting the script and sitting right down in the hotel and reading it and loving it. Just absolutely loving it. There were rewrites but it was fantastic."

The women hit a snag in November 1996, when Warner Bros. merged with Turner Pictures, pushing out Amy Pascal as president. Pascal had dozens of films in development, including theirs. To compound matters, Warner's co-presidents, Lorenzo di Bonaventura and Billy Gerber, disagreed on whether to go forward with the romantic comedy; up until then, the studio had largely ignored the female audience.

"Lorenzo di Bonaventura was adamant that we would not make this movie," Lauren tells me. "Billy Gerber felt that absolutely we should make this movie. And it is a tribute to Billy Gerber that he fought to get the movie made. And that it did well. It was a bit of an uphill battle to even get it made and get the budget approved and everything. So it was particularly satisfying that we did well. And you can put that in the fucking book."

(Di Bonaventura, for his part, told me he presumed the movie would be successful when they greenlighted it. The fact that Tom Hanks was attached likely didn't hurt.)

Billy Gerber called Bob Pittman, president of America Online, about using the internet provider's logo and dial-up service in the movie then titled *You Have Mail*. Pittman set up an AOL tutorial and presentation so Nora could learn more. She was "communication-savvy," not necessarily tech-savvy, and instantly grasped the importance of IM-ing and chatrooms and how that would change the way we communicate, according to an executive involved in the unprecedented deal between studio and cyberspace.

In 1993, AOL unveiled its chatroom function, accessible through dial-up subscription, and four years later, Instant Messenger and its yellow "running man" mascot. Users could enter one of the roughly 19,000 chatrooms that sprouted within AOL, yet the social stigma remained: *at your own risk*. Though chat was growing popular among lonely stay-at-home moms—"Beats doing housework, don't you think?" an Omaha homemaker joked to the *St. Louis Post-Dispatch*—there lingered the perception, not without a shred of truth, that only techies, teens, and creeps lurked online. Hollywood of that era exploited these fears to portray the internet as a subterranean freak show populated by sexy young cybercriminals (Angelina Jolie in *Hackers*) and cyberterrorists (Jeremy Northam in *The Net*). A movie had yet to be made that represented its benevolent place in people's everyday lives—not their wildest nightmares. Over at AOL, skeptical staffers raised concerns about how the company would be portrayed and whether spending millions to plug itself was worth the risk. What if the technology wasn't seamlessly integrated into the story? How much brand identification would they get? Could they trust Nora and Warner Bros.?

Pittman, a marketing whiz who came from MTV, could identify no cons in granting Tom Hanks and Meg Ryan dial-up access—especially when AOL was the industry leader. That kind of exposure did not come cheap, but the internet was rolling in cash. The terms of the deal, according to an insider, required the company spend $5 million, though in actuality, it shelled out $10 million on TV and $40 million on online ads.

Funny thing, though.

"I had hired a consultant for the movie who was involved, trying to make sure WB understood exactly what [AOL] was," says Lorenzo di Bonaventura. "And he discovered that AOL had not trademarked 'You've Got Mail.' Which is pretty wild when you think about it. So, he actually trademarked it and gave it to them. So, even in the modern age the modern company forgot the thing they were building equity in."

When informed, an AOL exec looked at the producer as though he were crazy.

You Have Mail then changed to *You've Got Mail*, reflecting the famous salutation recorded by Elwood Edwards in 1989. The Cleveland-based voice actor chirped three other phrases: *Welcome. File's done. Goodbye.* During AOL's heyday, his peppy voice was heard upward of 35 million times per day. Edwards's William

Morris agent tried unsuccessfully to snag his client an acting credit on *You've Got Mail*, which used his vocals. Edwards, who goes by El, was a bit down about that. But those corporate residuals surely softened the blow. Asked how much money he's made overall, Edwards demurs, "I have a good relationship with AOL."

So did Joe and Kathleen. The two connected to the internet using AOL software version 4.0, then in beta testing. Where many real-life users experienced dial-up delays, accompanied by that grating screech, the secret loves magically logged on without ear bleeds. And when a legal problem arose upon discovery that some other woman had claimed Kathleen's screen name, AOL moved to persuade the rival Shopgirl to give it up. "She actually worked at an autobody shop," Nora said.

When Nora Ephron asks you to be in her movie, don't you clear your schedule and sign the dotted line right there and then?

"Yeah, kind of," Meg, dancing around the question, told me with a smile in her voice. "Had we done the other one yet? . . . So yeah, I knew her already."

The actress felt stifled by romantic comedy, though turning down Nora—and Tom Hanks, for that matter—would seem pretty foolish. "I really loved the script and wanted to work with Tom and Nora again," she said. "But people were starting to get the idea that all I could do was romantic comedies. I've done something like 30 movies and only 7 have been romantic comedies. But I was getting locked into that. It was starting to get irritating."

The truth was she loved doing them. "Oh, man, is this something I should be doing again?" she would ask herself. But she would always get drawn back in. Around the time she started *Mail*, Meg began to mull a hiatus from acting to spend more time behind the scenes with her production company, Prufrock Pictures. "Just watching a little more and not so much being out there," she said.

Tom Hanks, dogged by Jimmy Stewart comparisons his whole career, tabled his issues in this instance. "I mean, you'll never see me remake *Mr. Smith Goes to Washington* or *It's a Wonderful Life*," he said. "But *Shop Around the Corner* is very different. This is a very young Jimmy Stewart. This is Jimmy Stewart before Jimmy Stewart was Jimmy Stewart."

While 1997 saw Tom film *Saving Private Ryan* in the UK, Meg spent three months in LA shooting *City of Angels*, a romantic melodrama that boasted the most overwrought soundtrack to emerge from the late '90s (Goo Goo Dolls' "Iris," Alanis Morissette's "Uninvited," and Sarah McLachlan's "Angel," to name just a few). The picture resonated worldwide, pulling in $200 million.

Meg named her production company Prufrock Pictures for the T. S. Eliot poem "The Love Song of J. Alfred Prufrock," which she liked because it was a "meditation on life" and "that's kind of what maybe movies are—different meditations on parts of life." With partner Kathryn Galan, she set up Prufrock at 20th Century Fox as a way to determine a bit more of her own stake in the movie business.

At Prufrock, Meg developed a spectrum of projects that interested her and parts for her to star in as well. One was a Sylvia Plath biopic. Another was a postfeminist remake of the 1939 George Cukor comedy *The Women*, for which she and Julia Roberts had been in talks to star. "We love that these women could slay with a word," the two said in a joint statement circa 1994. "Our goal is to make this new version as sharp for today's audience as the original was in the '30s."

Entertainment Weekly buzzed that Nora Ephron and *Angels in America* director Tony Kushner were on the director shortlist, with Galan teasing: "Meg would probably love to play the bitch-goddess character." *Murphy Brown* creator Diane English conceived the project, writing a less catty spin on the classic screenplay by Anita Loos and Jane Murfin; as buzz mounted, James L. Brooks became attached to direct, with Meg and Julia to co-star and co-produce. The project, insanely difficult to get off the ground, began unraveling around 1997 when Brooks went off to helm the Jack Nicholson–Helen Hunt romantic comedy *As Good as It Gets*.

The actresses reportedly eyed the same part—presumably the bitchiest, which would allow Meg to cast off her America's Sweetheart image and Julia to trade on her intrinsic spunk. (Though Julia has been dubbed "sweetheart" by the press, she breaks the mold. She might be sparkly and fun, but she's definitely not *sweet*.) That year they separately headlined the nontraditional romcoms *My Best Friend's Wedding* and *Addicted to Love*, featuring each as a devious antiheroine scheming to break up an ex's happy new relationship. Benefitting from better writing, casting, and marketing, *My Best Friend's Wedding* raked in $127 million domestically; *Addicted to Love*, which teamed Meg and Matthew Broderick, was dark and anxious, floundering at $35 million. If you were a mainstream soccer-mom type, it was hard to identify with Meg's possibly sociopathic SoHo rule-breaker, who wore heavy eye makeup and raver clothing and squatted in an abandoned building to spy on her former lover. The actress had bigger success voicing orphaned Russian princess Anastasia opposite John Cusack in the animated film of the same name. (Oddly, Meg and Cusack's Dmitri, a cartoon, had hotter chemistry than she and Broderick.)

In 1995, Meg produced and starred in the charming romantic comedy *French Kiss*, playing a structured, unadventurous schoolteacher whose fiancé (Timothy Hutton) travels to Paris and falls in love with a French beauty (Suzan Anbeh). Meg's character overcomes her fear of flying to chase him down and becomes entangled in the petty crimes of a Frenchman and jewel thief (Kevin Kline), who shows her how to loosen up. Meg hired Lawrence Kasdan to direct and Kline to co-star after Gérard Depardieu bowed out; fortunately, she and Kline worked very well together.

French Kiss opened to mixed reviews. The *Washington Post* called it chaste yet seductive: "Doris Day and Rock Hudson had sexier scenes, but none this romantic." Ebert complained, "The characters in this movie may look like adults, but they think like teenagers."

As romantic comedies go, *French Kiss* did OK, seizing $38 million domestic to rank below genre rivals *Sense and Sensibility* (Hugh Grant), *Nine Months* (Hugh Grant again), and the Sandra Bullock sleeper *While You Were Sleeping*. Propelled by positive word of mouth, the latter was Sandra's *Sleepless in Seattle*. She was entirely believable as a dowdy "L" train operator pretending to be engaged to a man in a coma. Meg was probably the only other actress who could escape with such trickery while remaining noncreepy. Of course, if the genders were reversed, you'd have to cast Tom Hanks as the trickster. The actor was otherwise preoccupied: His astronaut drama *Apollo 13* and animated feature *Toy Story* topped the box office, continuing Tom's post–*Forrest Gump* hitmaking streak. Next came his 1996 directorial debut, *That Thing You Do!*, a low-key dramedy about a one-hit wonder pop band. The same year, Tom Cruise dominated action (*Mission: Impossible*) and romantic comedy (*Jerry Maguire*), a role Cameron Crowe initially saw Tom Hanks playing.

Lining up his 1998 slate, the time was ripe for Tom to alternate *Saving Private Ryan*, a guaranteed blockbuster, and That Thing He Stopped Doing: romantic comedies. Tom, signing on to Nora's latest, pocketed $20 million plus some of the back end, while Meg reportedly earned $10.5 million against 10 percent of the gross profits.

Could they re-create *Sleepless*'s magic—and deliver upon those gigantic, if wildly unequal, paychecks?

"You never know if that magic chemistry is going to strike again," Warner Bros. chairman Terry Semel said at the time. "But two people falling in love—especially these two people—has international appeal. If there is such a thing as a perfect couple, Tom and Meg are it. They're like Mr. and Mrs. World."

Just don't call them Mr. and Mrs. Sweetheart.

"The thing I liked about working in these movies with Nora is that they were about grown-ups," says Tom. "They're about adults who had already witnessed bitter compromise, some degree of pain, varying degrees of loss, and they weren't the kind of people who were hoping aliens will make their lives happy. They had gone through something and knew what it was like to be alone. They also knew what it was like to be with someone they were not meant to be with. And that's grown-up stuff. I gotta tell you, we were billed for a while as America's Sweethearts, which was something that made our stomachs turn. Inside that there is a forceful presence. A very, very forceful presence."

The America's Sweetheart label, once bestowed upon silent film legend Mary Pickford, was primarily a woman's burden to bear. Pickford was popular in young-girl roles, even as a powerful adult who formed United Artists with Charlie Chaplin and Douglas Fairbanks. "America's Sweetheart" had its perks—*Who wouldn't want to be loved and adored?*—but with wide adulation came great pressure. Even if you *are* a decent person, the constant, unrealistic expectation to be kind, cheerful, and proper 24/7—or risk public backlash—must indeed churn the stomach. If Meg Ryan felt boxed in, or exhausted from keeping up appearances, or limited in the kinds of roles she could play, that's because she was America's Sweetheart.

"It's a lazy encapsulation of what is hard and more serious work that we do," says Tom. "It just ends up being a pigeonhole description of what the movies are. What the movies meant."

The movie business, meanwhile, was on a kick of remaking classics. There was *101 Dalmations. The Parent Trap.* The Ephrons' loose interpretation of *The Shop around the Corner.* After Nora, Tom, and Meg's involvement was announced, Rick Jewell, a professor at the USC School of Cinematic Arts, expressed skepticism in an interview with the *LA Times.* "That film is so much a part of its time," Jewell told the paper. "It's such a sweet kind of sentimental picture made by a master—Lubitsch. Who are you going to get to direct the material like that anymore?"

CHAPTER 11

Pride and Prejudice and Perfect Hair

Pre-production was under way, with so many fires to put out and plans to arrange, and NY152—offering up *The Godfather* as the sum of all wisdom—might advise Nora as he did Kathleen: "Go to the mattresses."

After locking Tom and Meg, Nora worked with casting director Francine Maisler to round out the supporting roles. Conan O'Brien, five years into his gig hosting NBC's *Late Night*, auditioned for Frank Navasky, but Nora and Delia were eyeing Greg Kinnear. After seeing his Oscar-nominated performance as a gay artist in *As Good as It Gets*, the Ephrons wondered if there was a chance they could get the handsome 34-year-old actor for *You've Got Mail*.

"I got a call from my agent to go meet Nora on the Upper East Side," says Kinnear. "I hadn't met her before. She showed up looking smashing, as usual, and took me to eat at E.A.T. [café]....I was a little unsure about it. I liked the script and I liked the character, but you know, young actor, you angst, you ask a lot of questions. But, really, all I remember is she just wanted me to try the knishes and the salads. She was less interested in my big, heady questions about who Frank was." Charmed, Kinnear thought, *Oh, this'll be a blast.*

"When Greg Kinnear committed to this movie, the character he played did not break up with the character that Meg Ryan played," Nora explained. "And he came into the movie and he was very concerned. He didn't want to be that stock Ralph Bellamy character who kind of is the butt of every joke.... And so we came up with the idea of having him break up with her—which led to the idea that the person interviewing him on television was a woman rather than the man that it had been in an earlier draft."

Actress Jane Adams filled the role of the cable-access TV host who shamelessly makes a pass at Frank on the air, and Nora amended a plotline in which he and Patricia wound up together. Nora brought in Parker Posey, one of her favorites, as Patricia. Parker, then 29, had cheekbones as high as Katharine Hepburn's and a personality as outrageous as Diane Keaton's. She could make coffee nervous. Since traumatizing freshmen as queen bee senior Darla in *Dazed and Confused*, the downtown Manhattanite garnered a cult following as the star of independent films, including *Party Girl*, *House of Yes*, and *The Daytrippers*; in February 1997, *Time* magazine crowned her "Queen of the Indies." Christopher Guest, who cast her in his mockumentary *Waiting for Guffman*, was another to notice Parker's offbeat comic gifts. Nora must have known how much Parker disliked auditions because all they did was talk about Patricia rather than read lines.

"I was just thrilled that she liked me," Parker says. "I remember running into her in London in my 20s and she said—and I was young enough not to be intimidated by her—'You'll continue getting older, but you'll always feel the same.' That's so true! And I think about that a lot." They shared a therapist, Mildred Newman, whom Nora saw in the 1970s. "We would talk about Mildred, who she described as the White Witch. She was like being at a party, a nice cocktail party on the Upper West Side. She had classy Hollywood style in romantic comedy, which isn't made anymore, with chemistry between actors. Financiers and producers don't seem to care about that anymore. She also got extremely lucky with Meg Ryan and Tom Hanks who were like the perfect male and female counterparts for each other. I remember thinking, like, 'Wow, if Meg was a man, she would kind of look like Tom Hanks, and maybe be a little bit like him.'...They just had this compatibility that was kind of so easy and remarkable."

As in any office environment, co-worker compatibility is paramount—after all, Joe and Kathleen spend more time offline, at work, than typing email love letters. For Kathleen's employees, Nora staffed Jean Stapleton as maternal, mischievous bookkeeper Birdie Conrad (the reverse of Conrad Birdie in *Bye Bye Birdie*); Steve Zahn as silly sales guy George; and Heather Burns as serious sales gal Christina. When casting director Maisler brought Heather in to see Nora, the 22-year-old NYU grad affected a deadpan style that she figured would balance out Meg's sunniness. Nora "pulled up a chair right, like, knee-to-knee with me and read with me, right in my face," Heather remembers. "And then I got the part. And it was my first movie so I did not know what to expect. I barely knew how to hit a mark so she was very supportive in general with me because I think she was aware of that."

For Kevin, Joe Fox's co-worker and sounding board, Nora cast Dave Chappelle before he was Dave Chappelle. The 24-year-old stand-up comic, five years away from breaking ground on his eponymous Comedy Central sketch show, was an inspired choice on her part. In January 1998, Chappelle headlined the stoner comedy *Half Baked*, which he wrote and produced. He was wicked smart and on the edge, but knew to rein himself in as the laid-back foil to Tom's wired Joe Fox. Several years earlier, Chappelle rejected the role of Forrest Gump's army buddy Bubba, which would've been huge for him, though off-brand in terms of his comedy. He reportedly regretted his decision when *Forrest* smashed records (and made Tom super rich). Nora "just reached out and said, 'Look, I know I can cast this guy,'" script supervisor Dianne Dreyer told me. "I don't think there was anybody else on the list. He said, yes, he was gonna play the part. He was a delight, and proved to be everything she thought he was."

For William Spungeon, the reclusive author, Nora called upon Monty Python actor and sketch comedian Michael Palin—a verified legend and something of a Britain's Sweetheart, though he doesn't think of himself that way. "Legend really doesn't mean anything," says the self-effacing Palin. "Legend is something that is created around you." When Nora called with an enthusiastic offer, "I was my usual 'doubting Thomas' self," he recalls. "'Am I going to do this? I'm not sure. We got lovely people doing it. It will be fine.' They paid for me to go over there on Concorde."

What was not to like, really? But Palin would soon become disillusioned with his character.

As president of Marvel Studios, Kevin Feige oversees superhero franchises from *Iron Man* to *The Avengers*. Nine years before assuming that position, the University of Southern California film major and comic book fanboy was assistant to Lauren Shuler Donner on *You've Got Mail*.

Feige's "earliest memories of it were going to Meg Ryan's house and teaching her how to use America Online," he says, chuckling. "Teaching her how to actually use email. Which I found very entertaining—and, by the way, I had probably only learned to use email the summer before that."

Over two or three days at the Ryan-Quaid household in

Brentwood, Jack running in and out of the room, Feige showed Meg the basics: *"This is an inbox. And this is the start-up sound. And this is when you get an email that says 'You've Got Mail.'* And I think we were using these Apple laptops, which had been sent over, which ended up being the ones that were used in the film. And I just thought it was very exciting to be in a movie star's house teaching them how to use email. I also remember on the first day on set, which must have been months later, that I was at the craft service table or something and heard, 'Hi, Kevin!' and I turned around and it was Meg arriving on the set that day and I thought, *She remembered my name."*

In the late 20th century, not everyone had a personal computer—Meg included. She did without until receiving a Mac PowerBook on *You've Got Mail.* She told me: "I mean, I hadn't even ever emailed anybody until I emailed Tom." And she wasn't the sort to voluntarily check into a chatroom at two a.m. "I'm not interested in that at all," she said at the time. "I don't want to talk to anybody I don't know."

Tom, who typed on a PC as Joe Fox, once entered a *2001: A Space Odyssey* chatroom, but it was empty. Nora attempted entry, but didn't stay for long. "The spelling was so horrendous," she said. "I had to leave immediately."

Now email, *that* she could get behind.

When *You've Got Mail* script supervisor Dianne Dreyer decried the evils of electronic mail, Nora turned into a techno-evangelist.

"I said to her, this is going to change everything for the worst!" said Dianne. "And she's like, 'You couldn't be more wrong! It's going to make everything better. To be able to quickly respond and say hello, blah blah blah,' and I said, 'No, it's gonna stop people from writing. People aren't going to write letters anymore. It's really sad.' And we argued about it. Didn't argue but she was like,

'Dianne, you have to grow up! You have to embrace this technology,' and she already had the giant Apple computer at her house and I was lamenting having to buy a laptop to continue to work in the motion picture industry. Of course I ended up doing all of those things, but when you read her memoir *I Remember Nothing*, if you look at the things that she 'won't miss,' she [said] 'email' twice. Twice.... Because I think when you have such a big life as Nora, you are inundated every day. She looked at her inbox and there's 2,000 things in it."

Though she appreciated classic traditions and history—recall her obsession with the Beverly Hills Hotel's fading palm-print wallpaper—Nora remained absolutely contemporary.

"She was not one to yearn for the simplicity of the past," says Tom. "She was the first one I knew who had an iPhone.... She was never one to make an editorial comment about how the past was better, fresher, more pure, or anything like that. Same way my kids don't view the onslaught of technology as anything other than the currency of the day.... Nora was awfully current in the making of these movies. Still held the magic, the whimsy, the cinema of the falling-in-love construct that movies will always return to. She was doing it with grown-ups that were falling in love. It wasn't young kids trying to figure things out, high schoolers or whatnot."

You've Got Mail was a love letter to the Upper West Side. "[Nora] grew up in Los Angeles, right, but she had a love and a loyalty to New York that exceeded any native New Yorker that I ever met," John Lindley, the film's cinematographer, said to me, recalling: "And one of the things that I remember her saying is that many people think of New York as this monolithic, intimidating place. But when you live there, you realize that's what it is: a bunch of little villages. And her little village was the Upper West Side. One of the examples she always used about how unfrightening it was, was that bakeries would deliver bags of bread in the morning and leave them outside of delis and little restaurants and luncheonettes and things—and they would be there three hours later when the guy shows up to work to open the door. And, she said, 'You know, everybody thinks everything here gets stolen and people are being assaulted all the time. But look, here's this bread that nobody steals.'"

Nora put Randy Sweeney in charge of scouting locations, explaining: "Meg Ryan, Tom Hanks, and New York are the stars of the movie." She did not want Randy to hunt down exteriors in SoHo that resembled West 86th Street; she wanted West 86th Street. While she wasn't specific about venues, she did single out gourmet grocery store Zabar's at 80th and Broadway and Parisian-style Cafe Lalo on West 83rd. As it happened, Randy lived in a walk-up apartment above Cafe Lalo, which had served cappuccino and cake since 1988. Owner Haim Lalo was "extremely difficult," she says. "He just wanted to take us for a ride. He wanted tons and tons of money. I was able to negotiate with him finally. That was one of those long arduous negotiations, where, for lack of a better word, [I] had to kiss his ass a whole long time to get what we wanted. But we did."

If Lalo was tough, try dealing with Zabar's. "They loved the idea that Nora Ephron was going to film there but 'We're as famous as Nora. We don't care,'" Randy recalls. "They just wouldn't flex on anything. It was their game, their rules. . . . I kept having to go to Nora. She kept saying, 'I want this and that' and I kept saying, 'I can't. They won't budge.'" Taking matters into her own hands, Nora, a regular customer, picked up the phone and pressured Saul Zabar into letting her take over the market after closing time. He agreed on one condition: the crew had to be out by six a.m.

Seeking a Fox Books stand-in, Nora actually approached

brothers Leonard and Steve Riggio, who ran Barnes & Noble. "We had a couple of experiences with movie crews in our stores during opening hours," Steve, the more bookish of the two, says. "It was very disruptive, so we weren't very enthusiastic when Nora reached out to us. She then came to see us to ask if she could film scenes at our store on 82nd Street and Broadway. She was very nice and she talked about how much she loved the store. But she wanted us to close the store for two days, which was not possible. We'd simply never deny our customers access." Besides, he says, "The store in the movie was a mythic construction of Nora Ephron's in order to serve the David vs. Goliath theme of the subplot. It was a transmogrification of a Barnes & Noble bookstore that bore little resemblance to the soul of the store itself or the people that worked there."

When one store closes, another opens: In 1997, Barneys shuttered its first-ever department store on 17th Street and Seventh Avenue when it went bankrupt, leaving Fox Books a convenient vacancy. Warner Bros. shelled out a significant amount of money to rent the space for several months. The extra time allowed production designer Dan Davis and his team to build a stunningly realistic set from scratch. Nora would incorporate its construction in her movie to show a hard-hatted Joe and Kevin surveying the site. Davis: "I remember going into Barnes & Noble after we'd done the set thinking, 'Well this is kinda depressing because they use all that dark green everywhere.' Ours wasn't like that. Ours was a much friendlier version. And we had that great children's department with all the little cutout spaceships and stuff."

And a *lot* of work. Davis lugged "truckloads and truckloads and truckloads of books"—about 25,000 from some 30 publishers. Networking at a library conference that winter, set decorator Ellen Christiansen was barraged: "Everyone wanted to be involved," she said. The crew requested nonspecific titles across general categories, like travel, for which they received a batch of dated *Let's Go* guides. Nora made sure books were stocked in their rightful sections. Standing 200 feet away, the hawk-eyed director would notice two mismatched hardcovers side by side on a shelf.

The set had a functional coffee bar. People on the street would walk in thinking it was a real bookstore.

Over on West 18th Street, customers at Books of Wonder, one of the city's last independent children's booksellers, warned owner Peter Glassman a new chain was opening three blocks away. "I said the day any chain can afford to put leaves in the trees [as the filmmakers did in winter 1998], they're over-financed!" Glassman recalled at the time.

Books of Wonder inspired the Shop around the Corner. In fact, Nora had shopped there since it opened its original Hudson Street location in 1980. The store, which had its own imprint with publisher William Morrow and Company, garnered wide respect for its carefully curated selection of classics. To Nora's delight, it reprinted L. Frank Baum's Oz books in their original glory, with full-color illustrations by Baum's artist-collaborators. Surprising staffers, *You've Got Mail*'s designers showed up asking permission to take photos and measurements in order to best mimic Books of Wonder on a stage at Silver Screen Studios in Chelsea Piers. One morning, Glassman's assistant manager was given a fright. "She shows up to open the store—we have one of those pull-up gates—and all of a sudden five people jump out of a van across the street from her and say, 'Hold it! Wait, wait, wait!'" Glassman recalls. "They wanted to see her open the gate. They wanted to see how the gate worked and what it looked like when someone is opening and closing it."

He embraced their efforts as exposure to forward a worthy

cause. "A lot of people have not stopped to realize that when they make the choice between an independent and a chain store, they are not just making a decision today but on the future of literature," he told *Publishers Weekly*. The store loaned about 250 books, including 70 timeless titles; Shop around the Corner contained some 7,000 books in total. Nora wanted the shop "to be cheerful, to look friendly and West Side. We wanted most of the books to be classics and hardcovers, and for there to be a feeling of a rather strong editorial presence on the part of the proprietor," she said. "We made a list of the books that we thought no store should be without: Robert McCloskey, Ferdinand, Curious George, all of Maurice Sendak."

Her other shop inspirations were the Corner Bookstore on 93rd and Madison and "that fantasy bookstore that we all have in our brains."

Kathleen was a walking children's book encyclopedia: her late mother, Cecilia, founded the shop in 1956, passing it down to her daughter. So lovely was she that even Joe Fox's money-grubbing grandfather (John Randolph) found her "enchanting." (They carried on a pen-pal correspondence.) Kathleen inherited Cecilia's warmth, kindness, and wholesome blond looks. Nora "didn't want Meg Ryan to look like she didn't shave her armpits," Davis told me. "We had to make it charming and old and stuff but not dowdy, right? It shouldn't look like some old, dowdy person ran the place. So it was a fine line to keep it charming and funky and stuff without making it look like a total bag lady worked there."

Books of Wonder staff came to the set to give guidance on displays; touches of Wonder could be seen throughout the shop. The bookshelves were by the same company, Franklin Fixtures, that furnished its inspiration, and the shop followed suit in expressly selling twee illustrations and merchandise that tied in to the books. (Godzilla bobbleheads need not apply.) The shop, though, was smaller in scale, with warm woodwork and checkerboard floors. You not only wanted to shop there; you wanted to *live* there. "She was really pleased, and Delia, who was always with her, was very complimentary," Davis added. "And she liked the Fox Books too, even though she didn't like the two books that were beside each other."

Back on the Upper West Side, Randy Sweeney pounded the pavement to locate the exterior of Kathleen's storefront. Nora requested it be on a side street. That was important. Randy and her scouts snapped numerous photos of different shops, and Nora picked Maya Schaper Cheese and Antiques at 106 West 69th Street. Schaper once sold Nora vintage wineglasses. She opened her quirky store in 1994, pushing the cheese to the front and spreading the antiques throughout. When Hollywood repainted the outside a shade of bright green, Schaper went away on vacation; when she returned, everything was back to normal.

Nora ruled out Apthorp addresses for Joe and Kathleen. They found Joe's apartment at 210 Riverside Drive, a prewar elevator building with a marble lobby. As an added bonus, it was pet-friendly, which worked out because Joe had a golden retriever, Brinkley. Since Joe, in Nora's view, was "slightly Republican," they gave his apartment an expensive gloss that also managed not to be stuffy.

Nora, meanwhile, saw Kathleen living in a brownstone on a side street. The address: 328 West 89th Street. Like much of the Upper West Side, the stony façade had lost its shimmer but none of its charm. The interiors of Joe's and Kathleen's homes were constructed on stages at the Teaneck Armory in Teaneck, New Jersey. Nora and Davis collaborated on a floorplan for Kathleen that had a kitchen nook and a big bay window.

"It's sort of based on an apartment I used to live in," she said. The decor was very English cottage, with a palette of Easter egg pinks, yellows, and whites. Floral patterns abound: Pinky-red blooms on a couch. Daffodils on a stained glass window. Daisies, which Kathleen favors as "the happiest flower," on her pillowcase. The apartment, cozy yet spacious, occupied an entire floor—a step up from Sally and Annie, whose living quarters were no match for Harry's loft and Sam's houseboat. But in *You've Got Mail*, Meg scored the apartment that would later get pinned to oblivion on Pinterest.

At an actor read-through, 10-year-old Hallee Hirsh really went for it when her character, Annabelle Fox, the daughter of Fox & Sons founder Schuyler Fox and Joe's aunt, was supposed to have an epic crying fit in a scene Nora dropped later. She was too young to realize you're not supposed to go *all the way* at a table read. During a pause in the scene, Nora looked around at the smug smiling faces and said, "Can't I pick 'em?"

Meg, though, couldn't figure out her part. That was the worst thing about starting a film. She wondered: *What am I doing?*

Whereas Tom demanded character alterations on *Sleepless*, this time Meg insisted upon additional changes to strengthen Kathleen Kelly. "She was just the more demanding one on that movie!" said Delia, who recalled writing lots of emails for Kathleen at Meg's request. "She just needed more stuff, and she wasn't totally happy." Meg had nixed Kathleen's original moniker, Betsy, because that was the name of her *As the World Turns* alter ego. Meg's ideas ranged from the sweet (Kathleen's memory of twirling with her mother) to the darkly comic (Kathleen points a kitchen knife at Joe during their heated confrontation at Vince Mancini's book party). "I remember saying [to Nora], 'This is my interpretation of this character. She's finding her voice. She's finding herself,'" Meg later told me. "None of these things are things that, like, you share when the movie comes out initially. You just know it. You have this confederacy with the director about intention when you're making it....It's just a very subtle thing underneath that just percolates up. This [push] of becoming herself, of finding her voice, with this anonymous person."

When it came to wardrobe, Meg was agreeable but did push back at wearing what *You've Got Mail* costume designer Albert Wolsky calls a "jumper": a utilitarian shift dress, the sort a nine-to-five children's bookstore owner might pair with a turtleneck or blouse in a tasteful neutral color.

"Well, she wore a jumper," said Wolsky, an elegant and easygoing gentleman with a twinkle in his eye and two Oscars to his name for *All That Jazz* and *Bugsy*. "She didn't wear as many as I would've hoped. But there was a compromise there. She wore it once or twice if my memory serves me. I never quite understood why she didn't like it. I thought it was such an easy garment." Something Kathleen could slip on without thinking too much. "I think she was getting to a point, really, where she was beginning to feel 'I don't know if I still want to be Meg Ryan,'" he observed. "You know, it was a funny period for her, where she began to think, 'How long can I play these ingénue parts?'"

Wolsky wanted Kathleen to look fresh rather than prim. Nora wanted Wolsky to capture the authentic look of a working New York woman. The designer, heralded for his sophisticated taste and attention to detail, stayed close to Kathleen's middle-class background by dressing Meg in a variety of urban uniforms: a simple black dress to take her from Shop around the Corner to soft cheese and merlot reception. Roomy khakis for her day off. And a cozy sweater—that romcom staple—to keep her bundled during a chilly walk to work. Wolsky generally ignored designer brands save for a specific Marc Jacobs dress, which Meg requested for the Riverside Park finale. It was light gray and swooshy, hitting just below the knee, conservative yet still cool. "She'd been quite cooperative and she'd agreed to most of what I asked for," Wolsky said. "So, 'Aw, c'mon, she wants to wear that dress.' I finally added a little sweater and that saved me. That saved the dress for me. I felt the color was photographing a little 'eh' and [that] was why it was dyed [to appear brighter]. Plus, I had to do a little bit of finagling because you could see right through it and that was not what the scene was about. And I had to convince Nora. . . . I said, 'It will be fine, Nora.' Because I knew Meg really wanted it so badly."

The director held reservations about the actress's bedhead haircut: a short, scrunchy, artfully messy shag created for Meg by celebrity hairstylist Sally Hershberger, who styled her tresses on *I.Q.*, *French Kiss*, *Courage under Fire*, *Addicted to Love*, and *City of Angels*. Consider the crop an heir apparent to Sally Albright: while it fancied itself low maintenance, the truth was the opposite. "There's actually a lot of work that goes into making it look like a really good fucked-up mess," says Hershberger protégé Matthew Shields. Alongside the Rachel, the layered shag-bob Jennifer Aniston made famous on *Friends*, the Meg was arguably the most trendsetting hairstyle of the 1990s.

"She had a feeling the hair should be neater, cleaner," Wolsky says of Nora. "It was all that kind of jumbled [scrunch] that made Nora crazy. Nora came from another period where that's not the way you wore your hair. That was the issue. . . . I don't even know if there was any compromise. And then Nora is smart enough; after a while, she has got to move on."

There was a hair emergency a week into production when a stylist on set failed to re-create Hershberger's scissor skills. In other hands, Meg's *Fraggle Rock* locks became flat and lifeless.

Witness: her first scenes ordering morning brew at the Starbucks on 81st and Broadway and walking past Verdi Square eight blocks south. "Meg was uneasy because her hair was becoming iconic," Shields recalls. Hershberger, who'd just opened an LA salon, asked Shields, "Would you like to do a movie?" He wasn't too jazzed—*those epic hours*—but came back the next day prepared to go to New York for the remainder of the four-month shoot.

This was his first time working on a film, so he got a union waiver. Hershberger tweaked Meg's shag to add fullness on top in a perkier, Kathleen Kelly–ified variation; Shields upheld the 'do with trims every three weeks.

"Sally's a bit more of a freehand hairdresser," he says. "I'm much more of a technical hairdresser. I'm a very precise hairdresser." His meticulous approach made him a natural on a Nora-led operation as the director would sit behind the monitor and detect wayward strands. He snapped photos of Meg's hair to maintain continuity and admittedly went a bit overboard during touchups to ensure her coif appeared the same as it did in the previous take. Toward the end of a 14-hour workday, he would go to dailies and rewatch every scene and study each strand. Where Shields felt timid around powerful women like Nora and Lauren Shuler Donner, Meg put him at ease. Sometimes she worried about her performance, asking, "You are going to dailies tonight, aren't you? Did you go to dailies yesterday?"

Contrary to Meg's hair, Tom Hanks's brown curls never set off a stampede to the barber. Nor did his film fashion set any trends; he was indifferent. "He just stands there and you just put it on him," says Wolsky, who outfitted Tom in Armani and Calvin Klein. "He has no opinions at all." Nor did he have any major script notes for Joe Fox.

"I just got a guy," Tom says. "Sam Baldwin was damaged. His

wife died of cancer and he had this kid. He was doing a good job. But at the end of the day, there's an emptiness and loneliness that goes along with that. Joe Fox had none of that. Joe Fox came from a fucked-up, goofy family. The scene with Dabney Coleman that we had together, oh my God, it was so reflective. Dabney plays my dad in the movie, explaining why he got another divorce. Dabney Coleman is defining my character for me right now. All I have to do is sit here and listen to this guy, and Joe Fox comes to life. Joe Fox lives in this disconnected place. He's not a bitter man or a cynical man, but he doesn't have any real faith in the connection with members of the opposite sex."

Tom and Parker Posey displayed very little chemistry, making Parker's casting as his chilly, self-absorbed girlfriend all the more spot-on. The imbalance underscored Kathleen's rightness for Joe and how wrong he was about Patricia in the first place. Tom explains Joe's New York state of cohabitation thusly: "First we'll start fucking and then the living together phase. We'll skip any sense of real connection and commitment. Fine, let's do it. Because Joe Fox comes from a realm of, never meant anything anyway. Getting married never meant anything. Having kids never meant anything. It was just like living status of 'baggage claim,' waiting for your bag to come down the ramp. The liaison that he has online, with Kathleen—it held. It was perfect because it was their own original constructs. Their email pen pal was as they imagined it. That imagination was perfect. It's not until they actually figure out who's who that you start living in the real world, everything gets fucked up. I got that right off the bat."

By *You've Got Mail*, Tom and Meg and Nora and Delia had developed a potent professional shorthand. "The whole of it I remember was just so much fun," Meg told me. "It's just so much fun. Even waiting. . . . Just sit in the director's chair next to Nora and Tom and don't really talk about anything, but whatever it is you're talking about just seems like the best possible thing that you could possibly be talking about. Really! I mean, it was simple and fun and she knew what she wanted and she was organized and in a way that everybody had faith in."

Her fifth time behind the camera, Nora felt she'd finally got the hang of this directing thing. She brought in *Sleepless* crew members Don Lee as co-producer and Maggie Murphy as her second AD. Lee was associate producer on *Michael* and others from that film joined *Mail*, including executive producer G. Mac Brown, script supervisor Dianne Dreyer, and production designer Dan Davis, who replaced Tony Walton after Walton's other projects stretched him thin. John Lindley, *Michael*'s affable cinematographer, came to the rescue when the first guy flamed out. "He had a way of working with her and discovering what is funny," Brown remembers. "What is it in the scene that we're trying to find that is charming or warming or romantic? How do we shoot the film, design the set, costume the actor, so it's all in the same team? John was really good at listening to Nora and hearing that. They appreciated each other and they had a history. John was really patient and really interested. And when John wasn't there, it didn't work as well. With *You've Got Mail* we started with a different DP [director of photography]. John wasn't available then became available, and thank goodness."

Nora, who storyboarded every shot, worked with John to establish an homage to Ernst Lubitsch at the beginning of *Mail*, when the unseen camera seems to soar through the trees outside Kathleen's apartment and into her window. That cut, a dissolve, was similar to a move Lubitsch had done in film, "using much less technology," said Nora.

While she frowned upon *sad* faces in the background of her

productions, Nora encouraged authenticity, with a rose-colored veneer. The extras had New York energy, Hollywood style. Nobody was seen folding up a slice of bodega pizza and eating messily on the street. Or stopping to snap a photo of a rat dragging a pizza down the sidewalk. According to Dianne Dreyer, "She was challenging to the ADs...because she wanted to repeat people in the background action. Like, she wanted to recognize people on the street that you'd seen before. She didn't want just anybody and she didn't want them to be random. She wanted them to have a purpose and walk past Meg when she's walking to work and then walk past her when she's going home from work, so that you would have this idea that there are people who live in the neighborhood."

Poor Jimmy Mazzola, the prop man, "had to have a truck full of stuff for people to carry around," remembers Maggie Murphy. One extra who played a pregnant florist was given a pad to place on her belly; later, when Kathleen is buying flowers, a sign in the window reveals, "It's a girl."

"If you shoot too much in a certain neighborhood in New York, they ban people from shooting there for a while," says Maggie, explaining that's what happened after *Mail*. "The neighbors just get sick of it. Lots of trailers, because it was a big movie. Nora said you had to behave on the street."

That meant talking down pissed-off locals. There had been some fuss when *Mail* took over the Starbucks on Broadway. But nothing like the guy who went ballistic the day they were filming inside an Upper West Side restaurant. Suddenly, "there was somebody pounding on a plate glass window, screaming, and it was arresting," said John Lindley. "And then the next thing I know I can hear the guy screaming, 'Nora Ephron! Nora Ephron! I thought you loved this neighborhood! Why are you fucking with us?!? Blah blah blah.' The guy is just screaming at the top of his lungs, but

I couldn't really see him. I could see a body against the window and hands pounding and this guy screaming. I just happened to be standing next to Nora, who grabbed my arm—I'm like six-one and she's like five-nothing, I mean she was tiny—and she said, 'What should I do?' And I said, 'Just stay here. It's fine. Don't worry about it. Someone will take care of it and the guy will be placated and he'll move along and don't worry about it, it's fine.' And she said, 'OK.' And 10 seconds later, she let go of my arm and walked outside to talk to the guy. And I was so struck by her fearlessness but also her integrity. She really felt like it was her neighborhood. And she didn't know this guy. But in some ways, he was a neighbor. And she wanted to say, 'Hey, look, I'm sorry if you were inconvenienced and what can I do to help you?' And meanwhile, he's a screaming maniac."

"Tom said immediately the first day of shooting: 'Nora, you're the only director I've worked with, ever, who knew the Upper West Side and is not sending me to Staten Island to do the next scene,'" says costume designer Albert Wolsky.

The actor spent more time on the set of *Mail* than *Sleepless*, rarely disappearing into his trailer. He seemed to enjoy the humanity of it. Maggie Murphy took the opportunity to remind Tom about his "production weenie" comment, as relayed to her in 1992 by Colin Hanks.

"So, Tom, you called us production weenies."

"I did not."

"You did too."

"Did I really?"

"Yeah, you did."

Though new to Nora's movie family, Greg Kinnear was made to feel part of things. The Los Angeleno hadn't spent much time in New York, and she introduced him to the city. Nora would invite

Kinnear over to her and Nick's for dinner. "She cooks! She does it. *She* does it," he marvels. "I had a ham there one time. And it was *amazing*." He noticed that she operated with greater efficiency than directors who were younger, greener, and constantly over-thought a scene. She had her well-sharpened number 2 pencil out during rehearsal and jotted down ideas as actors talked and joked; she'd get them to expand on things she found amusing. Sometimes, Kinnear recalls, she'd "work in a story of her own life, or something she saw that morning." Rehearsing is "not an indulgence," he says. "It was a necessity. It wasn't out of wastefulness. It was out of the importance of finding real voices in the people who are populating her movies."

Meg kept Greg guessing. "As you expect her to go right, she was very likely gonna go left," he says. "And yet it always felt right. It never felt contrived. In my experience, she'd just show up with a wonderful attitude every day."

Her positive spirit seemed to bounce off Nora's. "They would just be laughing their ass off for most of the day.... It was joyous to watch the two of them, actually," he says, recalling of Meg: "She would get the giggles and she would not be afraid to let it just come out. Just let it come out. I think that's part of her process. She kind of *has* to do that. At least in that kind of movie.... There was a little joy in her that she had to keep percolating right at the top. It didn't feel manufactured. It didn't feel forced or fake. But she needed to keep that happening up there."

Hallee Hirsh tried to get Meg's attention by humming Sarah McLachlan's "Angel" from the *City of Angels* movie trailer. It didn't work because Meg, among other activities, was too busy reading Roald Dahl's *Boy: Tales of Childhood* to a group of kids during the Storybook Lady scene. Hallee's mind was blown. She was beginning to learn what acting really is, and watching Meg maintain enthusiasm take after take hammered home the importance of living in the moment.

Heather Burns, who played shopgirl Christina, learned to work a cash register alongside Meg at Books of Wonder. They got to know each other during rehearsals, which made their comradery in the bookstore scenes appear genuine. "I remember thinking it was like, she's this person and then they say 'action' and it was like a switch would go on and this light would come out of her eyes and this Meg Ryan that we all know just emerged immediately and I remember being fascinated by that. Because she could just turn it on and it was like a glow."

Some other New Yorker might have shrugged. "So what? Who cares?" While schooling Meg in the ways of customer service, Peter Glassman's assistant manager encountered one very jaded shopper who could not have cared less about a celebrity.

"Hi, this is Meg Ryan," it was explained to the customer. "She's preparing for a role in a film as a bookseller and we're just training her on how to make a sale, so it might take an extra minute or two—but we'll get through this very quickly with you."

"I understand but I'm in a bit of a rush," the woman responded. "Could someone else ring me up?"

Parker had only to walk down the block to film her scene at the Chelsea loft posing as fictional author Vince Mancini's apartment. She and her friends threw a "lava lamp kind of wine party" during the shoot, recalls Tom, who swung by in his downtime. He found cocktail scenes as arduous as wedding scenes: "You don't really get to eat the food. You've got to stay really dressed up, pretend you're having a great time." The center of the scene was Kathleen and Joe's verbal duel at the food table. The two then awkwardly introduce Frank and Patricia to one another, with Frank coming to Kathleen's defense: "Joe Fox? Inventor of the superstore, enemy of the mid-list novel, destroyer of City Books—tell me something: How do you sleep at night?" To which Patricia responds, "I use a wonderful over-the-counter drug, Ultrasom."

The four didn't rehearse in pre-production; they merely talked about the social dynamics of it. "We were pretty humming by that point," says Tom. "We were making the movie for quite some time. We were all in very good places. We were all awake."

As always, Nora was focused on culinary presentation.

"We shot that scene at night because the apartment had views and we wanted to use the windows in that location," Dianne Dreyer said. "And so they spread out this whole buffet and the food is beautiful and the prop people have brought it in and dressed it and presented it and laid it out. Nora looks at Jimmy Mazzola who was the prop manager and she says—she's pointing at the avocados— and she says, 'Jimmy, are these Hass?' And Jimmy goes, 'Nora, they're avocados.' He had no idea the difference between a regular avocado or a California avocado and a Hass avocado. And she said, 'Did I write Hass in the screenplay?' And I said, 'No, you didn't.' And she went, 'Oh, that is so sad.'"

The good news: her molded egg salad with caviar garnish turned out great. And unlike the other treats on the tableau, there seemed to be an unlimited supply of egg salad to feed cast and crew between takes. "It was quite delicious and, as I recall, when the cameras weren't rolling, most of the conversation was about her recipe," Kinnear says. "I probably had a pound of that stuff."

The dish was not mentioned in the original script but proved an essential, if smelly, ingredient. "I love when he swoops up all the caviar garnish," says Julie Durk, the *You've Got Mail* producer who first proposed remaking *The Shop around the Corner.* "And then while they're talking, and they're enemies, she takes her spoon and puts some of it back from his plate. Which feels like a very intimate moment; all those things where they just can't help themselves. They're so drawn to each other even when they're feuding."

Nora suggested Meg remind her adversary that caviar is a *garnish*. Nora thought the word had a humorous ring to it.

"This was very important to Meg, this scene, because she wanted to make clear that part of the movie was about this woman...finding her voice," Nora said. "Going from a person who really couldn't say what she meant to say to a person who could partly because of her relationship with him online. Because he helps her to say whatever she means to say at the moment she means to say it."

Kathleen and Joe's connection becomes more apparent still when the two exchange a knowing glance, as if to read each other's minds: *I can't believe I'm dating this person.* Their significant others:

> **PATRICIA:** Your last piece in the
> Independent, the one about
> Anthony Powell, was brilliant.
> I'm Patricia Eden, Eden Books.
> Joe, this man is the greatest
> living expert on Julius and
> Ethel Rosenberg—
>
> **JOE:** And this is Kathleen Kelly—
>
> *Kathleen glares at him.*
>
> **FRANK:** You liked my piece. God, I'm
> flattered. You know you write
> these things and you think
> someone's going to mention them
> and then the whole week goes by
> and the phone doesn't ring, and

> you think Oh, God, I'm a fraud, a
> failure—
> **PATRICIA:** You know what's always fascinated
> me about Julius and Ethel
> Rosenberg is how old they looked
> when they were really just
> our age.

"That's such a Nora thing when they're talking about the Rosenbergs," says Durk. "That's one of my favorite moments. It's very intellectual snobbery and a world that Nora knows, but you get it on every level. She has the upper hand; then he has the upper hand. Her boyfriend is preening, kind of like an ass. His girlfriend is sort of a dope. For some reason that feels sort of *Pride and Prejudice*."

As in that novel, the Ephrons' *Mail* screenplay contained a number of subplots featuring supporting characters. After the Rooftop Killer leaves a dead body on the roof of George's apartment, the shopguy falls in love with a detective who believes *he* is the murderer. ("There was a rooftop killer in mine and Delia's building," Nora once said, referencing the discovery of a woman's corpse atop the Apthorp in 1997.) Christina, desperate for a date, tries a professional matchmaker but ends up flirting with a fellow jogger in Central Park. Patricia hosts an event for author Veronica Grant (Deborah Rush), who's written a tragic memoir entitled *Am I Rising from Ashes, or Did I Just Forget to Dust?* "I can't talk about it without crying," Patricia tells a crowd of people. "Veronica and I have so much in common—well, not all the sad parts—but we were both famous by the time we were 29 and, believe me, that's rough." By *Mail*'s end, Patricia appears to have found God—and a new man—as a rabbi leads her in a folk dance at the local synagogue. Frank spies mysterious novelist William Spungeon (Michael Palin) on the subway and follows him to H&H Bagels on West 80th Street and a sporting goods store where Spungeon purchases six pairs of tube socks for $7.99. (Kathleen: "William Spungeon and tube socks." Frank: "I know. I don't want to dwell on it.") Spungeon later ignites a media frenzy when he comes out of hiding to help Kathleen fight Fox Books. Turns out he has a thing for her. One rainy night, as Kathleen walks home, he springs out of the darkness...

Spungeon suddenly puts his hand through Kathleen's hair. She stops, frozen in place.

> **SPUNGEON:** You have your mother's hair.
> Thick, wild, the color of
> Nebraska wheat.

He grabs her and tries to kiss her.

> **KATHLEEN:** What are you doing? Let me go.

He backs her into a wall.

> **KATHLEEN:** Stop it. Are you crazy?

She kicks him in the shins, wiggles free, and runs away.

> **SPUNGEON** (calling after her): If you
> change your mind, you can
> E-mail me. Hermit@AOL.com.

Palin, a founding member of Monty Python, extracted comedy in Spungeon's eccentricity but wasn't totally comfortable with the scene above. "He's kind of lustful," Palin says. "He makes a pass at Meg's character. I thought that was oddly broad. I didn't know if I could quite deliver it in a sort of debonair way." The script called for Palin to open an umbrella over Meg in dramatic fashion; Nora wanted Palin to twirl it, Gene Kelly style. It was tricky to strike the right tone given the character's aggressive behavior. "I think I wasn't quite the right person to do that," he tells me. "If he had been a bit more curious, a bit more blinking in the light, as it were. This man that doesn't come out much. The fact that he felt so at ease with it all seemed odd."

While the Palin scenes would prove too bizarre, sealing their fate on the cutting room floor, Meg didn't take to another vignette that referenced the Ephrons' dislike of boats:

KATHLEEN: The worst, the worst—I could never, under any circumstances, love anybody who had a sailboat.

CHRISTINA: Neither could I.

KATHLEEN: If I had to get up on Saturday morning knowing that I was about to go down to the pier and unravel all those ropes and put on all that sunblock—

CHRISTINA: All that talk about the wind.

KATHLEEN: And then you have to go out on the boat, and you sail and sail and sail until you are bored witless, and then, only then, do they say, let's turn around and you realize the trip is only half over, only it's not, because the wind has changed—

CHRISTINA: It hasn't changed. It's died.

KATHLEEN: So then there's more talk about
the wind. While you just float
up and down trying not to get
nauseous. And when you finally
get back, you have to clean up
the boat.

The joke's on Kathleen, of course, because Joe owns a boat that he docks at the 79th Street Boat Basin. "It didn't end up in its entirety in the final film I think maybe because Meg didn't feel the same way and couldn't make it that funny—but I think Meg could make anything funny," Dianne Dreyer says. "It just didn't resonate with her the way it resonated with some people."

❋ ❋ ❋

Meg Ryan to cheese! Meg Ryan to coffee!
Tom Hanks had gotten hold of the microphone at Zabar's, where the two stars—plus 100 extras—were gathered for an overnight shoot. The scene: Joe Fox sweet-talks a humorless cashier into letting Kathleen use her credit card in the cash-only line. The cashier was Sara Ramirez, a recent Juilliard grad who would go on to win a Tony for Broadway's *Spamalot* and play Dr. Callie Torres in TV's *Grey's Anatomy. You've Got Mail* was her first film credit. Nora's pal Diane Sokolow, who waited on Meg and Bill Pullman at Tiffany's, was a customer pissed at Kathleen for holding up the line.

Nora was inspired by the time when Jim Skotchdopole, her first AD on *Sleepless in Seattle*, used his good looks to charm a concierge who would not let their group of 20-some people occupy the first-class lounge at the airport. Nora watched the woman "lose her mind" and succumb to Skotchdopole; they all got through, just like that. If another woman had tried to pull what Skotchdopole pulled, there was no way she'd get those results. Nora channeled that frustration—injustice!—into Kathleen.

Zabar's longtime manager, Scott Goldshine, stressed to me that his cashiers were never as mean as Ramirez—but the store took her character's attitude in stride. While his boss, Saul Zabar, had been a bit difficult in allowing access, Nora and husband Nick Pileggi were regulars. Goldshine always found Nick to be charming and chatty, more gregarious than Nora. The director, wedded to the idea of flooding the background with authentically Upper West Side types, made Goldshine an extra, and amusingly, he had to change into a sweater vest after his outfit was judged too similar to Tom's suit and tie.

Filming ended right on time at 5:55 a.m. And that was the last time Zabar's let in a Hollywood crew.

* * *

At Nora's urging, Dave Chappelle changed a lot of his lines. "Please, please make this part more your own," she told him.

The before: "So you don't feel bad about basically destroying her livelihood, not to mention her legacy, not to mention her raison d'être?"

The after: "You don't feel bad about basically sending her ass back to the projects, with food stamps? Broke single white lady?"

On May 14, 1998, Tom and Chappelle filmed their scene walking down Columbus Avenue as Joe nervously prepares to meet Kathleen. That same night, *Seinfeld* had its highly anticipated series finale. In between takes, the two would sneak into the corner bar and watch. "It was kind of like the Super Bowl was on

TV," he says. "Everything became muted in the city. The noise level came down a few decibels. It was quieter. There was a hush."

Not everything about Joe Fox made sense to Tom. Even after extensive rehearsals, he struggled during the nighttime shoot for *You've Got Mail*'s showpiece: the Cafe Lalo square-off. He couldn't understand why Joe would go inside and antagonize Kathleen, the woman he secretly adored. What, exactly, did the character hope to get out of the dialogue? Why was he there?

Nora shared no insight on Joe's agenda. Perhaps she was busy overseeing the hardcore twinkle light display outside. Or conferencing with legendary cinematographer Haskell Wexler (*One Flew over the Cuckoo's Nest, Who's Afraid of Virginia Woolf?*), who replaced John Lindley on the Lalo sequence. (Lindley had flown home for the birth of his child.) More likely, though, Nora trusted Tom to discover it on his own.

He decided initially that alpha dog Joe was driven by the need to establish superiority over Kathleen. To put his enemy in her place through manipulation. To win. But this rationale ignored an inconvenient truth: *Joe Fox was in love with Ms. Wrong.* Given Joe's feelings toward Shopgirl, how could he arrive at Lalo knowing she'd been stood up and then proceed to make this wonderful woman's night even worse?

In a very quiet voice, script supervisor Dianne Dreyer told Tom: "You want her to know it's you."

"I just about shit my pants," he recalls. "That was the thing. I was too busy being Joe Fox, the guy who doesn't take the scene seriously. The guy who's waiting in baggage claim for the next one down. When she said that, I said, 'Oh, jeez, Joe Fox is actually the one putting himself so far out on the line.' Because if she realizes he's the one and rejects him, well then it's all over. The one time where he wanted to have a relationship with a woman is gone. Then he's back to the Parker Posey types."

Once that lightbulb went off, Tom was better equipped to go head-to-head with Meg. "Look, sometimes I was just trying to keep up with her," he says. "She's so fucking smart. She's an artist in a different way that goes beyond being an actress in some movies. You can tell that by a lot of the work she's done with her photography.... Meg does not suffer any fools. She's also low-maintenance. At the same time, you better be on your toes working with Meg. You better be willing to pony up the same amount of cash that she's bringing to the game. Otherwise, you'll get dusted. You'll lose. You got to be there."

Filming inside Cafe Lalo was a rigorous game of chess. Tom and Meg had to pull off super-specific choreography within super-tight quarters. Tom glided from Meg's table to the one behind her as gracefully as he'd landed atop FAO Schwarz's giant piano keys in *Big*. Meg held her makeup mirror at just the right angle so the camera could catch Tom's reflection. When Tom abruptly switched tables, grabbing a seat opposite Meg, the camera flipped 180 degrees to look toward Lalo's window rather than the back of the restaurant. The trick "makes you feel not that you have gone to a different set, but that you have moved into a different space or a different room," Nora said. "And it makes it possible to have a six- or seven-page scene not feel unbelievably lengthy."

In the script, a female impersonator was supposed to walk through the door, prompting Joe to snipe, "I am going to take a wild guess that this isn't him, either." In practice, the gag wasn't funny. Nora improvised. Albert Wolsky procured a red magician's cape and Peter Mian, the shy video assist operator, reluctantly agreed to wear it on camera. But not before raising his hand and saying, "Taxi!"

Cast and crew wrapped at about 4 a.m. Tom kept up with Meg, Mian won five seconds of movie immortality, and Haim Lalo's little café would become the most famous on the Upper West Side.

✳ ✳ ✳

During rehearsal, Frank and Kathleen's breakup morphed into a softer goodbye in the sense that both realized it was for the best. According to Kinnear, an earlier version had been more one-sided, with Frank flat-out dumping Kathleen for talk show host Sidney-Ann. Kinnear's friends would bug him about it either way. *What? You dumped Meg Ryan? This is the last girl any guy wants to break up with*, Kinnear thought. But it was also kind of empowering. Says Kinnear, "It's great fun living in movies and breaking up that way, let me tell you."

"I always read into it a bit more remorse, and a bit more awkwardness," Lauren Shuler Donner recalls. "But that's not how Nora played it. She played it that once the news came out that they both embraced it immediately—and if there was awkwardness, it was tucked way deep inside so that neither would know."

We don't get to see Joe cut Patricia loose, but we can guess she wasn't happy about the turn of events. "She had to be enough of a bitch so you aren't sad when Tom Hanks dumps her," Parker said.

Which happens after Joe and Patricia get stuck in the elevator of their apartment building along with the glamorous author Veronica Grant (Deborah Rush), clutching Nora's Chihuahua, Lucy, in a cameo. Everyone's talking about what they plan to do when the elevator gets unstuck—shallow Patricia wants to get her eyes lasered—and *boom!* Joe says nothing, but his defeated expression speaks volumes.

Goodbye, Patricia.

When Jimmy Stewart checks on Margaret Sullavan in *The Shop around the Corner*, his presence feels welcome—his character did not put hers out of business, after all. Ringing Meg's doorbell as Joe Fox, who did the unforgivable, Tom Hanks was forced to toe the delicate line between gallant and sinister. One false move, he'd lose both Kathleen (fighting a cold) and her sympathetic audience.

His mission was to avoid having the door slammed in his face. He disarmed Kathleen with a daisy bouquet and wiggled his way into her apartment, asking in a concerned voice, "What's that noise?"

"It's almost like taking Omaha Beach," Nora told Tom in a reference to *Saving Private Ryan*.

Tom and Meg rehearsed several days onstage in New Jersey, moving from den to kitchen to bedroom, working through the gauntlet of conflicting emotions that electrified Joe and Kathleen's relationship. While Kathleen was angry at Joe, she couldn't deny the heat she felt a few months before when he stepped into her store with Annabelle (Hallee Hirsh) and Matt (Jeffrey Scaperrotta), his child aunt and child brother. "We are...an American family," he joked. Her hungry eyes registered: *Mr. Darcy, is that you?*

"We shot that scene like gangbusters," Tom says. "I just went deeper. It went from the mechanics of moving the camera around— shooting the scene—to capturing the behavior of the scene. That's the high country when you can get there. We were so primed for it. The construct of the scene is so Nora and Delia."

The Lucille Ball of the coupling, Meg harnessed physical comedy while Tom played straight man. She pitter-pattered in pajamas, neurotically tidying up before answering the door, and stamped her foot upon sight of the daisies. "And it says so much 'cause there's just nothing worse than when you get flowers from someone because we're all suckers for flowers," Nora said. "It's just a terrible, terrible moment. Because you know you can't be too terrible to a person who gives you flowers."

Like a downed plane, Meg dove her head into a pillow when Tom asked about the man she meant to meet at Lalo. "I don't actually know him," she confessed. By this time, Tom had almost crashed Omaha Beach: her bed. "He's taking advantage, of course, of her grogginess to get this close to her," Nora said. When Tom pulled the covers over her legs and put his hand atop her lips, Nora told the actor, "This is a kiss."

> **JOE:** (inching closer up the mattress): I think you should meet him. No. No, no, wait. I take that back. Why would you want to meet someone you're crazy about?
>
> **KATHLEEN:** Hey, I hardly think I need to take advice from someone who—
>
> **JOE:** (covering her mouth): Now I can see that I bring out the worst in you but let me just help you to not say something you're just gonna torture yourself about for years to come.

As Nora explained, "It's the moment that she knows she's in trouble. It's the uh-oh moment. Sex has crept into this movie in its unbelievably gentle and innocent way." Meg was breathing sexually, noticed Lauren Shuler Donner. "It was a little, 'OK, I'm here in your bedroom, on your bed.... What are we going to do?' It was that kind of moment, which everybody felt. There's nothing better than sexual tension on the screen. It's better than watching sex."

In Tom's view, Joe Fox left Kathleen's knowing she was the woman for him. He even restrained the snark while she lectured him on how business *is* personal.

> **KATHLEEN:** And what is so wrong with being personal anyway?

JOE: Uh, nothing.

KATHLEEN: Because whatever else anything is,
it oughta begin by being *personal*.

If Joe had a smart remark, he bit his tongue. It was as though his curmudgeonly offline self had begun to merge with his menschy online persona.

In May 1998, Tom and Meg filmed their walking and talking scenes on the streets of the Upper West Side. There was the scene at the farmers market in Verdi Square, where they waved at people riding by on buses. The surrounding streets were eerily empty of taxis because cabbies had gone on strike for the first time in more than 30 years. The sidewalks, however, were teeming with locals, including a mom who reportedly got ticked off because the filmmakers refused her kid a piece of fruit. There was the exterior of Ocean Grill on Columbus Avenue. The exterior of Gray's Papaya on West 72nd Street and Broadway. Then, one of Nora's favorite blocks—West 78th Street between Columbus and Amsterdam Avenues—which was quieter than most and lined with lovely pear trees. It was the site of Joe's "If only" speech to Kathleen, who brushes him off to make her date with NY152.

"That was hard. That was a tough day," Lauren says. "When they say goodbye, after they've had lunch, they're talking about who [NY152] could be. He gets very close to revealing....Just striking the right tone so that it was a little revealing but not too revealing. If he were too revealing, then she would be stupid not to see it. And you wanted to always maintain her intelligence. And he wouldn't let his feelings out all the way because she would reject him. That dance we do when we're trying to figure out how the other person feels about us."

Nora was pleasantly surprised by an intimate moment that transpired when Meg rubbed her neck, chest, and collarbone after Tom tenderly touched her shoulder. The birds in those trees seemed to like it, too, because they were chirping like crazy, ruining the moment. Months later, the actors had to redo half their dialogue in post-production. The looping was done "so well that the performances were actually better than they were in real life," Nora said.

As script supervisor, Dianne Dreyer's job was to handle the details, keep things real. She argued with Nora over the fact that Kathleen, unlike every other woman in New York, was strolling about without a purse. Nora, who hated carrying purses, wasn't worried; she figured Kathleen had her keys in her pocket as well as a $20 bill. "I'm like, where are her keys? Where are they? Are they in her shoes? Are they in her bra? It just doesn't make sense that she doesn't have a purse," Dreyer says. Then again, she concedes, "any kind of encumbrance may have altered that final moment of, 'I knew it was you; I so wanted it to be you.' Meg didn't want it. That's the perfect example of choosing romance over reality."

Tom, meanwhile, had gained a few pounds after going away on vacation for a week or so. "You can see it in the movie," says producer G. Mac Brown. "He came back all chubby. In the end, when they find each other in the park, he's got a nice little roll. Very cute. You wouldn't notice until you look for it."

"Lauren had to make that phone call," Kevin Feige, her former assistant, recalls. "They were sitting in dailies. They were watching the footage. I guess they were like, 'Well, look, he looks different.' And it fell to Lauren, the producer of the movie, to make that potentially awkward phone call to the star of the movie."

Nora wanted Tom to shed the weight. "On camera it's deadly," costumer Albert Wolsky asserts. "She was very conscious of that. We're not talking humongous. Four or five pounds. Tom felt bad, because he's a nice man. It's totally natural what happened. Because it goes to the face; Tom's face doesn't need weight. It may not have been a problem any other time. He was playing a romantic lead."

The set decorators had little work to do in enhancing the natural beauty of Riverside Park's 91st Street Garden. A few red flowers were added to the purple, yellow, and white blooms planted by neighborhood volunteer gardeners. Two bicyclists whirred past the camera, which lingered upon a happy couple before capturing Joe Fox's long-delayed reveal. Brinkley the golden retriever, announcing his master's presence, entered the scene before Joe. Nora had big plans for that animal actor, named Clovis, who was supposed to jump into the air but pulled at Meg's sweater instead. In the shot she used, the dog had yanked Tom's brown jacket—there was a treat inside the pocket—before leaping upon the kissing meant-for-each-others.

When editor Richard Marks put the scene together the first time, he and Nora showed it to Lauren. "They knew they hadn't had it and we had to get [Tom] back and film it again. It wasn't joyful enough," the producer said.

Both needed to bring more emotion without seeming phony. Though Meg and Tom kissed in *Joe Versus the Volcano*, the actress was nervy at the thought of locking lips with the actor who had become her close—*platonic*—friend. Tom eased tension by discussing a Microsoft lawsuit that had been in the news. She knew what he was doing. He was transparent that way.

When *You've Got Mail* wrapped in early June, Nora joined Marks in the cutting room. The running time was 2 hours and 53 minutes. How mortifying! She had no choice but to remove the secondary plots involving Steve Zahn, Parker Posey, Heather Burns, and Deborah Rush. Nora dropped Michael Palin from the picture altogether. Palin joked that he outshone Tom Hanks, and that's why Nora Xed him out. His friend Basil christened the movie *You've Got Cut*.

Steve Zahn stewed. "It doesn't really bother me," he said at the time, "but the experience kind of makes you read scripts differently and figure out how important you are to the story."

Deborah was touched by Nora's good graces. "I just want to let you know that only one scene is left. But I owe you one," she wrote the actress. Lo and behold, Nora gave her a part in *Julie & Julia* a decade later. No other director on the face of the earth would have followed through on that promise, Rush thought.

While Nora shaved 53 minutes off the theatrical version, whittling the focus to Kathleen and Joe, the spirit of her original script remained intact. She could lose the moving parts, but the essence was still there.

Nora—surprise—was touchy about the music. Lauren, tired of using older songs, suggested the Cranberries' "Dreams," a tune the Irish band released in the early 1990s. Nora balked.

"This is the other side of Nora," Lauren says. "She was cranky over something; we didn't get a shot or whatever. She was sitting with Dianne and I came over and—it was out of the blue because I was urging her to use the Cranberries and she [didn't] want to use anything contemporary. I was saying, 'This is a great song.' So she said, 'Richie cut the scene to the Cranberries song,' but then she turned to me and said, 'Don't think we're going to use it.' And I was like, 'Uh...whatever.' And sure enough, not only did we use it, the theme of dreams inspired a lot of the other songs. It was very strange."

J. J. Sacha was beginning a stint as Nora's new personal assistant, and found himself swept up within her packed schedule: long days on set; dinners at night; writing, writing, writing. Always writing. "I had previously worked in television," Sacha says. "I didn't know anybody [on *Mail*], except Nora. I couldn't tell if she even liked me at that point. I thought, 'She's just barely tolerating me. I'm doing just enough to not fully annoy her.'...I was very nervous for probably the first six months [that] at any moment she was going to tell me that was it."

As it turned out, Sacha would outlast his predecessors and

work with Nora for a record 14 years. How did he pass the test? "One, I'm a guy," he explains, repeating an observation others have relayed to me: "Nora was a guy's girl. You don't have to look any further than the fact that she wrote *Lucky Guy*. She loved being in the room with a bunch of guys. Which isn't to say she wasn't super-girly, because she was kind of super-girly. But she loved... hanging out.... In terms of someone who ran her personal life, I was the only male assistant she ever had. I think it was a very different dynamic because I wasn't trying to be Nora Ephron. I had no interest in becoming the next Nora Ephron."

On December 10, 1998, *You've Got Mail* premiered at the Ziegfeld Theatre in midtown. Nick and Nora wore black suits. Tom and Meg posed together in neutral ensembles of the era: he paired his dark gray suit with a black shirt and tie; she slipped on a floor-length black leather jacket over her gray dress. Heather Burns went bold in a navy hooded dress, bright red coat, and on-trend Prada Mary Janes that resembled "witch shoes," she recalls, laughing. "It was just one of those New York sparkly moments."

After the screening, guests flocked to the Museum of Natural History, which hosted the after-party. Kevin Feige's mom was his date. She once scolded her son for ditching school to see *When Harry Met Sally* at the theater. Here they were, eight years later, at Nora's third movie starring Meg Ryan—and this time, Kevin was an ambitious production assistant with a promising future as head of Marvel Studios. While Tom Hanks and various above-the-liners socialized in the VIP area, Feige did what he always does: he hid in the corner. Later in the night, Tom left the event with a whole entourage of people. On his way out, he stopped, looked Kevin in the eye, and said, "Thanks for everything." "He did it because he knew my mother was standing right there," Feige suspects.

Elwood Edwards, unsung voice of "You've Got Mail," flew in for the occasion. He was happy to see Tom and Meg mouthing his catch-phrase. He got to see Alanis Morissette perform at the event. The only bigwig to notice him there was AOL co-founder Steve Case. In-the-know invitees likely recognized Sally Hershberger. She arrived with associate Matthew Fields, who was "excited-nervous" to see how Meg's shag looked on a grand scale. Other hair people in attendance: the two Russian stylists who blew out Nora's tresses on the regular.

Warner Bros. released *You've Got Mail* the week before Christmas. It made $116 million nationally and $251 million worldwide to rank number 14 among the year's biggest movies. The only other romantic comedy to come out ahead, at number 3, was *There's Something about Mary*, with $370 million in foreign sales. The Farrelly brothers flick unleashed ample gross-out humor to spin the classy genre on its head. Told from the guy's perspective, the movie puts boneheaded Ted (Ben Stiller) through the gauntlet of humiliating scenarios as he struggles to win over bone doctor/dreamgirl Mary (Cameron Diaz). While the film targeted young men, lots of women and older folks bought tickets and laughed at the raunchy episodes involving zippers, hair gel, and a border terrier. To some, *Mary*'s blockbuster bona fides seemed to signal the end of the verbal romcom that Nora revived and the birth of a slapstick generation. "Nora Ephron, take a cue," said the *Los Angeles Times*. "The romantic comedy, as we've known it, just took a radical turn." The paper quoted Jeff Arch for good measure: "This is scary," he joked. "They so effectively brutalized the [genre], how do you ever top that? They just lambasted what we do. You know this kind of romantic comedy is like taking your 13-year-old daughter to a concert backstage before she sees the show. You don't want her to see what's really going on before she gets there."

Bobby and Peter Farrelly, who co-wrote and co-directed *Mary*, felt romantic comedies—like 1996's *One Fine Day* with George Clooney and Michelle Pfeiffer—lacked suspense. Given low stakes and few obstacles, it was easy to foresee the leads hooking up in the end. Nora and Delia Ephron's solution: he puts her out of business! The Farrellys': he loses out on a 10! *Mary*'s high stakes hinged on the joke that someone like Mary would give someone like Ted the time of day. Ever. "Look, Mary's the perfect girl," Bobby said. "Drinks beer. Plays golf. Loves sports. She's smart. She's pretty. She's nice and she likes everybody, even geeky guys. She's got a retarded brother."

On the contrary, Kathleen Kelly loves books and drinks white wine. She's nice and likes everybody except Joe Fox, the butt of her killer insults. A Farrelly's "retarded brother" comment would make her wince.

Despite the infantile gags, the nation's critics tended to love *Mary* more than *Mail*.

The *Village Voice* sneered: "Nora Ephron can't direct her way out of a popcorn bag. . . . Ephron may claim inspiration from 1930s comedies, but her true model is 1950s Hollywood—in her world, men pick up the tab while women pick up the pieces. Classic screwball comedies fed on sex and class antagonisms, but Ephron's own starry-eyed formula precludes conflict: one minute Meg Ryan sets up a picket line in front of the competition; the next she's a spineless waif who makes googly eyes at the man who just wrecked her life."

Writing in Salon.com, Ron Rosenbaum, the original Frank Navasky, acknowledged the "benign caricature" and knocked "the chirpy sentimentalizing of terminally insipid emails by tragically insipid stars Meg Ryan and Tom Hanks."

Though reviews were "begrudging," as Delia put it, many glowed with praise. "Even if you already live on the Upper West Side, you might feel the urge to move there before the film is over," said the *New York Times*' Janet Maslin, writing: "Being firmly on the side of the angels, this film treasures the written word so proudly that the closing credits thank a long list of publishing houses. And they really ought to be thanking Ms. Ephron in return. The film's mix of romance and reading matter is seductive in its own right, providing comfy book-lined settings and people who are what they read and write. When they fall in love, they do it wistfully, as if not quite believing that real life can measure up to really good fiction."

Meg, opined Maslin, "plays her role blithely and credibly this time, with an air of freshness, a minimum of cute fidgeting and a lot of fond chemistry with Mr. Hanks. And he continues to amaze....Though he has none of Mr. Stewart's lanky grace or leading-man patina, the wonderful Mr. Hanks has all the same romantic wistfulness and the same poignant shyness when he learns who Kathleen really is. He shares Mr. Stewart's lovely way of speaking from the heart."

Late-night host Stephen Colbert would later confess to weeping throughout the movie. Quentin Tarantino, a guest on Colbert's show, said he once defended *Mail* while talking with "these really serious film critics" who were trashing it. "I thought that movie actually did a really good job of describing how big chain stores kill the little stores," Tarantino argued. "And I actually thought it was one of the only Hollywood movies to actually deal with that subject in a serious way."

"At the end she forgives him and she ends up being rich with the chain store guy," Colbert reminded. "She totally sells out."

If you found the bookstore's closure tough to stomach, perhaps you couldn't fully digest the paradoxical ending, as satisfying as it was. Though Nora admitted to guilt over shuttering the Shop Around the Corner (the saddest scene in the movie), she supported the union of Kathleen Kelly and Joe Fox. When Heather Burns voiced frustration over the unfairness of it all, Nora said to her, "Heather, the older you get, you're going to realize that things change and there's not very much that you can do about it. And the city changes, and that's just the way it is." The actress would come to realize Nora was correct: "That things change—especially in New York. It's just constantly changing, for better or for worse, both at the same time."

Doing press in London, Nora folded her arms and seemingly seethed when a *Guardian* reporter said he found the outcome "shockingly conservative."

Had *Mail* been released in 2017, its moral cloudiness would be less accepted by society at large. But this was 1998, when both Hillary Clinton and Monica Lewinsky were vilified by sexist newspaper columnists and cable TV pundits and there were no social media activists to shut them down. Feminism was largely a dirty word. You have to wonder what the feedback might have been if you crossed out "Nora Ephron" and subbed in "Richard Curtis." (Curtis's *Love Actually*—your ex-boyfriend's favorite romcom—depicted leading men Colin Firth and Hugh Grant finding love with their assistants while leading ladies Emma Thompson and Laura Linney got left in the lurch.)

"Critics were hard on her, much harder than on male directors who did half as good work," Delia wrote. "This country likes to take down strong women. Everyone loved Hillary more after Bill cheated during his own presidency."

The negative criticism stung. Even so, *You've Got Mail* became an instant classic, eternally replaying on television. These days, it provides some welcome comfort in uncertain times. Here's Dianne Dreyer:

"One of the things Nora's trying to say in the movie is that there are lots of ways to fall in love, and when you fall in love with someone, you want to fall in love with them truly. Because she loved words so much, she made it very clear that you could actually fall in love, even online to some extent, through revealing who you are by what you say and how you say it and your bravery in saying it, and saying it to that other person.... Write the letter. If it tells you anything, it says: 'Write the letter. Use your voice.'"

CHAPTER 12

A Heart in New York

Shortly after *You've Got Mail* hit theaters, Meg Ryan began film-ing her next Ephron film, *Hanging Up*, a dramedy based on Delia's 1995 novel of the same name. The semiautobiographical book revolved around the relationship between a troublesome father and his caretaker daughter. Eve Mozell, a fictional version of Delia, had an older sister, Georgia, a self-absorbed New Yorker who runs her own glossy. "When you want to impress people, you must always wear Armani and you must compliment men on their ties," Georgia declares. "That's something not every women's magazine will tell you, but *Georgia* will. We're not afraid to sound stupid if it's smart."

And: "Round tables are better for conversation than square. We almost bought an apartment but didn't because the dining room was long and narrow."

And: "She'll never meet men if she doesn't go to college."

(As if a woman's sole purpose in seeking higher education is to land a man. Edited to better reflect her elitist perspective, Geor-gia's declaration could be taken to mean: "She'll never meet the *right* kind of man if she doesn't go to college." This all goes back

271

to Sally Albright saying she could never date a man who runs a bar, even if the man is Humphrey Bogart in *Casablanca*.)

In *Hanging Up*, Eve feels abandoned by Georgia, "the closest thing I have to a mother," and the fear of losing her sister keeps Eve from conveying the depth of her irritation.

Nora loved her alter ego. The sisters conspired to adapt *Hanging Up* into a movie, with Nora the director. But teamwork enflamed old wounds. Namely, Delia's grudge against Nora for leaving her and sibling Amy to handle Henry's death in 1992. "That history played out when we began writing," Delia wrote. "I was edgy, harboring resentment, and she was territorial as always, but also she needed this to be her story—it was her father, too.... At some point after completing the first draft, we disagreed about the script so much that we stopped speaking for at least a month—or at most we spoke when necessary. This was the only time in our lives that such a thing happened. We were both miserable."

In order to preserve sisterly affection, Nora and Delia mutually agreed that someone else should direct *Hanging Up*. Diane Keaton took the job, and the Ephrons remained as writers and producers. Keaton multitasked to play Georgia while directing Lisa Kudrow as kooky Maddy and Meg as good-girl Eve. With Keaton in control, the film "doesn't feel as if it belongs to me or Nora," Delia said. "I didn't recognize the tone. It was much broader than our script.... Keaton didn't enjoy collaboration the way Nora and I did. Like many directors, once she was in preproduction—from then on through shooting and the editing process—she didn't consult the writer."

In February 2000, *Hanging Up* opened to droopy box office and reviews. Still, it performed better than Nora's *Lucky Numbers*, released that fall.

Nora had chosen a black comedy from Adam Resnick, formerly a joke writer at *Late Night with David Letterman*. A Pennsylvania weatherman (John Travolta) hatches a scheme to rig the local lottery when uncommonly warm winter weather affects his side business selling snowmobiles. His partner in crime (Lisa Kudrow) is the flaky lotto presenter who draws the winning numbers. Their boss (Ed O'Neill) threatens blackmail. An assassin (Michael Rapaport) pursues Travolta. Making cameos: Bill Pullman as a dopey detective and documentarian Michael Moore as Kudrow's asthmatic cousin whose inhaler she swipes after he refuses to 'fess up to the whereabouts of the winning lottery ticket.

Lucky Numbers was as tedious to sit through as *Mixed Nuts*—possibly even more. It made only $11 million and earned Travolta the Razzie Award for worst actor along with his bizarre role in *Battlefield Earth*, adapted from a sci-fi book by Scientology founder L. Ron Hubbard. Roger Ebert quipped, "Travolta survived this experience with his sense of humor still intact. How can I be sure? He has announced he wants to make a sequel to *Battlefield Earth*."

J. J. Sacha recalls: "We made that movie and we all thought it was one of the most hilarious things we've ever been a part of. We loved it every day. Then the movie came out and nobody wanted to see it."

While Nora's move to do something new and gritty backfired, Meg was caught up in tabloid scandal. Her cutie-pie image was ripping apart at the seams. In the spring of 2000, Meg—still married, unhappily, to Dennis Quaid—began a passionate affair with Russell Crowe on the set of *Proof of Life*. The thriller, filmed in Ecuadorian forests and English soundstages, followed Alice Bowman (Meg) and engineer husband Peter (David Morse) as they moved to the fictional South American country of Tecala for his job. When Peter gets kidnapped by guerrilla fighters, Alice takes matters into her own hands and hires brawny negotiator Terry Thorne (Russell) to rescue him. Working cheek by jowl in exotic locations, the two pretty people develop sexy feelings. The plot thickened off the screen. Meg, 38, became enamored of the 36-year-old New Zealand native, a decade Dennis's junior. Russell, moody and intense, was the action star of the moment. His role as Roman general Maximus Decimus Meridius in *Gladiator* made him a global superstar. His fiery temper made headlines. Like Dennis, he fronted a rock band. (Russell called his 30 Odd Foot of Grunts.) "He's a tough thing to resist," Carrie Fisher said. "I was just glad I had a friend that got him."

When the media got wind of the showmance, Meg went from America's Sweetheart to Hester Prynne overnight and Dennis from reformed bad boy to noble victim. Russell, the bloke caught in the middle, couldn't dodge the "homewrecker" label more often pinned on women who get involved with married men.

Meg and Dennis separated in May 2000. On July 12, Dennis filed for divorce in LA, citing irreconcilable differences; several weeks earlier, Meg was spotted cozying up to Crowe on a Concorde jet bound for London. A stunned passenger detailed the scene to *People*: "He was leaning over her, kissing her on the neck and stroking her hair—and it went on that way the whole flight.... The guy next to me and I, we were just like, 'I guess that's what goes on in Hollywood.'" The magazine splashed the love triangle on that week's cover, with the headline MEG RYAN'S SHOCKING SPLIT.

Later that month, Meg and Russell were snapped acting couple-y at a David Bowie concert in London. In September, they surfaced in Santa Monica and Australia. By December, they had broken up because Meg reportedly got cold feet about jumping into another relationship.

She was obviously in love—and out in the open about it. Rather than celebrate their heroine, her fans recoiled, airing the sort of grievances that saw Ingrid Bergman flee America amid outrage over her affair with filmmaker Roberto Rossellini in the 1950s.

"Meg Ryan's cuckolding of her husband is shameful and heart-breaking," said a letter in *People*, Meg's one-time safe space for scandal-free coverage. "As for the suggestion that all this won't affect her box-office popularity, this is one former fan who won't be paying to see any more Meg Ryan movies," huffed another.

Though Meg put up a silent front at first, letting rumor run wild instead of answering directly to the press, anonymous friends turned up in print to explain that crazy work schedules drove the Quaids apart. But the actress grew more candid over the years. In a 2006 interview with Oprah Winfrey, Meg called the tabloid coverage "heartbreaking." She was ever more distrustful of report-ers and the snitches who snitch to them. She wondered: "If I say something to someone, is she gonna tell someone else and is that person gonna talk to the *National Enquirer*?"

Meg knew five years in that she and Dennis weren't working. She chose to stick around. A child was involved, deepening her guilt.

"It was a very unhealthy marriage, and it was pretty much not a happening marriage for a very long time," she revealed, choos-ing her words carefully so as not to hurt Jack, then 13 years old. "I probably should have left much earlier. I was very sad actually that it all had to come apart the way that it seemed to have. It was never about another man. It was only about what my and Dennis's relationship just couldn't sustain."

Defending Russell, she added, "He wasn't a homewrecker. He took a lot of heat for that, and he had a lot of grace, frankly... not talking about things that he knew were going on in my marriage." She made clear: "I didn't leave my marriage for Russell Crowe. I left my marriage."

In 2008, Meg dropped the diplomacy act and gave a straight answer. "Dennis was not faithful to me for a long time, and that was very painful," she told *InStyle*. "I found out more about that once I was divorced."

Following that rare moment of candor, Dennis—remarried with twins and a reinvigorated acting career—fired off a statement. "It was eight years ago," he complained, "and I find it unbelievable that Meg continues publicly to rehash and rewrite the story of our relationship."

The story turned Meg into the bad guy and made Dennis look amazing. Why would he want that rewritten? By saying nothing, Meg had perpetuated a narrative she could never totally undo; by opening up, she filled in the plot holes and stood up for herself.

"I am not a victim," she said. "My time as a scarlet woman was really interesting. As painful as it was, it was also incredibly liberating. I didn't have to care about what people thought."

The millennium was a turning point for Meg. *Proof of Life* tanked. The actress shut down her production company. She moved out of the Brentwood home she shared with Dennis and into new digs in Bel Air. She embarked on a new life as a single mom. In the spring of 2001, she stayed at her Fifth Avenue apartment while filming *Kate & Leopold* in New York. The romantic comedy, directed by James Mangold (*Girl, Interrupted*), teamed Meg and Hugh Jackman as a modern-day Manhattan marketing professional and a dashing Englishman who time-travels from 1876 to shake up her all-work, no-play world. In the end, Kate chooses Victorian England over Corporate America and chases Leopold back to the 19th century, which is a terrible idea all around unless you don't care about lack of access to modern medicine and dentistry.

Kate & Leopold grossed a decent $47 million in a year that saw bigger hits like *Bridget Jones's Diary* (perfection) and *The Wedding Planner* (please skip this soulless focus-group dud). It would be the last splashy Meg Ryan romcom before she took a break from roles she felt she'd outgrown. Around the time she turned 40, in 2001, studio execs began questioning her bankability. "I'm probably too old to do romantic comedies," she told *Newsweek*, two years before Nancy Meyers disproved ageist notions that give actresses an expiration date by pairing Diane Keaton and Jack Nicholson in the blockbuster *Something's Gotta Give*.

"I mean, who wants to see me trying to decide about a guy?" said Meg. "I want to do more complicated movies anyway, smaller movies anyway, so I'm trying to catch up with myself."

She played against type in grittier films. There was the 2003 erotic thriller *In the Cut*. Meg earned good reviews as a high-school English teacher who hooks up with a homicide detective (Mark Ruffalo) she suspects of brutally murdering a young woman. The next year, she starred in *Against the Ropes*, a biopic about Jackie Kallen, the boxing manager who cracked the glass ceiling in a male-dominated sport.

When Nicole Kidman dropped out of *In the Cut*, written and directed by Jane Campion, Meg auditioned to replace Kidman. "I was scared of the sexuality, and I was scared I couldn't be the kind of actor who did nothing," she said. "I'm not a likely choice for that kind of material, and Jane took a huge chance on me."

Campion advised Meg not to worry about being liked. A tall order, considering that what attracts many actors to the profession is that thing they did not get too much of during childhood: love. Even if it's coming from strangers. Even if they downplay their reaction to strangers' opinions on their work and life choices.

Sometimes, if Campion offered help on a scene, Meg would

brush her off. The director, learning Meg's personality, glimpsed a sensitive and independent person. "Meg is actually sort of a wily thinker," Campion said. "She's pretty cunning."

Fans ignored Meg's against-type detours, preferring the purity of her 1990s persona. She threw back to Hollywood's Golden Age, and while some compared her to Carole Lombard, Doris Day, or Lucille Ball, none of those comparisons really stood up. Like a Carole Lombard, Meg was an iconic product of her own time, which made her timeless. But Meg was singular. Unmistakably different from any other actress. There is still nobody like Meg. They are still looking for the next Meg Ryan to replace the real Meg Ryan. That's what it means to be an original.

"America will never forgive Meg Ryan for growing old," says Harley Jane Kozak, with a sigh in her voice. "There are people who are born old and people who are eternally young. I think that Meg was the perfect ingénue. I think ingénues have a very tough time when they move into the role of motherhood or beyond. So you don't think of Meg Ryan, like Sigourney Weaver, being cast as the president. She's not Robin Wright. She's not a political figure. She's not ever going to be Margaret Thatcher. But then where does an ingénue go after they hit 50? I guess they have to go into character roles. A lot of us do. I'm not saying there are no parts for Meg Ryan, but it's unlikely that she will be able to grow old in the spotlight that she had in her 20s and 30s because that was her prime. That was the perfect storm of genre, decade, style, and her particular form of youthfulness."

Combine that with Tom Hanks, and suddenly you're wrapped up in a warm blanket on a snowy night, sipping hot cocoa by the crackling fire. That's what it means to give off sparks. "That these two have made only three movies together feels like a rip-off," film critic Wesley Morris later wrote.

They are right for each other, even when what Ephron has them do at the end of You've Got Mail *is notoriously wrong. But Hanks had different gears, which makes you wonder whether Ryan's attempts to find gears of her own—as a depressive good-time girl, an alcoholic guidance counselor, and the first woman to (posthumously) receive the Medal of Honor—was, in a sense, a way of keeping up with him. And she maybe...could have kept trying, but a chameleon star like Nicole Kidman (never the same role twice), honed in on at least some of Ryan's dreams of actorly seriousness. In any case, despite understandable attempts to diversify, her brand was love, and you could feel the search for it turning her bitter.*

After wrapping *Against the Ropes*, Meg went away for a while to experience life off the Hollywood grid. To really catch up with herself.

✳ ✳ ✳

Lucky Numbers put Nora in movie jail.

A Paramount Pictures exec blocked Lynda Obst from having Nora write an adaptation of the Sophie Kinsella chick-lit novel *Can You Keep a Secret?*—with romcom ingénue du jour Kate Hudson as the lead. It was something Nora could direct while getting her hair blown out. It had potential to become her Get Out of Jail Free card.

Lynda assumed the studio would be thrilled that Nora was interested in developing the project. Incredulous, she stumped on Nora's behalf. "Yes, you know we have great faith in you, and we love Nora, of course, but she just made *Lucky Numbers* for us, and it didn't work," the exec explained.

Nora, meanwhile, had two scripts in development at Columbia

Pictures: one about birdwatchers and Pale Male, the majestic red-tailed hawk that nests atop a fancy building neighboring Central Park. The other focused on the sexually charged romance between Korean War correspondents Marguerite "Maggie" Higgins and Keyes Beech. The two shared the Pulitzer Prize for international reporting for their coverage; Higgins was the first woman to win the honor. "She was completely fearless," Nora said. "She was all of our basic nightmares—she did sleep with someone for a story." Higgins drove Beech nuts on the job. "In her quest for fame, she was appallingly single-minded," he wrote. "Almost frightening in her determination to overcome all obstacles. But so far as her trade was concerned, she had more guts, more staying power, and more resourcefulness than 90 percent of her detractors."

Higgins, a difficult woman, was interesting to Nora and therefore personal. Her screenplay, co-written with Alice Arlen, had been waiting to be made for quite some time. Tom Hanks enjoyed what he read when Nora sent him the screenplay, though doubted its prospects. At one point, Meg considered playing Maggie. Michelle Pfeiffer and Richard Gere were attached in the early 1990s. In 1996, Elisabeth Shue was up for consideration. George Clooney was a candidate for Beech until he saw that Higgins had the starrier role.

Back when Pfeiffer was involved, distributor United Artists reportedly feared going over budget. And while Nora and Alice embraced Higgins, warts and all, as they had with Karen Silkwood, her unlikable qualities proved risky. Said Alice, who died in February 2016 following a long illness, "I honestly think that Maggie Higgins was an impossible character because as much as we tried to make her endearing she finally had the nasty habit of selling people out."

Nora, heartbroken that *Higgins and Beech* never got the greenlight, was also developing a film project for HBO dubbed *Stories about McAlary*. Her subject: a difficult man. A guy who might fit in among the macho antiheroes on the premium cable network that brought us Tony Soprano. Mike McAlary was an actual person, not a mobster but a journalist. A son of a gun who made some bad mistakes but left this world on a high note. McAlary offered Nora the chance to remind her peers that, yes, she was capable of mastering material beyond the romantic comedy.

She turned to Broadway. Her subjects: difficult women, specifically novelist Mary McCarthy and playwright Lillian Hellman. The two were mortal enemies, and Nora imagined the literary lions hashing it out in *hell*, mixing low blows with heady conversation. Her smart and playful debut stage play, *Imaginary Friends*, starred Cherry Jones as McCarthy and Swoosie Kurtz as Hellman. She got *A Chorus Line* composer Marvin Hamlisch to write some musical interludes. There were puppets! And yet, the production opened at the Ethel Barrymore Theatre in December 2002, shuttering after 76 performances and a spate of unfavorable reviews.

Earlier that year, Nora ended her 22-year attachment to the Apthorp. She and Delia moved out in the spring after management jacked up their monthly rents (Nora's to $12,000) amid a push to attract tenants richer than they. A marble nude statue was installed near the entrance. The elevators were spray-painted gold. The Apthorp was losing its soul. The building was run by this "completely insane man," says Delia, and "maybe someone from Silicon Valley could afford to live there but we couldn't."

Delia and her husband departed for Greenwich Village, and Nick and Nora found a place on the Upper East Side with views of the Chrysler Building. What irony: Nora admittedly built a religion out of the Upper West Side, then defected to swankier territory. She regretted not leaving the Apthorp sooner once the honeymoon period ended. "On the other hand, I'm never going to dream about this new apartment," she wrote. "It's not love. It's just where I live."

As Nora moved on, so did romantic comedy. Her influence was everywhere. Sally Albright helped popularize the trope of the urban single-girl journalist that traces its origins back to 1940 and Rosalind Russell's portrayal of Hildy Johnson in Howard Hawks's *His Girl Friday* (1940), one of Nora's favorite love stories ever. Hildy was an anomaly, ahead of her time; only male characters played by Cary Grant and Jimmy Stewart were written as rascally reporters.

After Sally, we saw Renée Zellweger the hapless broadcast reporter in *Bridget Jones's Diary*, Kate Hudson the sneaky magazine columnist in *How to Lose a Guy in 10 Days*, and Eva Mendes the cynical tabloid tomboy in *Hitch*. On HBO, Sarah Jessica Parker wrote sex columns for a New York City newspaper. She worshipped Manhattan, leaned on her friends, and unapologetically hunted love—often, in the wrong places. She was messier than Meg Ryan's haircut, but just as trendsetting: her tutus, big flower pins, and Manolos stood for individualism, romance over reality. While *Sex and the City* set out to subvert the romantic comedy, with nakedly unlikable characters like Carrie Bradshaw, viewers adored Carrie in spite of her flaws. They wanted her to get that happy ending—with Mr. Big, a Joe Fox–ian playboy who treats her poorly. Over its six-year run, the show morphed into a love letter to New York and a romcom about the quirky singletons who were products of the city in which they lived and nostalgic for what it used to be.

Female wish fulfillment prevailed.

During the aughts, Tom's biggest movie romance was with Wilson the volleyball in *Cast Away*.

The multihyphenate icon, now in middle age, had dedicated himself to dramatic roles that ultimately burnished his brand: ordinary men thrust into extraordinary circumstances. Men of action, integrity, and mystery. Good men (*The Terminal*) and bad men

(*Road to Perdition*). Weird men (*The Ladykillers*). Long-haired men (Robert Langdon in *The Da Vinci Code* film franchise).

Newspaper men: not applicable. Tom turned down *Stories about McAlary*, renamed *Lucky Guy*, because of his low opinion of the real-life tabloid columnist. Around 2005, journalist Jim Dwyer—one of the many McAlary colleagues Nora interviewed as part of her research—ran into her at a party and inquired about the status of the script. He'd heard great things about it. "I can't get the person I want to play the lead," she teased, later pulling Dwyer aside to leak the name.

"Tom Hanks."

"Tom Hanks what?"

"Tom Hanks really doesn't like certain people in your profession."

Tom reportedly earned an enormous paycheck on 2009's *Angels & Demons*, and his producing endeavors rained money as well. Tom, with wife Rita, produced the 2002 international sensation *My Big Fat Greek Wedding*, which remains the top-grossing romantic comedy of all time.

With that kind of credential, plus the legacy Nora Ephron movies, why would he need to star in another romcom?

Four years after *Lucky Numbers* crashed and burned, Nora returned to the director's chair for her fourth romantic comedy: Columbia Pictures' high-profile update of the TV classic *Bewitched*, co-starring Will Ferrell and Nicole Kidman. Nora and Delia co-wrote the script, injecting some originality into the boring trend of remaking retro series like *Scooby-Doo* and *The Dukes of Hazzard*.

In the 1960s sitcom, doofy Darrin is married to clever witch Samantha. Shenanigans ensue in the suburbs as she tries to hide her supernatural powers from mortals. The Ephrons modernized this plot gimmick to jab at Hollywood's unease around powerful women—in this case, a woman with magic at her fingertips. Jack Wyatt, a washed-up actor and insufferable narcissist, suggests that a non-famous actress play second fiddle to his Darrin in a TV remake of *Bewitched*. Jack discovers Isabel Bigelow twitching her nose, just like Elizabeth Montgomery, in a bookstore; unbeknownst to Jack, Isabel is a witch. She nails her audition and becomes the star of the show—outshining Jack. He'll have none of that. He's the blowhard who yells, "Guys! Make me 200 cappuccinos! Bring me the best one!"

An angry Isabel casts a spell that turns Jack into her number one cheerleader. When she reverses it, romantic feelings transpire—no witchcraft required. Jack accepts Isabel as an equal partner and proposes (before she can come to her senses and ride off on her broomstick).

The Ephronized *Bewitched*—sweet and sophisticated and a little bit airy, like a macaron—incited a bonfire of critical groupthink: almost every reviewer slimed it. The film "exhibits a fondness for the original series but doesn't click as a romance—in part because the miscast Ferrell's character is such a self-absorbed boor it's hard to fathom what Isabel sees in him," *Variety* opined.

Nora fired her agent Jim Wiatt. "She wanted to make other decisions and have other people try to help her because that movie was very tough," Wiatt says of *Bewitched*. "That was very tough for her. And she was afraid that she wasn't getting to work and she was very concerned about it."

Time was of the essence. After experiencing fevers, among other health issues, Nora had been diagnosed that year with myelodysplastic syndrome, a disease that quashes the development of healthy blood cells and may turn into leukemia. Nora, who had long feared dying of cancer, which had claimed her uncle Dickie at age 28, was given medication and blood transfusions that stabilized the disorder, prolonging her life. She kept her MDS secret from all but her sons, her sisters, selected close friends, and Nick. She did not want this to define her, to make people feel bad for her, to compel studios to remove her from their director shortlists.

She continued to work, work, work.

She was prolific. She had established herself as the no-bullshit expert on aging and a funny, wise voice for women of her generation in the 2006 essay collection *I Feel Bad about My Neck*, a national best seller. "If anyone young is reading this, go, right this minute, put on a bikini and don't take it off until you're 34," Nora, your new best friend, confided.

She wrote magazine articles for *Vogue* and the *New Yorker*. She wrote another book's worth of blog posts for the Huffington Post. She recounted the time Steve Wynn accidentally poked a hole in a Picasso. She analyzed Condoleezza Rice as skilled at "making nice, which is the opposite of being funny. I've always believed that women of my generation (and hers) were literally trained to make nice." She lit into the 2008 Democratic primary in Pennsylvania, down to Barack Obama and Hillary Clinton: "This is an election about whether the people of Pennsylvania hate blacks more than they hate women. And when I say people, I don't mean people; I mean white men. How ironic is this? After all this time, after all these stupid articles about how powerless white men are and how they can't even get into college because of overachieving women and affirmative action and mean lady teachers who expected them to sit still in the third grade even though they were all suffering from terminal attention deficit disorder—after all this, they turn out (surprise!) to have all the power."

She and Delia partnered on the play *Love, Loss, and What I Wore*, a set of witty and poignant monologues exploring women's lives through their wardrobes. Not one man graced the stage when the show opened off-Broadway at the Westside Theatre in October 2009. Rosie O'Donnell and Rita Wilson were among the revolving cast. The show, a smash success, won a Drama Desk Award and was soon performed all over the world, from Buenos Aires to Cape Town.

Two months before *Love, Loss* launched its long run, Nora had released her seventh movie and what many considered her finest. If anyone distrusted the director's skills behind the camera, *Julie & Julia* would prove them wrong.

It was going to be an independent film, but became something bigger once Nora got involved. She had first read about Julie Powell in a 2003 *New York Times* profile of the 30-year-old blogger. Julie, an office secretary with a refreshingly unladylike trucker's mouth, lived in a modest Queens apartment. Her roommates were her husband, Eric, and three cats. In a professional rut, Julie conceived the Julie/Julia Project, challenging herself to cook every single recipe—524 in total—from Julia Child's *Mastering the Art of French Cooking*. She documented her ups, downs, and adventures in aspic in a blog that gained a loyal readership and, eventually, a deal to write her bestselling memoir, *Julie & Julia*.

Intrigued, Nora wondered whether there was a movie in Julie's story. Could she stretch it into two hours? She thought not.

Later, Amy Pascal, co-chairman at Sony Pictures, shared the concept of mashing up Julie and Julia's stories into a parallel structure. "Oh my God, that is, that's brilliant!" Nora said. At the time, "another writer was on the project, and I was stricken by this news and very much hoped that something terrible would happen so that she wouldn't be able to write it," she recalled. "And it did! She got a big hit television show, and I got to write it."

Julia Child was 51 years old when she debuted her TV cooking show, *The French Chef*, in 1963; Nora directed *This Is My Life* when she was 50. Both glimpsed God in a pat of butter. Both had loving husbands. Nora was thrilled "that one could write about how sweet it can be if you have a husband who thinks it's great that something good is happening to you."

To friends and colleagues, this instance of domestic bliss—a rarity in the movies—was a way for Nora to acknowledge the Paul Child of her life.

Nick joined Nora on location in Paris with Meryl Streep, who embodied Child to an uncanny degree, and Stanley Tucci, a sort of thinking woman's sex symbol.

One day on set, Nora turned to producer Larry Mark and said: "I just want to say how much I love you and love having you here."

It was out of the blue. They hugged. Nora wasn't a hugger. In retrospect, Larry thought that was her way of showing appreciation before it was too late.

In January 2006, Meg Ryan confirmed her adoption of a baby girl from China. She planned on the name Rae, or Charlotte, but decided upon Daisy True about a month after bringing the one-year-old home. "She's a really ridiculously happy person," Meg later said. "It was the happiest word I could think of."

The next year, Meg stepped back into the limelight as Kristen Stewart's mother in the forgettable drama *In the Land of Women*, following up the role with two straight-to-DVD comedies that paired Meg with William H. Macy (*The Deal*) and Antonio Banderas (*My Mom's New Boyfriend*). On a higher profile, Meg headlined 2008's *The Women*, which finally hit theaters a decade after a version starring her and Julia Roberts went nowhere. The remake co-starred Annette Bening, Debra Messing, Eva Mendes, and Jada Pinkett Smith. Meg played clothing designer Mary Haines, whose husband is cheating on her with Saks Fifth Avenue saleswoman Crystal Allen (Eva Mendes).

Only one scene of Meg stress-eating a stick of butter gave her the "chance to remind us that she is still the spitfire who won America's heart when she faked an orgasm at Katz's Deli," wrote A. O. Scott in his review. "In *The Women*, she certainly works at faking something—pluck? distress? belief in the script?—but table-pounding ecstasy, or even simple, modest pleasure, is beyond the movie's range."

For Meg, quietly raising Daisy in the cozy-bohemian bubble of downtown New York, reminders of *When Harry Met Sally* were inescapable. Twenty years had passed, yet her performances were still being graded against her most famous character. Her changing looks were picked apart in the magazines and on the internet and social media. With good roles harder to come by, Meg poured her creative energies behind the camera as a serious photographer and first-time director, helming the World War II homefront drama *Ithaca* on an indie budget. Tom Hanks stepped in to produce her 2015 adaptation of the William Saroyan novel *The Human Comedy*, which tells the story of a teenage boy telegram messenger who comes of age while delivering bad news to fallen soldiers' families. Meg starred as the boy's widowed mom, and Tom reported to the set to film a few scenes as her late husband.

"He just did me such a solid, it just takes my breath away," Meg told me while editing the film and longing for Nora's advice. "He really didn't have to come and do this little cameo, but he did it. And he was gracious and at the end he thanked everybody for having him. I mean, *really*? He's fantastic and it was fun and easy. Easy. It's just easy with him."

✳ ✳ ✳

Tom Hanks was rethinking his first impression of Mike McAlary.

In the summer of 2011, he'd come around after having dinner with Nora and Jon Hamm at the Wolseley in London. He was in town to promote *Larry Crowne*, a romantic comedy he directed, co-wrote with Nia Vardalos, and acted in opposite Julia Roberts—his first love story since *You've Got Mail*. Julia played a community college professor who ditches her deadbeat husband upon meeting Tom's Larry Crowne, a kindhearted Navy vet and her student. Reviews were middling. Opening weekend numbers were underwhelming. When the demographics rolled in, it was reported that a whopping 71 percent of *Larry Crowne*'s audience was over 50 years old. Hollywood doesn't want to hear that. One flabbergasted studio exec told the *Hollywood Reporter*, "My goodness, there are bristlecone pines younger than this movie."

Jon Hamm was pop culture's shiny new thing and a critical darling for his portrayal of antihero Don Draper in *Mad Men*. During dinner, Hamm told Tom he'd traveled overseas to read a play for Nora.

"Hey, Nora, what play is he reading that you are doing?"

"Oh, I'm doing that thing that I sent you a long time ago about the tabloid reporter that you thought was a jerk, Mike McAlary."

"Oh, is it a play now?"

"Well, yeah."

"Oh, OK. Can I read it?"

Tom, feeling in competition with Hamm, the young-ish whippersnapper, began to view the character in a different light. "It's about somebody who is almost good enough to deserve what he achieves," he said. "And I understand that....I still feel sometimes that I'd like to be as good as so-and-so actor. I see some other actors' work, and I think I'll never get there. I wish I could."

Back in New York, Tom took a stab at reading *Lucky Guy*. No tears were shed in Tom's performance, yet he delivered a bittersweet emotional punch that impressed witnesses. He was invigorated. And he loved any old excuse to hang with Nora.

McAlary was a piece of work: a tough-talking, hard-drinking, wannabe Jimmy Breslin creature of the newsroom, back in the day when an ink-stained *Daily News* journalist held sway over a citizen reporter with an iPhone. Back in the day when a lucky guy like McAlary could become New York's highest-paid columnist. Working the police beat, he schmoozed sources, burned bad guys, earned a bloated paycheck, and made enemies along the way. In 1994, he fanned outrage when he incorrectly reported that a woman faked her rape in Brooklyn's Prospect Park. Four years later, he won goodwill—and the Pulitzer—for his career-saving coverage of Abner Louima, a Haitian immigrant who was brutally beaten by NYPD officers at a Brooklyn precinct. "This is not about the police force," McAlary seethed in print after landing the first interview with Louima. "This is about a group of cops who are sadistic racists. Be afraid, be very afraid if this story is true, and I am afraid it is." McAlary logged seven columns on the 1997 crime while battling colon cancer, the disease that killed him one year later.

"I remember asking her specifically: What's so fascinating about Mike McAlary? Did he write great columns?" Tom recalled. "She said, 'Some, but not particularly.' I said, 'Well, you know, was he a crackerjack writer that you absolutely had to read?' And she said, 'No, not really.' And George Wolfe at one point said, 'Well then why ya telling this story?'"

Nora told Wolfe, *Lucky Guy*'s director, "This play is about somebody who has more luck than talent.... And I know something about that."

Tom Hanks, who had signed on for the part, his Broadway bow, was stunned to hear this. "It's the last sort of thing you would think you'd get from Nora," he said.

She and Wolfe would meet each week to hone the script, which featured actors addressing the audience and swapping stories about McAlary. Nora submitted drafts at a turbo pace, baffling Wolfe.

What was fueling her rapid, self-imposed deadlines?

By early 2012, Nora's blood count was destabilizing. She kept appointments and appearances in New York. On May 16, she accompanied Nick to CBS's unveiling of *Vegas*, a crime series he wrote, as part of the network's fall lineup. "There was *Vegas* as big as life," Nick recalled of the Carnegie Hall to-do, "and Nora leaned across to me in the theatre and said, 'This one is for real...you can't just phone it in.' She was very hopeful for it. This was in the spring. Nora was mad for the series *The Good Wife*, and the whole cast of that show was there too, and she gushed over them because she really wanted to hire Julianna Margulies for her own next movie."

While Nora remained mum on her own battle—not everything was copy, especially this—she inserted clues into her work. In her 2010 book *I Remember Nothing*, she listed the things she won't miss—"Funerals," "Illness everywhere," "Panels on Women in Film"—and what she would: "My kids," "Nick," "Twinkle lights," "Coming over the bridge to Manhattan."

"Absolutely, she planned for it," Jacob Bernstein wrote. "She redid her will earlier in the spring when her blood counts were going the wrong way, typed an exit letter on her computer, spelling out what she wanted after she died: a party in the apartment with Champagne and cucumber sandwiches from William Poll; a memorial held days after. 'Get it over with' was the gist of her instructions. She even supplied the speaker list....Nevertheless, as she ran out of time, she chose not to acknowledge, at least explicitly, what was happening to her."

"The last time I saw her was at a small dinner party at a mutual friend's apartment on the Upper East Side. It was funny and fun...," Meg said. She, along with many others, had seen Nora's secret sickness soften her. "She was easier and easier and easier about her own flaws, about mine, about other people's. She laughed easier about things. She just got so porous."

One by one, Nora reached out to friends who weren't privy to her declining health, arranging lunches and dinners that, in hindsight, were also goodbyes. Nearing Memorial Day, she checked into NewYork-Presbyterian Hospital. Nora's MDS had advanced into leukemia, and she was started on chemotherapy. Weeks later, when she had hours left to live, "Nick sat beside her and wept," Jacob recalled.

She said, "This is it," "in a tone that seemed to be half-question, half-declaration," he wrote. "It occurred to me later that it might have been the first uncertain moment she'd had in her entire life."

She died there on Tuesday, June 26, at the age of 71, leaving stunned reactions and a trail of tributes in her wake. For those who knew her, and those who did not but felt they had, New York was never quite the same.

Expectations were high for *Lucky Guy*, and Tom Hanks worried he might not meet them. The demands of getting McAlary right, of conveying the reporter's flaws, of making Nora proud, hovered like a foggy mist. As usual, he cut through the uncertainty with a joke. "We're just resorting to imagining the headlines for bad reviews— 'Lucky Guy, Unlucky Audience!' 'Yucky Guy!'" he cracked at the time, several days before the show's sell-out run at the Broadhurst Theater on March 1, 2013. "Look," he explained, "I have just as impressive a track record of movies and projects that didn't work out."

Scratch *Sleepless in Seattle. You've Got Mail*. And soon, *Lucky Guy*, to be lavished with Tony nominations, including one for Tom.

Leading up to his high-pressure debut, Tom would think of Nora as he walked home from the theater at the end of the day. Out on the street, absorbing the heartbeat of the city, he heard her voice.

Afterword

It's true that Nora once laughed off the preposterous idea that she, an acid-penned, thrice-married writer, could become better known for her romantic comedies than anything else. But I suspect that underneath it all, and even as she challenged herself to try out new, darker material, she deeply relished her unlikely status as a leading expert of a genre beloved by zillions—from your next-door neighbor to the many Chinese tourists who booked flights to Seattle after seeing their country's *Sleepless*-inspired blockbuster, *Finding Mr. Right*.

(Had Nora lived to hear about her legacy in China, I strongly believe she would have excitedly emailed Delia a link to the news story.)

Even in death, Nora continues to set a high standard for excellence in romantic comedy, serving as a twinkly fairy godmother figure—a Julia Child of love—who had found the perfect husband for her and nurtured the hope that something good, somebody *great*, was out there somewhere.

Nora's optimism—her belief in second, and third, chances—trickled into Kathleen Kelly, whose clean break with Frank Navasky freed the resilient bookstore pixie to start over and seek a new life.

"What about you? Is there someone else?" wonders Frank, to which Kathleen demurs: "No. But there is the dream of someone else."

While earlier films threw cold water upon that dream—a single career woman foolishly attempting to have it all will end up alone, or homicidal—*You've Got Mail* showed a single career woman undergoing significant life changes. Kathleen's self-worth came neither from a man nor from her status as a girlfriend-*of*, but from her professional achievements. A soulmate? That's the cherry on top. Kathleen was looking for a best friend to share her life with, even if he broke her heart by bankrupting her proudest accomplishment and the last vestige of Cecilia Kelly: the Shop around the Corner.

But in choosing to forgive Joe Fox, aka NY152, Kathleen demonstrates that she's the brave one of the two. *She* is embarking on an exciting, scary, brand-new life. Joe, meanwhile, must prove that he can deserve her because Kathleen, like Elizabeth Bennet, is good and fair and whip-smart. Though Nora was mostly nothing like Kathleen, she created a woman whom she could admire, an homage to Austen's beloved heroine.

And similar to Nora, Kathleen—not to mention Annie and Sally—stood up for what she believed in and opened herself to the possibility of romance in the unlikeliest of places, with a friend, a stranger, or a chatroom buddy, each an equal partner with whom she shared equal screen time. What Kathleen lacked in the full rainbow of Nora's dynamic, complicated personality, she made up for with pluck, perseverance, and personal style. Yes, she was uncool, but her twee squareness felt charming and individual. Kathleen did not follow trends: she made them, right down to her perfectly mussy hair.

The snappy energy between Tom and Meg, or Meg and Billy, are reason enough for these movies to resonate as they have.

Though, let's not discount the power of Nora's insistence that a female character gain the privileges afforded to men: Hopes. Dreams. Humor. Pathos. An inner struggle that makes us root for the hero and identify with her, as women have identified with heroic male characters throughout history. The Ephron woman, even at her most Pollyanna, makes us feel less alone in a man's world—and inspires us not to give up.

Her fatal flaw, and Nora's as a filmmaker, was living within a bubble. While Nora created worlds in which we all wanted to live, her daffy, urban universes included mainly straight white people and couples at the unfortunate expense of diversity.

Nevertheless, Nora persists as an icon in the same big league as equally complex, multifaceted romcom pioneers Woody Allen, Preston Sturges, and Ernst Lubitsch, the master himself. People talk wistfully about her movies the way Frank Navasky types remember the good times before everyone became glued to their cell phones and stopped living life.

She reigned over a romcom golden age I've dubbed After Nora, AN, an era when big, splashy, starry romances found renewed success and so did the writers and directors who specialized in them. Garry Marshall (the Julia Roberts breakout *Pretty Woman*), Nancy Meyers (the upscale dream *Something's Gotta Give*), and Judd Apatow (the bro-centric *Knocked Up*) often eclipsed Nora at the box office. But Nora's boldfaced name outshone everybody else.

As an architect behind three beloved romantic comedies, Nora refreshed a stagnant film genre and stamped it with her own image, even yanking *When Harry Met Sally* away from Rob Reiner. As a feminist writer-director whose one-liners rivaled any high-speed car chase, she broke barriers and cleared the way for the Lena Dunhams, Mindy Kalings, and Tina Feys of the world to have a voice in patriarchal Hollywood, where men call most of the shots. As an uptown New York institution who knew all the best restaurants, she was a mascot for living well. As Diablo Cody said, "Her body of work is an eternal reply to the questions 'Are women funny? Can women direct?' Everything she did was unbelievably elegant, hilarious, and warm—basically everything anyone aspires to when they're writing a romantic comedy, but I don't think anyone will ever do it as well as she did."

Alert the *Annie Hall* police, the Lubitsch army, the Billy Wilder brigade: it's as if the mainstream romantic comedy Before Nora—BN—had ceased to exist, according to her fans.

Meanwhile, media headlines spell gloom and doom: *Whatever happened to the romcom? Is it dead? DID KATHERINE HEIGL KILL IT?*

No, sillies, it's alive and well on television and streaming services, with a few standout films rekindling the flame (notably, Chris Rock's *Top Five* and Amy Schumer's *Trainwreck*). Series like *Catastrophe* affect an astringent realism that Nora might have attempted if she were alive today. While sweetness and serendipity had been recipes for romance in Nora's time, they're all but lost amid a cynical Facebook age where dating apps rotate an assembly line of potential mates on continuous loop.

Given the overwhelming array of potential life partners (and mistakes) made possible by technological advances, more romcoms should be produced—as it stands, however, the really big stars, like Jennifer Lawrence and Ryan Reynolds, tend to steer clear of material that could diminish their respectability and pigeonhole them, a la Matthew McConaughey circa *Fool's Gold*.

Speaking of material: Maybe you've got a concept that might change their minds? If so, go ahead, write it!

What are you waiting for?

Acknowledgments

Four years ago, when I was living in downtown Manhattan, Jennifer Armstrong and I partnered on a romantic comedy location tour of the Upper West Side, something we did on the weekends. We tended to view ourselves as the movie heroines of our own lives, and while dating presented a number of frogs, we never gave up on the dream that some smart, funny guy could surprise us—and show up when we least expected him to, like in the self-help aisle at Shakespeare & Company. We loved Nora Ephron, and we loved New York. On our walking tour, which stopped at Cafe Lalo (obviously), I would reenact the scene where Dave Chappelle identifies Meg Ryan through the window. Jennifer would talk to the group about *Heartburn* and Nora's early years in the neighborhood. The *Wall Street Journal*, which tagged along one afternoon, described the event as a meetup for like-minded romantics. Some came from out of town, and it was wonderful to share in their excitement while visiting the Apthorp, Kathleen Kelly's brownstone, and Riverside Park.

I've since moved to the West Coast, and this book, for me, was a way to return to a city I love, with like-minded romantics. I could not have done it without the encouragement and support of Jennifer, my first reader, who was there for every up, down, twist, and turn. She answered all of my annoying questions over countless phone calls, texts, and emails. She kept me sane! I'm honored to call her a friend.

Kristin McGonigle tirelessly transcribed most of my epic interviews, and gives the funniest and most amazing notes—because of McGonigle, I know how *not* to drag out an interview talking about the weather. McGonigle is now the world's greatest living expert on Sven Nykvist. Thanks go out to my super-cool stepdad, Tom Chivari, for his additional transcribing work: Tracy Reiner, if you're listening, he loves you best.

I am forever grateful to my agent, Daniel Greenberg (not to be confused with Dan Greenburg), for accepting my proposal and to Mauro DiPreta, Michelle Howry, and the team at Hachette Books for making my Empire State dreams come true. Michelle, the Marie Kondo of editors, helped calm my nerves, assuage my self-doubt, and structure the book while leaving a number of extraneous subplots on the cutting room floor.

The Nora Ephron romcom universe is overflowing with warm, smart, and funny people, and I thank everyone who took the time to discuss a remarkable woman and the Valentines she and her collaborators created. People like: Tom Hanks, Rob Reiner, Delia Ephron, Rita Wilson, Parker Posey, Greg Kinnear, Bill Pullman, Victor Garber, Heather Burns, Michael Palin, Barbara Garrick, Lisa Jane Persky, J. J. Sacha, Gary Foster, Lynda Obst, Alice Arlen, Lauren Shuler Donner, Mike Medavoy, John Patrick Shanley, Julie Durk, Pat Crowley, Jane Jenkins, Caroline Aaron, Jim Skotchdopole, Jeffrey Townsend, Amanda Maher, John Lindley, Andy Scheinman, Diane Sokolow, Betsy Sokolow-Sherman, Larry Mark, Charley Beal, Bob Reitano, Richard Marks, Kevin Feige, Nora Eckstein, Jim Wiatt, Jane Adams, Randy Sokol, Maggie Murphy, Jane Musky, Jane Bartelme, G. Mac Brown, Albert Wolsky, Steve Nicolaides, Bob Bookman, Lorenzo di Bonaventura, George

Fenton, Paul Levin, Harley Jane Kozak, Tracy Reiner, Buffy Shutt, Kathy Jones, Ed Russell, Bob Pittman, Matthew Shields, Steve Riggio, Marc Shaiman, Janey Bergam, Susan Bode, Bob Riggs, Elwood Edwards, Glen Brunman, Bobby Colomby, Kathryn Galan, Alisa Lepselter, David Rogow, Sally Swisher, Scott Stambler, Scott Goldshine, Laura Rosenthal, Juliet Taylor, Tony Malkin, Fred Austin, Jake Dell, David S. Ward, Jeff Arch, Brick Mason, Connie Sawyer, Clay Griffith, Carey Lowell, LaTanya Richardson, Mike and Brenda Badalucco, Judy Ruskin, Dana Ivey, Mary Kelly, Le Clanché Durand, Valerie Wright, Brian W. Armstrong, Bob Beuth, Kyle T. Heffner, Robin Joy Allan, John Kirby, Aaron Barsky, Kerry Lyn McKissick, Carl-Gustav Nykvist, Deidre Pibram, Peter Glassman, Maya Schaper, and Jim and Loretta Healy.

Another round of thanks to the agents, managers, and communications professionals who connected me with sources, and to the wonderfully organized and helpful researchers at the Margaret Herrick Library in LA and the Paley Center for Media in New York. Hat tip to the New York Public Library, where I would have pulled all-nighters had it not been for Judy Tomkins and Meggie Sramek, who let me sleep—and drink wine—on their respective couches while watching *Crazy Ex-Girlfriend*.

Much love to advisers and sanity-keepers Tom Polansek, Caroline Waxler, Pauline Millard, Anna Davies, Debbie Newman, Chelsea Farley, Adam Seidel, Andrea and Russell Pearlman, Jessica and Mark Sampson, Marlo and Larry Beeman, and Sue and Larry Yellen. To Rex Sorgatz, Rick Webb, and Andrew Cedotal: thanks for explaining the technology behind chatrooms to a person who did not own an iPhone until 2014.

Thanks to a legal addictive stimulant, Starbucks, for keeping me awake.

Thanks to my extraordinary mother, Laurel Chivari, for

accompanying me to *Ithaca*'s premiere at the Savannah Film Festival and—from childhood—teaching me a thing or two about resilience.

Thanks to my pop culture–loving father, Babe Carlson, for indulging my childhood fascination with movies, TV, and Hollywood awards ceremonies.

Thanks to my little brother, Tim, for being the greatest living expert on Tom Hanks.

Thanks to my handsome guy, Dave Beeman, who loves Tom Hanks but isn't so sure about Joe Fox, for being my rock and making me a better human being.

Secret of life: marry a Midwesterner.

Notes

This book is the result of dozens of interviews, multiple library visits, dozens more interviews, and months of sleuthing to discover such tidbits as the identity of *Sleepless*'s first Jonah and the whereabouts of Amanda Maher, a.k.a. Clarise the babysitter, who, turns out, is not Anne Hathaway! To take readers behind the scenes of these romantic comedies and reunite Nora, Meg, and Tom on the page, I combined personal interviews as well as information from books, magazines, newspapers, and video recordings, among other sources. I interviewed several people for a 2015 *Vanity Fair* story on *You've Got Mail*, and their attributed quotes are in the past tense to make clear that they were not interviews for the book. Meanwhile, behold a comprehensive list of sourcing:

Introduction: MFEO (Made for Each Other)

page 1 *"God, are we gonna get away with this?":* "An Affair to Inspire," *Premiere*, July 1993.

Chapter 1: It Was a Sign

page 5 *Suddenly it all made sense:* Nora Ephron, "The D Word," Huffington Post, November 8, 2010, http://www.huffingtonpost.com/nora-ephron /the-d-word_1_b_779626.html.

page 5 *a sharp-witted Texan:* Campbell Robertson, "Jay Presson Allen, 84, Writer of Adaptations for the Stage, Dies," *New York Times*, May 2, 2006.

page 5 *wrote her way out:* Pat McGilligan, *Backstory 3: Interviews with Screenwriters of the 1960s* (Berkeley: University of California Press, 1997), p. 19.

page 5 *"Male characters are easier to write":* Ronald Bergan, "Jay Presson Allen: Writer of Screen Adaptations True to the Original's Essence," the *Guardian*, May 4, 2006.

page 5 *"It was so awful":* Nora Ephron interview by William Price Fox, *Writers Workshop*, PBS, first aired January 28, 1982. Accessed in November 2015 at the Paley Center for Media in New York.

page 6 *"Forget journalism—that's power":* Ibid.

page 6 *an apartment at the Ontario:* Ralph Vigoda, "Washington's Present Meets the Past in Adams-Morgan," *Baltimore Sun*, June 25, 1995.

page 6 *vowed before marrying Nora:* Dolly Langdon and Martha Smilgis, "Can Carl Bernstein Handle Deep Troth? Nora Ephron Leaves Him over an Ex-P.M.'s Daughter," *People*, January 14, 1980.

page 6 *page 8:* Ephron, "The D Word."

page 6 *"It began with a married couple at a dinner party":* Ibid.

page 7 *seven months pregnant with their second child:* James Atlas, "The Glorious Days of Nora Ephron," *Newsweek*, July 9, 2012.

page 7 *"an incredibly stupid inscription":* Ephron, "The D Word."

page 7 *"What am I doing here?":* Nora Ephron, "The Story of My Life in 3,500 Words or Less," *I Feel Bad about My Neck* (New York: Random House, 2006), p. 97.

page 7 *landed a seven-year contract:* Nell Beram, "The Troubled Marriage That Inspired Nora Ephron," Salon, August 18, 2013, http://www.salon .com/2013/08/18/the_troubled_marriage_that_inspired_nora_ephron/.

page 8 *110th Street:* Henry Ephron, *We Thought We Could Do Anything* (New York: W.W. Norton & Company), p. 1.

page 8 *irony observed by daughter Delia:* Delia Ephron, "Why I Can't Write about My Mother," *Sister Mother Husband Dog: Etc.* (New York: Penguin Group, 2013), p. 170.

page 8 *"I don't go in the kitchen very often":* "Henry Ephron, 81, Screenwriter for 'Desk Set' and Other Works," *New York Times*, September 7, 1992.

page 8 *lasted 497 performances:* "Three's a Family," International Broadway Database, https://www.ibdb.com/broadway-production/threes-a-family-1291.

page 9 *chose to name Nora:* Hallie Ephron, "Coming of Age with the Ephron Sisters—and Their Mother," *O, The Oprah Magazine*, March 2013.

page 9 *Jane Austen:* Ephron, *We Thought We Could Do Anything*, p. 26.

page 9 *plucky female protagonists:* Ephron, "Coming of Age with the Ephron Sisters—and Their Mother."

page 9 *Nora's first memory of Phoebe:* Nora Ephron interview by the Academy of Achievement in Washington, DC, June 21, 2007, http://prodloadbalancer -1055872027.us-east-1.elb.amazonaws.com/autodoc/page/eph0int-4.

page 9 *in a Spanish stucco home with 14 rooms:* Ephron, "Coming of Age with the Ephron Sisters—and Their Mother."

page 9 *a bit of trivia that fascinated Delia:* Delia Ephron, "Delia Ephron on Hollywood: 'It's Still Better as a Fantasy,'" *Vanity Fair*, March 2015.

page 9 *nightly at six thirty:* Ephron, "Coming of Age with the Ephron Sisters— and Their Mother."

page 9 *"That's a great line. Write it down":* Ephron, *Sister Mother Husband Dog: Etc.*, p. 85.

page 9 *"Never buy a red coat":* Nora Ephron, "The Legend," *I Remember Nothing: And Other Reflections* (New York: Alfred A. Knopf, 2010), p. 34.

page 9 *"Don't worship celebrities":* Masha Leon, "Delia Ephron Dishes on Life and Marriage," Forward.com, May 8, 2013, http://forward.com /schmooze/176236/delia-ephron-dishes-on-life-and-marriage/.

page 9 *"Don't join sororities":* Ibid.

page 9 *Nora paid witness:* David Remnick, "Nora Ephron," *New Yorker*, July 9, 2012.

page 10 *"My mother took me to a screening in Westwood, and I just lost it":* Lawrence Frascella, "On the Front Lines with Nora Ephron," *Rolling Stone*, July 8, 1993.

page 10 *Mark Eden Bust Developer:* Nora Ephron, "A Few Words about Breasts," *Esquire*, May 1972.

page 10 *She'd catch a matinee: The Good, the Bad, the Beautiful: Women in the Movies*, TNT, first aired May 17, 1996. Accessed in November 2015 at the Paley Center for Media in New York.

page 10 *"She was as close as you could get to someone who was interesting and quirky and smart":* Ibid.

page 10 *side job at a local bookstore:* Susan L. Weis, "BEA: The Celebration of Bookselling," Shelf Awareness, June 4, 2007, http://www.shelf-awareness.com /issue.html?issue=448#m2923.

page 10 *once gift-wrapping a book for Cary Grant:* Tom Hanks's speech at the 2013 Women in the World Summit in New York, April 5, 2013, http://livestream.com/WomenInTheWorld/womenintheworld/videos/15573840.

page 10 *"Most Likely to Succeed":* Leslie Bennetts, "Nora's Arc," *Vanity Fair*, February 1992.

page 10 *number one out of 309 students:* According to Jacob Bernstein's documentary *Everything Is Copy*, first screened September 29, 2015, at the New York Film Festival.

page 10 *fire future billionaire Barry Diller:* Ibid.

page 11 *"There was not a lot of feminine about Nora":* Ibid.

page 11 *impressed the judges:* Ephron, "The Story of My Life in 3,500 Words or Less," *I Feel Bad about My Neck*, p. 99.

page 11 *"You will have a career like me":* Ephron, *Sister Mother Husband Dog: Etc.*, p. 49.

page 11 *"Everything is copy":* Ephron, "The Story of My Life in 3,500 Words or Less," *I Feel Bad about My Neck*, p. 98.

page 11 *"If you came back to her with a sad story, she had no interest in it whatsoever":* Matt Weinstock, "Nora Ephron's Potato-Chip Legacy," the

Paris Review's website, June 28, 2012, https://www.theparisreview.org
/blog/2012/06/28/nora-ephron%E2%80%99s-potato-chip-legacy/.

page 11 *"When you slip on a banana peel":* Ephron, "The Story of My Life in
3,500 Words or Less," *I Feel Bad about My Neck*, p. 102.

page 11 *referenced her letters home from Wellesley College:* Ephron, "The Legend,"
I Remember Nothing: And Other Reflections, p. 37.

page 12 *the table had to be set just so:* Beram, "The Troubled Marriage That
Inspired Nora Ephron."

page 12 *"When she found out my father was fooling around with other women, she
didn't walk out on him like Ibsen's Nora":* Ephron, "Coming of Age with the
Ephron Sisters—and Their Mother."

page 12 *"It was hard to change forty years of thinking that sex is a private thing":*
Ephron, *We Thought We Could Do Anything*, p. 205.

page 12 *She died on October 13, 1971:* Beram, "The Troubled Marriage That
Inspired Nora Ephron."

page 12 *"You're a reporter":* Nora Ephron, "The Mink Coat," *Esquire*, December
1975.

page 13 *"My sister Delia says this, and it's true":* Ephron, "The Story of My Life in
3,500 Words or Less," *I Feel Bad about My Neck*, p. 106.

page 13 *The retelling of their first date ended with a punchline: Everything Is Copy.*

page 13 *outlined requirements for her ideal husband:* Rachel Samstat, Nora's alter
ego, describes her ideal man on page 83 in the 1996 paperback edition of
Heartburn (New York: Alfred K. Knopf, 1983).

page 13 *Twenty-five years and 11 months old:* Ephron, *Heartburn*, p. 80.

page 14 *dating a journalist, too:* Ephron, "Journalism: A Love Story," *I Remember
Nothing: And Other Reflections*, p. 17.

page 14 *got married in the Rainbow Room:* Richard Cohen, *She Made Me Laugh:
My Friend Nora Ephron* (New York: Simon & Schuster, 2016), p. 69.

page 14 *lavender apartment:* Sally Quinn, "Sally Quinn shares memories of her
friendship with Nora Ephron," *Washington Post*, June 27, 2012.

page 14 *they spoke in high-pitched voices:* Nora Ephron, "Forget the Hamsters,"
the *Guardian*, November 5, 2004.

page 15 *bestselling nonfiction book of 1965:* Alice Payne Hackett, *70 Years of
Best Sellers* (New York: R. R. Bowker Co., 1967), p. 227.

page 15 *"We would have dinner parties":* Everything Is Copy.

page 15 *stung the pioneering* Cosmopolitan *editor as oversensitive, "Almost but
not quite tasteless":* Nora Ephron, "Helen Gurley Brown: 'If You're a Little
Mouseburger, Come with Me...,'" *Esquire*, February 1970.

page 15 *"silly," "frothy," and "giddy":* Nora Ephron, "Dorothy Schiff and the *New
York Post*," *Esquire*, April 1975.

page 16 *"almost unbearably girlish sensibility":* Nora Ephron, "Dorothy Parker,"
Esquire, October 1973.

page 16 *While Gloria Steinem represented:* Nora Ephron, "Miami," *Esquire*,
November 1972.

page 16 *rape fantasy involving "faceless" men:* Nora Ephron, "Fantasies," *Esquire*, July 1972.

page 16 *"I am skinny and have a long face, long chin, and dark hair and a snaggletooth that I've worked very hard to get":* Michael S. Lasky, "Nice to See Nora Ephron Happy in Her Work," *Writer's Digest*, April 1974.

page 17 *"He's like on this plane—it's terrible—and then I get to marry Mike Nichols!":* From footage of Nora's *Dick Cavett Show* appearance in *Everything Is Copy*.

page 17–18 *at Marie Brenner's party: Everything Is Copy.*

page 18 *in 1973:* Langdon and Smilgis, "Can Carl Bernstein Handle Deep Troth? Nora Ephron Leaves Him over an Ex-P.M.'s Daughter."

page 18 *made better life choices:* Alicia C. Shepard, "Woodward and Bernstein Uncovered," *Washingtonian*, September 1, 2003.

page 18 *University of Maryland dropout:* Michael Olesker, "Paying, parking and getting pilloried," *Baltimore Sun*, February 25, 1996.

page 19 *briefly dated Carl: Everything Is Copy.*

page 19 *Marie Brenner gets a phone call:* Ibid.

page 19 *secular Jew:* Clare Lennon, "Watergate reporter urges residents to dig deep for truth in UF speech," *Gainesville Sun*, April 13, 2013.

page 19 *FBI scrutiny:* Walt Harrington, "He Went from Watergate to 'Heartburn,' from Investigative Superstar to Celebrity Dinner Guest. Now Bernstein's Back with an Evocative Book on His Embattled Childhood, but He's Still Carl after All These Years," *Washington Post*, March 19, 1989.

page 19 *The Feds even crashed Carl's bar mitzvah:* Ibid.

page 20 *She found the notion of going dateless to a dinner party a distraction:* Lasky, "Nice to See Nora Ephron Happy in Her Work."

page 20 *she hated Washington: Everything Is Copy.*

page 20 *"As happens in great love affairs, you want the other person to know who you are at the most intimate and deepest levels": Everything Is Copy.*

page 20 *"so intense in his aura": Everything Is Copy.*

page 20 *"Carl! Nora is right across the room":* Liz Smith, *Natural Blonde* (New York: Hyperion, 2000), p. 228.

page 21 *People talk, and people said:* Langdon and Smilgis, "Can Carl Bernstein Handle Deep Troth? Nora Ephron Leaves Him over an Ex-P.M.'s Daughter."

page 21 *shortly after Nora's group therapy session:* Richard Cohen, *She Made Me Laugh: My Friend Nora Ephron* (New York: Simon & Schuster, 2016), p. 121.

page 22 *"Can you believe they served that lettuce?":* Shepard, "Woodward and Bernstein Uncovered."

page 22 *"She was really a well-known journalist and she was really successful at it and a lot of people were jealous of that":* Ariel Levy, "Nora Knows What to Do," *New Yorker*, July 6 and 13, 2009 issue.

page 23 *admitted that she and Carl should not have attempted to revise an expert's draft:* Rachel Abramowitz, *Is That a Gun in Your Pocket?: Women's Experience of Power in Hollywood* (New York: Random House, 2000), p. 229.

page 23 *"does things so economically that you can't believe it":* Ibid.

page 23 *"the daughter of a singer who outdoes her mother by becoming a rock star":* Ibid.

page 23 *"shared an easygoing equality of status":* Robert Bookman, "Nora Ephron: The First Modern Woman I Knew," Daily Beast, June 28, 2012, http:// www.thedailybeast.com/articles/2012/06/28/nora-ephron-the-first-modern -woman-i-knew.html.

page 24 *patronized incestuous writers' hang Elaine's:* Langdon and Smilgis, "Can Carl Bernstein Handle Deep Troth? Nora Ephron Leaves Him over an Ex-P.M.'s Daughter."

page 24 *startled close friends like* New Yorker *writer Ken Auletta and* Washington Post *columnist Richard Cohen: Everything Is Copy.*

page 24 *reportedly questioned Carl that summer:* Langdon and Smilgis, "Can Carl Bernstein Handle Deep Troth? Nora Ephron Leaves Him over an Ex-P.M.'s Daughter."

page 24 *"I Love You Truly":* Ephron, "The D Word."

page 25 *"We didn't know each other at the time":* Nancy Griffin, "That's the Way Love Goes," *Premiere*, July 1993.

page 25 *"I just took my head and smacked it into his stomach":* Rachel Abramowitz, "Private Meg," *Premiere*, May 1996.

page 25 *She was a popular and magnetic student:* Karen S. Schneider, "Educating Meg," *People*, August 2, 1993.

page 26 *"Usually in high school":* Ibid.

page 26 *original queen was kicked out of school:* Abramowitz, "Private Meg."

page 26 *"Inane Happiness":* "Meg Ryan School Days," Meg Ryan Co UK, http:// www.megryan.co.uk/meg-ryan-schooldays.htm.

page 26 *15-year-old Meg:* Kevin Sessums, "Maximum Meg," *Vanity Fair*, May 1995.

page 26 *"My husband told me":* Ibid.

page 26 *"The thing I want to be clear about":* Ibid.

page 26 *at the New England boarding school Choate Rosemary Hall:* Schneider, "Educating Meg," *People*.

page 27 *assisted a casting director:* Ibid.

page 27 *changed her last name from Hyra to Ryan:* Ibid.

page 27 *dropped out of New York University's journalism program:* Julie Miller, "Meg Ryan Is Moving Past Her Movie Star Days, and You Should Too," VF.com, September 8, 2016, http://www.vanityfair.com /hollywood/2016/09/meg-ryan-ithaca-interview.

page 27 *20 million viewers:* Ann Tatko-Peterson, "Top Five: Supercouples reigned on 'As The World Turns,'" *Mercury News*, August 13, 2016.

page 27 *dated movie husband Anthony Edwards:* Abramowitz, "Private Meg."

page 28 *"I remember thinking I had to stay away from him":* Ibid.

page 28 *"We went to dinner, I think once, as friends":* George Kalogerakis, "When Dennis Met Meg," *Vogue*, November 1993.

page 29 *Lightning struck on the movie's Austin shoot:* Here, I re-created a scene from a quote Dennis Quaid gave to the May 1996 issue of *Premiere*, saying: "We were in this place in Austin one night. The music was playing really loud, in this really rowdy place. People were dancing on the tables. We found ourselves in a corner table with a bunch of other people. For some reason, I just put my arms around her and it was like a thunderbolt. Both of us felt, 'This is it; we're gonna be together,' without saying a word."

page 29 *one of Nora's biggest fears:* Ephron, "The D Word."

page 29 *"Head over heels":* Nora Ephron, "Moving On," *I Feel Bad about My Neck*, p. 66.

page 29 *landmark status in 1969:* Mike Claffey, "Body Found on W. Side Roof," *New York Daily News*, February 12, 1997.

page 30 *five-bedroom abode on the fifth floor:* Ibid.

page 30 *"male nightmare":* Leslie Bennetts, "Nora's Arc."

page 30 *Nora dreamed of being Barbara Walters:* Nora Ephron, "A Star Is Born," *New York*, October 1, 1973.

page 31 *quoting Lillian Hellman:* Ibid.

page 31 *"I think probably the feeling I like least in the whole world is feeling dumb":* Leslie Bennetts, "Nora's Arc."

page 31 *"I'm 100 percent for her having written the book":* Jesse Kornbluth, "Scenes from a Marriage," *New York*, March 14, 1983.

page 31 *"Obviously, I wish Nora hadn't written it":* Ibid.

page 32 *"kind of Joan Rivers sensibility":* Tony Schwartz, "Playboy Interview: Carl Bernstein," *Playboy*, September 1986.

page 32 *suggested Nora to her agency colleague and boyfriend Sam Cohn:* Abramowitz, *Is That a Gun in Your Pocket?*, p. 230.

page 33 *"Meryl wanted to do it":* Lizzie Francke, *Script Girls: Women Screenwriters in Hollywood* (London: British Film Institute, 1994), p. 106.

page 34 *"It's like when you were in high school and nobody would choose you":* Frascella, "On the Front Lines with Nora Ephron."

page 34 *read the transcript:* Abramowitz, *Is That a Gun in Your Pocket?*, p. 231.

page 34 *"I couldn't believe what Meryl wanted to wear as Karen Silkwood":* Frascella, "On the Front Lines with Nora Ephron."

page 35 *Dustin declined out of respect for Carl:* Shepard, "Woodward and Bernstein Uncovered."

page 36 *They were a celebrity couple: Everything Is Copy.*

page 36 *tried to kill the film:* Bennetts, "Nora's Arc."

page 37 *"portrayed at all times as a caring, loving and conscientious father":* Johanna Steinmetz, "'Heartburn' Loses Some of Its Acid in Screen Version," *Chicago Tribune*, July 25, 1986.

page 37 *correctly guessed Deep Throat's identity:* Nora Ephron, "Deep Throat and Me: Now It Can Be Told, and Not For the First Time Either," Huffington Post, May 31, 2005, http://www.huffingtonpost.com/nora-ephron/deep-throat -and-me-now-it_b_1917.html.

page 37 *"wasn't pleased with Heartburn":* Abramowitz, *Is That a Gun in Your Pocket?*, p. 310.

page 37 *Tom escorted her down the aisle:* A re-creation of Bill Zehme's observations of the *Big* screening in his article, "Tom Hanks Is Mr. Big," *Rolling Stone*, June 30, 1988, http://www.rollingstone.com/movies/features/mr-big-19880630. Tom had been a few weeks away from marrying Rita Wilson, and on the cusp of bigger stardom. Zehme was there. His reporting was invaluable as I sought to capture this then-rising star, with his oddball energy and feet planted firmly on the ground.

page 38 *$100 million at the box office:* Penny Marshall, *My Mother Was Nuts: A Memoir* (New York: Houghton Mifflin Harcourt Publishing Company, 2012), p. 327.

page 38 *"Once Bobby wanted to do it, then Tom wanted to do it":* Abramowitz, *Is That a Gun in Your Pocket?*, p. 301.

page 38 *"insh":* Beverly Walker, "Hanks to You," *Film Comment*, March/April 2009 issue.

page 38 *"He was such a great kid":* Tom Hanks interview by Barbara Walters for her celebrity-interview special, which was first aired January 31, 1989, on ABC. Accessed in November 2015 at the Paley Center for Media in New York.

page 39 *"It's just a movie, hon":* Zehme, "Tom Hanks Is Mr. Big."

page 39 *"I'm glad my movies have met with some success":* From footage of Hanks's October 8, 1988, *Saturday Night Live* appearance at the Paley Center for Media.

page 39 *"I don't threaten any man's sense of virility":* Ingrid Sischy, "New Again," *Interview*, March 1994.

page 39 *he took five-year-old Tom:* And other details from Tom's early life reported by Karen S. Schneider, "Tom on Top," *People*, August 3, 1988.

page 39 *Male Class Cutup:* Christopher Connelly, "Tom Hanks Seriously," *Premiere*, April 1989.

page 39 *"horribly, painfully, terribly shy":* Zehme, "Tom Hanks Is Mr. Big."

page 40 *"I was attracted to acting because it was fun":* Richard Corliss, Cathy Booth, and Jeffrey Ressner, "Tom Terrific," *Time*, December 21, 1998.

page 40 *"Nobody on my track team was funny":* Patrick Healy, "Tom Hanks, Broadway's New Kid," *New York Times*, February 20, 2013.

page 40 *graduated from Skyline High to study at Chabot:* And other Hanksian history in Connelly's "Tom Hanks Seriously."

page 40 *earned $800:* Ibid.

page 40 *"You see pictures of it":* Hanks's interview with Johnny Carson on the *Tonight Show*, airing February 4, 1982, on NBC. Footage accessed at the Paley Center for Media in November 2015.

page 40 *number of murders rose during the 1970s:* Chris Mitchell, "The Killing of Murder," *New York*, January 7, 2008.

page 40 *an increase in the crime rate:* Kevin Baker, "'Welcome to Fear City'— the inside story of New York's civil war, 40 years on," the *Guardian*, May 18, 2015, https://www.theguardian.com/cities/2015/may/18 /welcome-to-fear-city-the-inside-story-of-new-yorks-civil-war-40-years-on.

page 40 *the migration of thousands of New Yorkers:* Richard D. Lyons, "New Study Finds More People in the City," *New York Times*, May 24, 1987, http://www.nytimes.com/1987/05/24/realestate/new-study-finds-more-people-in-the-city.html.

page 40 *"I lived around the corner from Broadway":* Healy, "Tom Hanks, Broadway's New Kid."

page 41 *commiserated over their not-great married lives:* Greg Braxton, "'Bosom Buddies still close to Tom Hanks' heart,'" *Los Angeles Times*, April 19, 2010.

page 41 *$100,000:* Kurt Andersen, "The Tom Hanks Phenomenon," *New Yorker*, December 17, 1998.

page 41 *"He came in wearing these 501 Levi's":* Ibid.

page 42 *"You can't put all the blame on the film business":* Patrick Goldstein, "Tom Hanks, New King of Cutups," *Los Angeles Times*, August 1, 1986.

page 42 *separated in 1985:* David Blum, "Tom Hanks's Real Splash," *New York*, July 28, 1986.

page 42 *"It was very When Harry Met Sally":* Bronwen Hruska, "'Seattle' Sob Story," *Entertainment Weekly*, July 9, 1993.

page 42 *engaged to a man she didn't love: People* staff, "Tom Hanks & Rita Wilson," *People*, February 12, 1996.

page 42 *"we were holding hands and we were waiting for the traffic light to change":* Rita Wilson interview by Piers Morgan on a CNN broadcast that aired May 11, 2012. Video: http://www.cnn.com/videos/bestoftv/2012/05/11/piers-morgan-rita-wilson-tom-hanks.cnn.

page 42 *New Year's Eve 1987 in St. Bart's:* Josh Eells, "A League of His Own: Tom Hanks, American Icon," *Rolling Stone*, December 10, 2012.

page 43 *at Saint Sophia Greek Orthodox Cathedral:* Trina Yannicos, "Hollywood's Greek Super Couple: Hanks and Wilson," Hollywood Greek Reporter, September 15, 2008, http://hollywood.greekreporter.com/2008/09/15/hollywoods-greek-super-couple-tom-hanks-and-rita-wilson/.

page 43 *"all the change I experienced at home made me feel ahead of everybody else":* Kristine McKenna, "The 'Philadelphia' Story," *Chicago Tribune*, January 9, 1994.

page 43 *Mort Zuckerman:* Alessandra Stanley, "Nora Ephron's Hollywood Ending," *New York Times*, June 27, 2012.

page 43 *"I realized I don't want to die with Joe Fox":* Kathy Henderson, "Maria Tucci and Carol Kane on *Lucky Guy* Scribe Nora Ephron's Unblinking Honesty and Love of Theater," Broadway.com, March 7, 2013, http://www.broadway.com/buzz/167856/maria-tucci-and-carol-kane-on-lucky-guy-scribe-nora-ephrons-unblinking-honesty-and-love-of-theater/.

page 44 *"Not unlike Henry Hill, I grew up in Bensonhurst":* Nick Pileggi interview by Tony Guida for *Tony Guida's NY* on CUNY TV. Published to YouTube on December 2, 2015: https://www.youtube.com/watch?v=kj5r9OpQaiY.

page 44 *"By the third date I had no questions":* Bennetts, "Nora's Arc."

page 44 *"instantly caught pinkeye":* Levy, "Nora Knows What to Do."

page 44 *surprise wedding:* Levy, "Nora Knows What to Do."

page 44 *March 28, 1987:* Moira Mulligan, "Personalities," *Washington Post*, March 28, 1987.

page 44 *"She had fallen in love":* Jacob Bernstein, "Nora Ephron's Final Act," *New York Times Magazine*, March 6, 2013.

Chapter 2: Transitional People

page 46 *1984:* Nora Ephron, "When Harry Met Sally dot dot dot," *Nora Ephron Collected*, p. 204.

page 46 *the Russian Tea Room:* A conversation between Nora Ephron and Rob Reiner for the *When Harry Met Sally* Collector's Edition DVD, released January 6, 2015.

page 46 *206 theaters, grossing $4.5 million:* Box Office Mojo, http://www.boxofficemojo.com/movies/?id=thisisspinaltap.htm.

page 47 *"I remember being slightly perplexed":* Ephron, "When Harry Met Sally dot dot dot," *Nora Ephron Collected*, p. 204.

page 47 *"you're the funniest person who doesn't get paid for it":* Robert Welkos, "Between a Rock and a Reiner Stand a Few Other Guys," *Los Angeles Times*, December 6, 1992.

page 48 *vetoed the first pitch:* Ephron and Rob Reiner discussion, *When Harry Met Sally* Collector's Edition DVD.

page 48 *"Two people become friends":* Ibid.

page 48 *"I can do that":* Ibid.

page 48 *February 1985:* "When Harry Met Sally dot dot dot," *Nora Ephron Collected*, p. 205.

page 49 *"I think I'm not ready for a relationship":* Ephron, "When Harry Met Sally dot dot dot," *Nora Ephron Collected*, p. 206.

page 49 *Rob clarified the project further:* Ephron, "When Harry Met Sally dot dot dot," *Nora Ephron Collected*, p. 207.

page 49 *brushes of Ingmar Bergman:* Reiner told me during our interview in November 2015 that he had been inspired initially by Bergman's *Scenes from a Marriage*.

page 50 *"He is the all-time gloom-and-doom guy, but he's funny":* George Stevens Jr., *Conversations at the American Film Institute with the Great Moviemakers* (New York: Alfred A. Knopf, 2012), p. 193.

page 50 *"I'm not precisely chirpy":* Ephron, "When Harry Met Sally dot dot dot," *Nora Ephron Collected*, p. 206.

page 51 *"she was Jewish and he was Gentile":* Abramowitz, *Is That a Gun in Your Pocket?*, p. 311.

page 51 *"every single time saying horrible things":* Nora Ephron commentary in *When Harry Met Sally* Collector's Edition DVD.

page 51 *"such a stupid thing to say":* Transcript from a June 7, 1993, press conference for *Sleepless in Seattle*, included the Argentina Brunetti papers at the Margaret Herrick Library in Los Angeles.

page 52 *"Once she put it in the movie, I couldn't throw it out":* Stanley, "Nora Ephron's Hollywood Ending."

page 52 *"probably began in* The Taming of the Shrew*"*: Stevens, *Conversations at the American Film Institute with the Great Moviemakers*, p. 194.

page 52 *one big long girls' night:* Hat tip to my friend Caroline Waxler, who had the original formulation of this joke in her 2005 standup comedy act and told it much better.

page 52 *"All of the guys I know"*: Ibid.

page 54 *"Harry and Sally belonged together"*: Ephron, "When Harry Met Sally dot dot dot," *Nora Ephron Collected*, p. 209.

page 55 *"I couldn't imagine how they could ever get together"*: Rob Reiner commentary in *When Harry Met Sally* Collector's Edition DVD.

page 55 *"I think for the story it really doesn't feel right"*: Rob Reiner commentary in *When Harry Met Sally* Collector's Edition DVD.

page 55 *"First of all, how was I going to do it with my kids?"*: Abramowitz, *Is That a Gun in Your Pocket?*, p. 362.

page 56 *differences with boss Barry Diller:* Al Delugach, "Horn Resigns as President of Fox Studio," *Los Angeles Times*, August 19, 1986.

page 56 *"sitting like a lox"*: Reiner's October 3, 2007, speech at an American Film Institute tribute to *When Harry Met Sally*, published May 5, 2009, on YouTube. Video: https://www.youtube.com/watch?v=Ke4qcrOX0nM.

page 56 *"He was sitting"*: Bruce Weber, "Can Men and Women Be Friends?," *New York Times*, July 9, 1989.

page 58 *"I loved it"*: Ephron, "When Harry Met Sally dot dot dot," *Nora Ephron Collected*, p. 210.

page 58 *"It was avocado and bacon and sprouts and cheese"*: Ephron and Rob Reiner discussion, *When Harry Met Sally* Collector's Edition DVD.

page 58 *"toasted and slightly burnt," the "bacon crisp"*: Ephron, "When Harry Met Sally dot dot dot," *Nora Ephron Collected*, p. 207.

page 58 *"My God"*: Ephron and Rob Reiner discussion, *When Harry Met Sally* Collector's Edition DVD.

page 58 *"I just like it the way I like it"*: Ephron, "When Harry Met Sally dot dot dot," *Nora Ephron Collected*, p. 207.

page 59 *Michael Keaton:* Abramowitz, *Is That a Gun in Your Pocket?*, p. 312.

page 59 *"I don't think Tom ever regretted not doing it"*: Ibid.

page 59 *hoped that Rob:* Sleepless in Seattle press conference transcript, June 7, 1993, Argentina Brunetti papers.

page 59 *worried the screenplay was too Woody Allen:* Bradford Evans, "The Lost Roles of Albert Brooks," Splitsider, June 30, 2011, http://splitsider.com/2011/06/the-lost-roles-of-albert-brooks/.

page 59 *"Richard Dreyfuss turned it down"*: Abramowitz, *Is That a Gun in Your Pocket?*, p. 312.

page 60 *tanked at the box office:* Box Office Mojo, http://www.boxofficemojo.com/movies/?id=letitride.htm.

page 60 *"I had to see everybody"*: Gregg Kilday, "When Billy Met Rob," *Los Angeles Times*, July 16, 1989.

page 61 *Billy didn't wait to consult his people:* Ibid.

page 61 *"It was always, 'Well, she could do it'"*: Sandra Gonzales, "Mindy Kaling Interviews Billy Crystal ahead of 'Mindy Project' Finale," *Entertainment Weekly*, May 5, 2014.

page 62 *"There was a really particular rhythm on the page"*: *Everything Is Copy*.

page 62 *Meg backed out:* Janet Hirshenson and Jane Jenkins, *A Star Is Found: Our Adventures Casting Some of Hollywood's Biggest Movies* (New York: Mariner Books, 2007), p. 287.

page 62 *One that could last:* Betsy Pickle, "Meg Ryan Is Trying Hard to Become Hip," *Chicago Tribune*, June 24, 1988.

page 62 *"What I love best about the movies is watching difficult choices being worked out"*: Hal Rubenstein, "Meg Ryan," *Vogue*, June 1988.

page 62 *"For the first time in my life I don't play the girl"*: Vintage interview with Ryan in *When Harry Met Sally—Special Edition* DVD, released January 31, 2006.

page 63 *"Well, why don't I just do it?"*: Ryan's recollection in *Everything Is Copy*.

page 63 *"Would you do that?"*: Ibid.

page 63 *"doesn't necessarily have punchlines in that script, but she's behaviorally funny. It came out of understanding that"*: Cohen, *She Made Me Laugh: My Friend Nora Ephron*, p. 193.

page 63 *"I don't know if we can get away with this"*: From Reiner and Billy Crystal's recounting of the orgasm scene's origins at the 2007 AFI tribute to their film. Crystal had suggested Estelle Reiner to deliver the famous line.

page 63 *At 65 years old:* "Singer-Actress Estelle Reiner Dies," Emmys.com, October 30, 2008, http://www.emmys.com/news/singer-actress-estelle-reiner -dies-jazz-vocalist-wife-carl-reiner-october-30-2008.

page 63 *"Marry someone who can stand you"*: Pat Gallagher, "Carl Reiner—the Art of Being Funny," Huffington Post, http://www.huffingtonpost.com/pat -gallagher/carl-reiner-the-art-of-being-funny_b_2567815.html.

page 64 *"Mom, we got a scene here"*: Before AFI's 2007 screening of *When Harry Met Sally*, Reiner recalled his exchange with Estelle while recruiting her to appear in what would turn out to be the most famous scene.

page 66 *MOD.55s:* Henry Allen, "Everything You Always Wanted to Know about Specs," *Washington Post*, December 16, 1991.

page 66 *Gloria Gresham:* Betty Goodwin, "Screen Style," *Los Angeles Times*, August 11, 1989; Elaine Louie, "Gloria Gresham, Costume Designer," *New York Times*, August 4, 1991.

page 67 *it would be funny if Sally's tresses got younger as she grew older:* Ephron commentary, *When Harry Met Sally* Collector's Edition DVD.

page 67 *August 29, 1988:* "When Harry Met Sally," Turner Classic Movies' production notes, http://www.tcm.com/tcmdb/title/95478/When-Harry-Met -Sally-/misc-notes.html.

page 68 *"It just fit my personality. . . . I didn't have to act"*: Carrie Fisher commentary, *When Harry Met Sally* Collector's Edition DVD.

page 69 *"We improvised our way into the scene"*: Lisa Jane Persky, "When Harry Met Sally, Remembered by Alice," Vulture, July 18, 2014, http://www.vulture .com/2014/07/when-harry-met-sally-remembered-by-alice.html.

page 71 *"resented that the girls would say, 'It was a boys' club'"*: Billy Crystal commentary, *When Harry Met Sally—Special Edition* DVD.

page 72 *"It's really not about you"*: Meg Ryan interview by James Lipton for *Bravo's Inside the Actors Studio* in an episode that aired July 27, 1997.

page 73 *"There is no question that everyone who complains about how little Hollywood cares about women characters is telling the truth"*: Francke, *Script Girls*, p. 110.

Chapter 3: The Orgasm and the Aftershock

page 74 *"What was I thinking?"*: The interaction between Reiner and Barry Sonnenfeld was based on remarks Sonnenfeld made when the filmmaker received the Film Society of Lincoln Center's Chaplin Award on April 28, 2014. I consulted Paula Schwartz's lovely write-up on reellifewithjane.com, http://www.reellifewithjane.com/2014/04/rob-reiner-film-society-lincoln-center-chaplin-award/.

page 74 *"happy denial"*: Broadcaster David Sheehan's 1994 interview with Meg Ryan, https://www.youtube.com/watch?v=x0ogvmrgVZU.

page 75 *"What's Dennis going to think?"*: Weber, "Can Men and Women Be Friends?"

page 75 *"Meg, it's in a deli. It's not a sex thing. It's comedy"*: Weber, "Can Men and Women Be Friends?"

page 77 *"They had sex, and she faked an orgasm"*: Ibid.

page 79 *around 30 takes:* Ephron commentary, *When Harry Met Sally* Collector's Edition DVD.

page 79 *mimicked her facial contortions:* In a *When Harry Met Sally—Special Edition* DVD featurette, Ryan described Reiner getting emotional while she filmed a crying scene.

page 79 *"That's as sexy as I get in any of my movies"*: Reiner commentary, *When Harry Met Sally* Collector's Edition DVD.

page 81 *"You know, you really shouldn't smoke"*: Sonnenfeld recounted the amusing banter between Reiner and Michele Singer during Reiner's Chaplin Award celebration in 2014.

page 82 *A script given to actors:* Actor Bob Beuth, who played Man on Aisle, was gracious enough to offer a copy of a script that was revised shortly before the shoot in late August 1988. Bob: You're a mensch.

page 82 *Nora had pulled for Harry to look up from his navel:* Abramowitz, *Is That a Gun in Your Pocket?*, p. 312.

page 83 *the ending that we all know and love:* Fun fact time! The late-August script addition of Harry's ode to Sally included the lines "I even loved when you used my sweater for a Kleenex" and "I love the way your mouth turns down just a little bit, right there." Those were removed, with Billy's changes, for the LA reshoot. View the original pro-Sally monologue here: http://www.dailyscript.com/scripts/whenharrymesally.pdf.

page 84 *walked home in high spirits:* Ephron regaled the audience at a 2009 TimesTalks panel with her memory of reacting to the raw footage of Harry and Sally's bungled reconciliation. Watch the filmmaker in her arch, suffers-no-fools glory on YouTube: https://www.youtube.com /watch?v=5Oqo_fFCkps.

page 84 *"It was the first time we shot the last scene in the movie":* Ibid.

page 86 *May 31:* Kilday, "When Billy Met Rob."

page 86 *grabbed hands:* Sandra Gonzalez, "Mindy Kaling Interviews Billy Crystal ahead of 'Mindy Project' Finale."

page 86 *As Nora suspected:* Alessandra Stanley, "When Nora Met Wendy," *New York Times*, January 24, 1991.

page 86 *This made her happy:* Ibid.

page 86 *Beverly Hills premiere:* Jeannine Stein, "Into the Night," *Los Angeles Times*, July 17, 1989; John Sellers, "The When Harry Met Sally Movie Premiere Was So 1989," Vulture, July 14, 2014, http://www.vulture .com/2014/07/when-harry-met-sally-premiere-photos.html.

page 87 *married in Hawaii on May 19:* "Harry and Sally Meet a Big Squeeze in Beverly Hills," *People*, July 31, 1989, http://people.com /archive/harry-and-sally-meet-a-big-squeeze-in-beverly-hills-vol-32-no-5/.

page 87 *"He must be 12!":* Stein, "Into the Night."

page 87 *stranded on the Hawaii set:* Ibid.

page 87 *$93 million:* That number and other details on the film's theatrical release and its competition can be found at Box Office Mojo, http://www .boxofficemojo.com/movies/?id=whenharrymetsally.htm.

page 87 *$51 million:* Box Office Mojo, http://www.boxofficemojo.com /movies/?id=broadcastnews.htm.

page 87 *$64 million:* Box Office Mojo, http://www.boxofficemojo.com /movies/?id=workinggirl.htm.

page 87 *$81 million:* Box Office Mojo, http://www.boxofficemojo.com /movies/?id=moonstruck.htm.

page 87 *"You seem quite wise":* Ephron, "When Harry Met Sally dot dot dot," *Nora Ephron Collected*, p. 211.

page 88 *"The truth is that men don't want to be friends with women":* Ibid.

page 89 *London premiere:* Getty Images' archive was a treasure trove of photographs from the UK outing. Diana and Meg were both coming into their own, but with dramatically different styles.

page 90 *"just belching it out":* Kelly Woo, "Billy Crystal Remembers Princess Diana's 'Belching' Reaction to the 'When Harry Met Sally' Orgasm Scene," Moviefone, September 20, 2013, https://www.moviefone .com/2013/09/20/billy-crystal-princess-diana-when-harry-met-sally/.

page 90 *Princess Di asked to screen the movie privately with friends—at Buckingham Palace:* Reiner's *When Harry Met Sally* DVD commentary.

page 90 *Nora happened to be on a plane:* Ephron recalled the moment when she watched a censored version of the movie, sans orgasm, on

a flight during an interview with Makers, http://www.makers.com
/moments/orgasm-scene-10000-ft.

page 90 *You're a Republican who's never had an orgasm:* Ephron's note to Meg
Ryan on playing Annie Reed, as relayed in her commentary in the *Sleepless in
Seattle—10th Anniversary Edition* DVD (1993).

Chapter 4: This Is Her Life

page 92 *claimed vacancies in the 1960s and 1970:* Katherine Marsh, "Palace
Revolt," *New York Times*, May 12, 2002.

page 92 *yuppie invasion:* Patricia Morrisroe, "The New Class," *New York*, May 13,
1985.

page 92 *on posh Fifth Avenue:* David Knowles, "Tom Hanks, Wife Rita Wilson
List Four Bedroom, 5.5 Bath California Mansion for $2.5 Million," *Daily News*,
June 14, 2013; Eells, "A League of His Own: Tom Hanks, American Icon."

page 93 *Soundstage 30:* Joy Horowitz, "Shanley's 'Volcano' Bubbles with Burning
Angst," *New York Times*, September 3, 1989.

page 94 *intense fear of death:* Horowitz, "Shanley's 'Volcano' Bubbles with
Burning Angst."

page 94 *New York University dropout:* Alex Witchel, "The Confessions of John
Patrick Shanley," *New York Times Magazine*, November 7, 2004.

page 95 *She thought that each character, a part of the whole, represented a
woman's growth through risk-taking:* Horowitz, "Shanley's 'Volcano' Bubbles
with Burning Angst."

page 97 *two days:* Ibid.

page 97 *"Meg is one of the all-time great people I know":* J. D. Reed, "Digital
Dish," *People*, January 16, 1995.

page 97 *Stage 24: My Blue Heaven* filming locations, IMDb, http://www.imdb.com
/title/tt0100212/locations?ref_=ttco_ql_6.

page 98 *a framed picture of John Gotti:* Levy, "Nora Knows What to Do."

page 98 *debuted at number one: Pretty Woman* box office, Box Office Mojo,
http://www.boxofficemojo.com/movies/?page=weekend&id=prettywoman.htm.

page 98 *She passed:* Meg Ryan interview by Barbara Walters for Walters's ABC
special airing March 21, 1994, and accessed in November 2015 at the Paley
Center for Media in New York.

page 98 *rejected* Ghost…Silence of the Lambs*:* Ibid.

page 99 *"It wasn't a druther situation":* Ibid.

page 99 *Casting decisions spelled agony:* "Casting is always a drama for Meg. She
agonizes," a talent agent said in the January 14, 1994, issue of *Entertainment
Weekly*, http://www.ew.com/article/1994/01/14/shes-just-girl-who-cant-say-yes.

page 100 *widened gender gap in 1989:* Abramowitz, *Is That a Gun in Your
Pocket?*, p. 335.

page 101 *Montana:* Kalogerakis, "When Dennis Met Meg."

page 101 *confessed his cocaine addiction:* Abramowitz, "Private Meg."

page 101 *1990:* Eric Richter, "Her Funny Valentine: Dennis Quaid and Meg Ryan Tied the Knot 10 Years Ago," *Entertainment Weekly*, February 16, 2001.

page 101 *went into therapy and Al-Anon:* Ibid.

page 101 *"I was probably as aware":* Barbara Walters's Meg Ryan interview, ABC, March 21, 1994.

page 101 *Hotel Bel-Air on Valentine's Day, 1991:* Kalogerakis, "When Dennis Met Meg."

page 101 *"I lost it so completely":* Barbara Walters's Meg Ryan interview, ABC, March 21, 1994.

page 101 *thought herself the most practical and least romantic of the two:* Sessums, "Maximum Meg."

page 102 *"a horrible experience":* Stephen Rebello, "Herbert Ross: The Man with the Tarnished Halo," *Movieline*, July 1, 1993, http://movieline .com/1993/07/01/herbert-ross-the-man-with-the-tarnished-halo/2/.

page 102 *"just destroyed in your opinion":* Stevens, *Conversations at the American Film Institute with the Great Moviemakers,* p. 182.

page 102 *like Mike Nichols and James L. Brooks:* Abramowitz, *Is That a Gun in Your Pocket?,* p. 362.

page 102 *1,794 studio movies issued between 1983 and 1992:* Ibid.

page 102 *women got more breaks during the silent film era:* Erin Carlson, "Outrageous sexism in Hollywood exposed in new blog," *Fortune*, May 8, 2015, http://fortune.com/2015/05/08/tumblr-blog-hollywood-sexism/.

page 103 *the first American woman to helm a full-length movie:* Lois Weber profile, Women Film Pioneers Project, https://wfpp.cdrs.columbia.edu /pioneer/ccp-lois-weber/.

page 103 *Universal Studios' top-earning director in 1916:* Carlson, "Outrageous sexism in Hollywood exposed in new blog."

page 103 *Dawn enlisted producer Lynda Obst:* Abramowitz, *Is That a Gun in Your Pocket?,* p. 362.

page 103 *"funniest person I know":* Jodie Burke, "Sisters Making Films: The Ephrons," *Los Angeles Times*, August 21, 2011.

page 104 *"Neither of us quite knew what we were doing":* Ephron, *Sister Mother Husband Dog: Etc.,* p. 196.

page 104 *wanted to be a* New York *director:* Nora Ephron and Lena Dunham in conversation, published to YouTube on June 27, 2012, https://www.youtube .com/watch?v=eqNPqCaxLE8.

page 104 *the executive resigned:* Times Wire Services, "Dawn Steel Leaves Columbia," *Los Angeles Times*, January 8, 1990, http://articles.latimes .com/1990-01-08/news/mn-252_1_dawn-steel.

page 104 *brought along his then-girlfriend Vendela:* Abramowitz, *Is That a Gun in Your Pocket?,* p. 363.

page 104 *slit her throat:* Joe Logan, "Nora's Vision," *Philadelphia Inquirer*, March 9, 1992.

page 104 *$9 million:* Stevens, *Conversations at the American Film Institute with the Great Moviemakers,* p. 182.

NOTES

page 105 *Dottie interested Bette Midler:* Nora Ephron's 2007 Academy of Achievement interview.

page 105 *"Jeffrey isn't really interested in women":* Ibid.

page 105 *"Several people turned it down and it really hurt my feelings":* Argentina Brunetti papers, Margaret Herrick Library.

page 105 *scared to death:* Logan, "Nora's Vision."

page 105 *"What they don't tell you":* Bennetts, "Nora's Arc."

page 105 *a big smile materialized on her face:* Ibid.

page 107 *"There is no answer to that question":* Ibid.

page 107 *"quite shocked":* Ibid.

page 107 *"Looking back on it":* Nora Ephron's 2007 Academy of Achievement interview.

page 108 *He said she was happier:* Bennetts, "Nora's Arc."

Chapter 5: Sleepless Nights

page 109 *35-year-old martial arts instructor:* Jessica Koslow, "Arch Focused on the Story Arc in 'Sleepless in Seattle,'" Playhouse Blog, May 31, 2013.

page 109 *lived in Los Angeles during his 20s:* "Sleepless in Virginia," Screenwriting from Iowa…and Other Unlikely Places, July 19, 2012, https:// screenwritingfromiowa.wordpress.com/tag/jeff-arch/.

page 110 *Jeff's Sleepless in Seattle:* I consulted Deidre Pribram's excellent, invaluable script analysis in her article titled "Sleepless in Seattle: Three Writers, Three Concepts," in a 1996 special issue of *Creative Screenwriting* 3, no. 4.

page 113 *"oughta have a mom. So I'm gonna find him one":* Pribram, "Sleepless in Seattle: Three Writers, Three Concepts."

page 114 *"high six figures":* Bennetts, "Nora's Arc."

page 115 *"I'd made a horrible financial error years earlier":* Stevens, *Conversations at the American Film Institute with the Great Moviemakers*, p. 183.

page 115 *"He's so weird and he's so serious":* Ibid.

page 115–116 *bounded from the mattress to sketch a map of the United States:* Argentina Brunetti papers, Margaret Herrick Library.

page 116 *"geographically correct moving montage in a movie":* Tom Hanks, "Nora Ephron: A Life of Voice and Detail," *Time*, June 27, 2012, http:// entertainment.time.com/2012/06/27/nora-ephron-a-life-of-voice-and-detail/.

page 116 *"real cars in real traffic":* Ibid.

page 116 *"She told Sally Quinn that the Kavner character was too Jewish":* Cohen, *She Made Me Laugh*, p. 189.

page 118 *$500,000:* Hilary De Vries, "A 'Peter Pan' for the '90s," *New York Times*, December 8, 1991.

page 118 *flopped hard:* Jack Mathews, "Four Studios Slice Up a $1.8 Billion Summer Pie," *Los Angeles Times*, July 6, 1989.

page 120 *Emotion:* Deidre Pribram, a media and communications professor at Molloy College who has written extensively on *Sleepless in Seattle*, described to me that Sam Baldwin's appeal to seemingly all women in the picture, not just Annie, is that he is in touch with his feelings—his emotions.

page 121 *"was not even attached":* Lawrence Grobel, "Kim Basinger: No Regrets," *Movieline*, January 1, 1994, http://movieline.com/1994/01/01/no-regrets/.

page 122 *"within inches of touching a green light":* Randy Sue Coburn, "An Affair to Inspire," *Premiere*, July 1993.

page 126 *rocked tweenage Delia to the core:* Delia Ephron detailed the effects of her girlhood addiction to *Seven Brides for Seven Brothers* in her essay "Blame It on the Movies," from *Sister Mother Husband Dog: Etc.*

page 127 *"hoped the line":* Nora Ephron commentary, *Sleepless in Seattle—10th Anniversary Edition* DVD.

page 128 *an editor at* New York Times Magazine: Lynda Obst, *Hello, He Lied* (New York: Little Brown and Company, 1996), p. 13.

page 129 *"I want to buy groceries":* Pribram, "Sleepless in Seattle: Three Writers, Three Concepts."

page 129 *"Do you like cats? I have 43":* Ibid.

page 130 *$100 million renovation:* Mathis Chazanov, "Beverly Hills Hotel to Close for Long-Overdue Face Lift," *Los Angeles Times*, December 20, 1992.

page 130 *Creative Artists Agency wooed:* From *Times* staff and wire reports, "Briefly," *Los Angeles Times*, April 12, 1991.

page 131 *"fuck-you money":* Kurt Andersen, "The Tom Hanks Phenomenon," *New Yorker*, December 7, 1998.

page 131 *Penny thought Tom was too cute:* Marshall, *My Mother Was Nuts*, p. 250.

page 132 *"motivation was immediately understandable":* Lisa Schwarzbaum, "The Nice Man Cometh," *Entertainment Weekly*, July 9, 1993.

page 132 *"one person's second chance can be the other person's first":* Coburn, "An Affair to Inspire."

page 133 *"Absolutely":* Griffin, "That's the Way Love Goes."

page 133 *"with a Madison Avenue type":* Michael Shnayerson, "Madcap with a Twist," *Vanity Fair*, 1999.

page 133 *emergency C-section:* Sessums, "Maximum Meg."

page 133 *"the baby bell wasn't ringing":* Barbara Walters's Meg Ryan interview, ABC, March 21, 1994.

page 133 *fretted for Jack's safety:* Kalogerakis, "When Dennis Met Meg."

page 133 *worried about her future:* Ibid.

page 134 *"Tom Hanks wasn't quite Tom Hanks":* Nora Ephron, 2007 Academy of Achievement interview.

page 135 *She knew:* Argentina Brunetti papers, Margaret Herrick Library.

page 135 *through emotional detachment:* Lindsay Kimble, "Rosie O'Donnell's Father Edward Joseph O'Donnell Has Died," People.com, August 23, 2015.

page 135 *"As I told Nora when I auditioned":* Griffin, "That's the Way Love Goes."

page 138 *"I asked Tom to watch it with me":* Hruska, "'Seattle' Sob Story."

page 142 *"That is such horseshit":* Francine Stock's interview with Tom Hanks for BAFTA's "A Life in Pictures" on October 19, 2013.

Chapter 6: Nearest Thing to Heaven

page 144 *The helicopter flew around the Empire State Building:* Nora described her harrowing ride and exchange with the late great Sven Nykvist in her commentary for the *Sleepless in Seattle—10th Anniversary Edition* DVD.

page 144 *"It was Sven's 102nd movie":* Argentina Brunetti papers, Margaret Herrick Library.

page 145 Winter Light: "Ingmar Bergman," the *Economist*, August 2, 2007, http://www.economist.com/node/9581178.

page 145 *loved photographing women:* I learned so much about Nykvist's innovative approach to cinematography (and love of the ladies) in the lovely documentary *Light Keeps Me Company* (2002), directed by his son Carl-Gustav Nykvist.

page 145 *"the only woman in Hollywood who had not slept with Sven Nykvist":* Lena Dunham, "Seeing Nora Everywhere," *New Yorker*, June 28, 2012.

page 149 *"every morning you would look out of the window":* Eileen V. Quigley, "The Queen and Her King," *Los Angeles Times*, April 25, 1988.

page 149 *When Leona met Harry in 1968:* Sewell Chan, "Remembering Leona Helmsley," *New York Times*, August 20, 2007.

page 149 *"'I'm Just Wild about Harry'–themed birthday parties":* Alan S. Oser, "Harry Helmsley Is Dead at 87; Amassed Billions in Property," *New York Times*, January 6, 1997.

page 149 *indicted on charges:* Chan, "Remembering Leona Helmsley."

page 150 *"Only the little people pay taxes":* Ibid.

page 150 *18 months:* Ibid.

page 150 *beat the record in 1972:* "Empire State Building," Skyscraper Center, https://www.skyscrapercenter.com/building/empire-state-building/261.

page 151 *"bought beautiful replicas of the Empire State Building encased in glass snowballs": Hello, He Lied*, p. 219.

Chapter 7: Sleepless, Stressed, and Addicted to Starbucks

page 163 *"The quality of life, right now, is not very good":* Nora as quoted by Maggie Murphy during our interview on January 14, 2016.

page 163 *"Do all these wires have to be here?":* From my interview with Dianne Dreyer in January 30, 2015.

page 166 *"When you're making a movie it's the one time you can control the experience":* Nora as quoted by Gary Foster.

page 166 *"I don't want to work with anyone that I wouldn't be willing to have dinner with":* Ibid.

page 166 *"Never walk barefoot on a hotel rug":* Nora as quoted by Mike Badalucco.

page 167 *"she was playing a Republican who had never had an orgasm":* Nora commentary, *Sleepless in Seattle—10th Anniversary Edition* DVD.

page 167 *dressed Meg:* Betty Goodwin, "Simple Clothes, Complex Hairdos," *Los Angeles Times*, June 25, 1993.

page 167 *"days going through clothes":* Stevens, *Conversations at the American Film Institute with the Great Moviemakers*, p. 165.

page 167 *She gave Meg a virginal nightgown:* Stephen Hunter, "Ephron balked at Pennsylvania, so…Baltimore!," *Baltimore Sun*, June 25, 1993.

page 167 *"She would wear that to bed?":* Ibid.

page 167 *"Do you know who you are?…You're the Breck girl":* Ibid.

page 168 *"Meg Ryan does not toy with men's feelings":* Peter William Evans, "Meg Ryan, Megastar," *Terms of Endearment: Hollywood Romantic Comedy of the 1980s and 1990s* (Edinburgh: Edinburgh University Press, 1998), pp. 188–206.

page 169 *"Christian" and "Jewish" romantic comedies:* Nora commentary, *When Harry Met Sally—Special Edition* DVD.

page 169 *"Annie is much more square than Sally":* Argentina Brunetti papers, Margaret Herrick Library.

page 170 *"You couldn't have sex in a movie in the '30s and '40s":* Ibid.

page 170 *"not such an easy thing to be empowered":* Ibid.

page 171 *"Standby on milk mustache!":* Coburn, "An Affair to Inspire."

page 171 *"That's the biggest laugh I ever heard onstage in five years of working":* Ibid.

page 171 *"Is that true?":* and ensuing Ephron-Malinger exchange: Ibid.

page 173 *always wanted that character to say NY for* no way: Delia Ephron commentary, *When Harry Met Sally—Special Edition* DVD.

page 174 *"like traveling in an armored vehicle":* Ephron, *Sister Mother Husband Dog: Etc.*, p. 200.

page 174 *"I often drove her crazy":* Ibid.

page 174 *"I don't think there's a million people that you can fall in love with":* Delia Ephron commentary, *When Harry Met Sally—Special Edition* DVD.

page 176 *driest on record in 90 years:* John Balzar, "Dry Northwest Gets a Taste of Water Rules, Fire Concerns," *Los Angeles Times*, June 3, 1992.

page 178 *"Rosie's last shot":* Griffin, "That's the Way Love Goes."

page 178 *"As a best friend":* Sessums, "Maximum Meg."

page 180 *perceived as hostile: Everything Is Copy.*

Chapter 8: Make Nora Happy

page 182 *handed Meg a red apple:* My re-creation of a scene from Randy Sue Coburn's "Affair to Inspire" feature in *Premiere.* "I don't have to interpret Nora's direction with that extra beat that I have to give it with a man," Ryan told Coburn.

page 188 I could have shot this movie forever: Ibid.

page 188 *A formal offer was made in mid-August:* Claudia Eller, "Rudolph, Altman Double-Park at Wm. Morris," *Variety*, August 11, 1992.

page 190 *a record 2,245 homicides:* Albert Samaha, "The Rise and Fall of Crime in New York City: A Timeline," *Village Voice*, August 7, 2014.

page 191 *by 250:* Ibid.

Chapter 9: Stardust

page 195 *"I have never felt so much like a celebrity"*: Griffin, "That's the Way Love Goes."

page 196 *"I was waiting by the phone"*: Ibid.

page 198 *weekend earnings of $17 million:* Box Office Mojo.

page 198 *$127 million domestically and $228 million worldwide:* Ibid.

page 198 *$900 million:* Mark Harris, "Park Effects: The Dark Impact of the $500 Million 'Jurassic World' Weekend," Grantland.com, June 16, 2015.

page 199 *two million VHS copies:* Chris Ball, "DVDs: 'An Affair to Remember' returns in a 50th anniversary, 2-disc collection," Cleveland.com, January 11, 2008.

page 199 *reaching number one:* Sheila Rule, "'Sleepless' Soundtrack Sends Vintage Durante Songs to MTV," *Baltimore Sun*, August 19, 1993.

page 200 *pulled from theaters in mid-November:* Box Office Mojo.

page 200 *"I find most movies today"*: Kalogerakis, "When Dennis Met Meg."

page 201 *"girl-next-door version of Nora"*: Coburn, "An Affair to Inspire."

page 202 *rejected a slew of major movies:* EW staff, "She's Just a Girl Who Can't Say Yes," *Entertainment Weekly*, January 14, 1994.

page 203 *shed 30 pounds:* Schwarzbaum, "The Nice Man Cometh."

page 203 *"the one I was most attracted to"*: Jesse Green, "The Philadelphia Experiment," *Premiere*, January 1994.

page 203 *$125 million globally:* Clifford Rothman, "'Philadelphia': Oscar Gives Way to Elegy," *New York Times*, January 1, 1995.

page 204 *someone walked up to her:* David Rogow, who worked on *Sleepless* in post-production, recounted to me how Nora responded to a comment about her newfound power with a witticism.

page 205 *$560,000:* Lesley Hazleton, "For Romance, There's No Sleep in Seattle," *New York Times*, September 29, 1994.

Chapter 10: "A Bouquet of Newly Sharpened Pencils" (Also Known as IM-ing with the Enemy)

page 208 *fleeing his homeland:* Myron Meisel, "Parfumerie: Theater Review," *Hollywood Reporter*, December 7, 2013.

page 208 *"Lubitsch had come to Hollywood from Germany"*: Mekado Murphy, "Critics' Picks Video: 'The Shop around the Corner,'" *New York Times*, December 20, 2010.

page 210 *"obey the logic set down in* The Shop around the Corner*"*: Ibid.

page 211 *$95 million:* Box Office Mojo.

page 212 *"What we were thinking?"*: Ephron, *Sister Mother Husband Dog: Etc.*, p. 204.

page 212 *$7 million:* Box Office Mojo.

page 213 *"they are not as compelling to the men who run studios"*: Dinitia Smith, "She's a Director with an Edge: She's a Writer," *New York Times*, December 13, 1998.

page 213 *"had only to cross a courtyard"*: Ephron, *Sister Mother Husband Dog: Etc.*, p. 208.

page 214 *"I said to Delia":* John Clark, "A Sisterhood of Writers," *Los Angeles Times*, November 8, 1998.

page 214 *Jacob Bernstein once worked:* Rebecca Keegan, "Jacob Bernstein Opens a New Window into the Life of Mom Nora Ephron in 'Everything Is Copy,'" *Los Angeles Times*, March 21, 2016.

page 214 *"After 15 years on West 81st Street":* Robin Pogrebin, "A Shakespeare & Co. to Exit the Scene," *New York Times*, June 13, 1996.

page 215 *"The truth is I love my local Barnes & Noble":* Karen Angel, "Superstore-Indie Conflict Gets Glamor Treatment," *Publishers Weekly*, May 18, 1998.

page 215–216 *"the Barnes & Noble bookstores are a part":* Nora Ephron's commentary, *You've Got Mail* DVD released 2008.

page 216 *"Can you fall in love with a Republican?":* Ibid.

page 218 *Nora used to date Navasky:* Cohen, *She Made Me Laugh*, p. 51.

page 218 *on West 69th Street:* Ephron's commentary, *You've Got Mail* DVD.

page 218 *"one lives in terror":* Pogrebin, "A Shakespeare & Co. to Exit the Scene."

page 219 *Judith Regan:* Angel, "Superstore-Indie Conflict Gets Glamor Treatment."

page 219 *four-bedroom apartment:* Jacob Bernstein, "Judith Regan Is Back. Watch Out," *New York Times*, February 6, 2015.

page 220 *"We are going to get Tom Hanks and Meg Ryan":* John Clark, "A Sisterhood of Writers."

page 220 *"He's doing a romantic comedy with you, Nora":* Ibid.

page 221 *19,000 chatrooms:* Caitlyn Dewey, "A Complete History of the Rise and Fall—and Reincarnation!—of the Beloved '90s chatroom," *Washington Post*, October 30, 2014.

page 221 *lonely stay-at-home moms:* Liz Doup, "Stay-at-Homes Have 'Coffee,'" *St. Louis Post-Dispatch*, June 5, 1996.

page 222 *35 million times per day:* Eun Kyung Kim, "'You've Got Mail' Guy: I Recorded Phrase on a Cassette in My Living Room," Today.com, March 27, 2014.

page 223 *"She actually worked at an autobody shop":* Ephron's commentary, *You've Got Mail* DVD.

page 223 *"I really loved the script":* Benjamin Svetkey, "Mail Bonding," *Entertainment Weekly*, December 18, 1998.

page 223 *"Oh, man, is this something I should be doing again?":* Jane Pratt, "We Like Meg," *Jane*, April 1998.

page 223 *"Just watching a little more and not so much being out there":* Ibid.

page 224 *"This is Jimmy Stewart before Jimmy Stewart was Jimmy Stewart":* Svetkey, "Mail Bonding."

page 224 *$200 million:* Box Office Mojo.

page 224 *"meditation on life":* Sessums, "Maximum Meg."

page 224 *"slay with a word":* EW Staff, "Julia Roberts and Meg Ryan in 'The Women,'" *Entertainment Weekly*, May 6, 1994.

page 225 *$127 million:* Box Office Mojo.

page 225 *$35 million:* Ibid.

page 226 *pocketed $20 million plus some of the back end:* Andersen, "The Tom Hanks Phenomenon."

page 226 *$10.5 million against 10 percent of the gross profits: You've Got Mail* miscellaneous notes, Turner Classic Movies website.

page 227 *formed United Artists:* "Mary Pickford," Women Film Pioneers Project, https://wfpp.cdrs.columbia.edu/pioneer/ccp-mary-pickford/.

Chapter 11: Pride and Prejudice and Perfect Hair

page 233 *"I'm not interested in that at all":* Svetkey, "Mail Bonding."

page 233 *"The spelling was so horrendous":* Ibid.

page 236 *"Everyone wanted to be involved":* Angel, "Superstore-Indie Conflict Gets Glamor Treatment."

page 237 *"the day any chain can afford":* Ibid.

page 237 *reprinted L. Frank Baum's Oz books:* Ibid.

page 238 *"rather strong editorial presence":* Ibid.

page 238 *"that fantasy bookstore that we all have in our brains":* Ephron's commentary, *You've Got Mail* DVD.

page 239 *"slightly Republican":* Ibid.

page 240 *"It's sort of based on an apartment I used to live in":* Ibid.

page 240 *couldn't figure out her part:* Pratt, "We Like Meg."

page 245 *"using much less technology":* Ephron's commentary, *You've Got Mail* DVD.

page 252 *corpse atop the Apthorp:* Marsh, "Palace revolt."

page 255 Meg Ryan to cheese! Meg Ryan to coffee!: Karen S. Schneider, "Ryan's Express," *People*, December 21, 1998.

page 255–256 *"lose her mind":* Ephron's commentary, *You've Got Mail* DVD.

page 256 *"Please, please make this part more your own":* Ibid.

page 258 *"Taxi!":* Ibid.

page 259 *"This is the last girl any guy wants to break up with":* Schneider, "Ryan's Express."

page 259 *"She had to be enough of a bitch so you aren't sad when Tom Hanks dumps her":* Al Weisel, "Parker's Poses," *Out*, February 1999.

page 259 *"It's almost like taking Omaha Beach":* Ephron's commentary, *You've Got Mail* DVD.

page 261 *"It's the moment that she knows she's in trouble":* Ephron's commentary, *You've Got Mail* DVD.

page 262 *"the performances were actually better":* Ibid.

page 264 *supposed to jump into the air:* Lauren Shuler Donner commentary, *You've Got Mail* DVD.

page 264 *"It doesn't really bother me":* Akin Ojumu, "Are You Being Surfed? Steve Zahn," *Neon*, December 1998.

page 267 *$116 million nationally and $251 million worldwide:* Box Office Mojo.

page 267 *$370 million:* Ibid.

page 268 *"Look, Mary's the perfect girl":* Judith I. Brennan, "'Mary': The Contrary Romantic Comedy," *Los Angeles Times*, August 1, 1998.

page 268 *"begrudging":* Ephron, *Sister Mother Husband Dog: Etc.*, p. 37.

page 269 *Late-night host Stephen Colbert:* This delightful exchange between Stephen Colbert and Quentin Tarantino, confessing his unlikely affection for romantic comedy and *Mail*. The video footage: https://www.youtube.com /watch?v=5JRQr4E8zkU.

page 270 *"shockingly conservative":* Xan Brooks, "Flaming Nora," the *Guardian*, February 19, 1999.

page 270 *"Critics were hard on her":* Ephron, *Sister Mother Husband Dog: Etc.*, p. 36.

Chapter 12: A Heart in New York

page 272 *"That history played out when we began writing":* Ephron, *Sister Mother Husband Dog: Etc.*, p. 213.

page 272 *"Keaton didn't enjoy collaboration":* Ibid., p. 214.

page 274 *"He's a tough thing to resist":* Karen S. Schneider, "Meg on Her Own," *People*, July 9, 2001.

page 274 *separated in May 2000:* Nicole Martin, "Hollywood's Golden Girl Meg in Marriage Split," the *Telegraph*, June 30, 2000.

page 274 *Dennis filed for divorce:* "Quaid Files for Divorce From Meg Ryan," ABC News, July 12, 2000, http://abcnews.go.com/Entertainment/story?id=116421.

page 274 *stunned passenger:* Karen S. Schneider, "Sweethearts Sour," *People*, July 17, 2000.

page 274 *reportedly got cold feet:* Stephen M. Silverman, "Meg Dumped Russell, Not Vice Versa," *People*, June 27, 2001.

page 276 *"I am not a victim":* "Meg Ryan on Divorce: 'Dennis Was Not Faithful,'" accesshollywood.com, September 23, 2008, https://www.accesshollywood.com /articles/meg-ryan-on-divorce-dennis-was-not-faithful-65433/.

page 276 *moved out of the Brentwood home:* Schneider, "Meg on Her Own."

page 276 *$47 million:* Box Office Mojo.

page 277 *"I was scared of the sexuality":* Sean Smith, "Love Is Dangerous," *Newsweek*, September 21, 2003.

page 278 *"She's pretty cunning":* Ibid.

page 278 *"feels like a rip-off":* Grantland Staff, "The Rom-Com Hall of Fame: Champions and Challengers," Grantland.com, July 22, 2014.

page 279 *A Paramount Pictures exec blocked:* Lynda Obst, *Sleepless in Hollywood* (New York: Simon & Schuster, 2013), p. 132.

page 279 *birdwatchers:* Kristin Sterling, "Acclaimed Screenwriter and Director Nora Ephron Offers Insights to School of the Arts Students," *Columbia News* website, November 15, 2001, http://www.columbia.edu/cu/news/01/11 /noraEphron.html.

page 280 *"She was completely fearless":* Smith, "She's a Director with an Edge: She's a Writer."

page 280 *"she was appallingly single-minded":* Kerrie Logan Hollihan, *Reporting under Fire: 16 Daring Women War Correspondents and Photojournalists* (Chicago: Chicago Review Press, 2014), p. 140.

page 280 *doubted its prospects:* Cohen, *She Made Me Laugh*, p. 254.

page 280 *Michelle Pfeiffer and Richard Gere:* Tribune Media Services, "'Higgins & Beech' May Be on Track Again," May 31, 1996.

page 280 *Meg considered playing Maggie:* Svetkey, "Mail Bonding."

page 280 *Elisabeth Shue:* Tribune Media Services, "'Higgins & Beech' May Be on Track Again."

page 280 *George Clooney:* Cohen, *She Made Me Laugh*, p. 236.

page 280 *over budget:* Michael Fleming, "Cost control: Making H'wood's tough calls," *Variety*, March 20, 1994.

page 280 *heartbroken:* Patrick McGilligan, *Backstory 5: Interviews with Screenwriters of the 1990s* (Berkeley: University of California Press, 2010), p. 39.

page 281 *76 performances:* Ernio Hernandez, "The End: Ephron's Literary Drama, *Imaginary Friends*, Closes on Broadway, February 16," Playbill.com, February 16, 2003.

page 281 *moved out in the spring:* Marsh, "Palace Revolt."

page 281 *$12,000:* "R.I.P. Nora Ephron, Upper West Sider," westsiderag.com, http://www.westsiderag.com/2012/06/26/r-i-p-nora-ephron-upper-west-sider.

page 281 *"I'm never going to dream about this new apartment":* Nora Ephron, "Moving On," *New Yorker*, June 5, 2006.

page 283 *inquired about the status of the script:* Jim Dwyer, "From Tabloid Myth to Opening Night," *New York Times*, March 28, 2013.

page 284 *diagnosed that year with myelodysplastic syndrome:* Bernstein, "Nora Ephron's Final Act."

page 284 *long feared dying of cancer:* Cohen, *She Made Me Laugh*, p. 11.

page 284 *uncle Dickie:* Ibid.

page 285 *Steve Wynn:* Nora Ephron, "My Weekend in Vegas," Huffington Post, October 16, 2006.

page 285 *analyzed Condoleezza Rice:* Nora Ephron, "Take My Secretary of State, Please," Huffington Post, December 9, 2006.

page 285 *lit into the 2008 Democratic primary:* Nora Ephron, "White Men," Huffington Post, April 20, 2008.

page 286 *wondered whether there was a movie:* Anthony Venutolo, "Nora Ephron on 'Julie & Julia,'" NJ.com, July 31, 2009.

page 287 *"that one could write about":* Katey Rich, "Interview: Julie & Julia Writer/Director Nora Ephron," cinemablend.com, 2009, http://www.cinemablend.com/new/Interview-Julie-Julia-Writer-Director-Nora-Ephron-14223.html.

page 287 *a baby girl from China:* People Staff, "Meg Ryan Adopts a Girl," People.com, January 25, 2006.

page 287 *"She's a really ridiculously happy person":* From Ryan's guest appearance on *Late Show with David Letterman*. It aired September 12, 2008.

page 288 *having dinner with Nora and Jon Hamm at the Wolseley in London:* Cohen, *She Made Me Laugh*, p. 255.

page 289 *71 percent:* Pamela McClintock, "Help! Save the Movies!," *Hollywood Reporter*, January 3, 2012.

page 289 *"Hey, Nora, what play is he reading that you are doing?":* Tom's question and the ensuing back-and-forth with Nora can be sourced back to page 255 of *She Made Me Laugh*.

page 289 *"almost good enough":* Healy, "Tom Hanks, Broadway's New Kid," *New York Times*, February 20, 2013.

page 289 *No tears were shed in Tom's performance:* Cohen, *She Made Me Laugh*, p. 256.

page 290 *"What's so fascinating about Mike McAlary?":* Everything Is Copy.

page 290 *"more luck than talent":* Ibid.

page 290 *baffling Wolfe:* Healy, "Tom Hanks, Broadway's New Kid."

page 291 *"There was Vegas as big as life":* Tim Adams, "Nicholas Pileggi: The Mob, Nora Ephron's Death and Vegas," the *Guardian*, February 3, 2013.

page 291 *"Absolutely, she planned for it":* Bernstein, "Nora Ephron's Final Act."

page 291 *"The last time I saw her":* Tim Appelo, "Meg Ryan Remember's Nora Ephron's 'Unbelievable Sweetness,' 'Ferocious' Love of Words," *Hollywood Reporter*, July 11, 2012.

page 292 *"Nick sat beside her and wept":* Bernstein, "Nora Ephron's Final Act."

page 292 *"This is it":* Ibid.

page 292 *worried he might not meet them:* Healy, "Tom Hanks, Broadway's New Kid."

page 292 *think of Nora as he walked home:* I crafted this scene from Hanks's evocative quote to Healy: "I'm not afraid of the end result because I think we'll have a very good production. But I am afraid of blowing it myself. I'm afraid of having something being my responsibility, yet not having the wherewithal or lack of self-consciousness or stamina to pull it off.... But when I walk home at night, that's when I hear Nora's voice the clearest, and that's when I feel the most excitement about taking on this play."

Index

About the Author

Erin Carlson is a journalist who has covered the entertainment industry for 13 years. She worked as a staff editor and writer at the *Hollywood Reporter* and established herself early on in her career as a reporter covering arts and entertainment at the Associated Press in New York City. She has written for *Glamour, Fortune, Vanity Fair*, and the Daily Beast. She lives in San Francisco.